The Way of the Actor

The WAY of the ACTOR

A Path to Knowledge & Power

■ ■ ■ ■ ■ ■ ■ ■ ■ ■

BRIAN BATES

Shambhala
Boston
1987

Shambhala Publications, Inc.
314 Dartmouth Street
Boston, Massachusetts 02116

9 8 7 6 5 4 3 2 1

First Edition
Printed in the United States of America
Distributed in the United States by Random House
and in Canada by Random House of Canada Ltd.

Library of Congress Cataloging-in-Publication Data

Bates, Brian.
    The way of the actor.

    Bibliography: p.
    Includes index.
    1. Acting—Psychological aspects. 2. Actors—Psychol-
ogy. 3. Actors—Interviews. 4. Self—realization. I. Title.
PN2071.P78B3   1987   792'.028'019   86-31332
ISBN 0–87773–384–8

Contents

To my Mother and Father

Acknowledgements

I first met Glenda Jackson in her dressing room at the Old Vic Theatre, London. And while we talked, she prepared the exotic make-up of a queen for her title role in Racine's *Phedra*. She talked to me of esoteric energies, while applying mascara. This seems entirely appropriate, for this marvellous actress combines the intellectual excitement and passionate energy of the actor's life with an unpretentious respect for the practicalities. The way of the actor is both esoteric and practical, and Glenda's work and ideas are an inspiration for this book.

Charlton Heston defies categories. A legendary film star who also tackles challenging stage productions, including the most demanding Shakepearian roles. While rightly asserting that acting is *doing* and cannot be captured in its 'smoky essence' by words alone, he then did his best to prove otherwise; his ideas on the actor's way were illuminating, entertaining and provocative.

Antony Sher is riding on a wave of acclaimed performances. His high-risk acting is a reinvestment in the magical power of the actor, and the tremendous response to his work demonstrates just how important is the role of the theatre in our lives. He talked with me about his work with quiet modesty and humour, and his presence informs many aspects of this book.

And Liv Ullmann shared with me ideas which were original, refreshing, frank and extremely perceptive. She talks about her work and life in ways which entertain, inspire, educate. Her commitment and sensitivity to other people lie at the heart of who she is. Liv embodies the sort of wisdom which I believe to be the legacy of the way of the actor.

While my discussions with these four actors helped me enormously, the basis of the book is the work I have done with hundreds of actors over the years. Much of that work happened in the Royal Academy of Dramatic Art (RADA), London, one of the world's leading centres for training actors. Hugh Cruttwell was the Principal of RADA when, ten years ago he invited me to give a lecture to his actors. It was my entry into the way of the actor. For subsequently, under Hugh's guidance I ran courses, taught tutorials, directed plays; in fact did the things that led to the writing of this book. Hugh was generous in his advice and encouragement, clear and frank in his judgements. Without him this book could never have been written.

One of the strengths of RADA is that in its intensive training courses it integrates a full range of perspectives from the world of acting: there is no narrow 'party line'. And it attracts an array of the best teachers and professional directors. As a result RADA is an institution bursting with vitality, and I am grateful to the staff of the Academy for their stimulating company, openness to new ideas, and commitment to the actor's way. In particular the new Principal of RADA, Oliver Neville, generously supported and encouraged the writing of this book.

While many of my explorations were carried out in RADA, the adventures I describe are my own responsibility, and the Academy is blameless where I had strayed onto paths of error.

Along the way there have been numerous individuals who have given advice, encouragement and practical support in my exploration of the actor's way. A few whose names should be recorded here include Elizabeth Watson Bates for many of the best ideas; John Goodman for the all-night discussions; and at RADA the Librarian, Claire Hope, for accurate advice; Elna Steinmann for organizing my workshops; and Gill Ingle for encouragement and the calls to Rome. Thanks also to Carol Malcolmson of the Royal Shakespeare Company, and Tracey Walker partly for the typing but mostly for the entertaining stories which kept me going.

My most important note of thanks, however, must go to the hundreds of actors I have worked with over the years. It would be invidious to name individuals, but those I have directed, taught closely in tutorials, and who have explored with me in workshops, are the people who taught me the way of the actor. In effect, they wrote this book with me.

Introduction

The Actor's Way

From the moment they met, Alec Guinness knew that James
Dean was about to die. It was not a rational prediction based
on Dean's wild reputation, nor even an intuition formed from a
snap judgement of the young man's character. It was a premonition as hard and sharp as a guillotine. Guinness warned
Dean that he would die within a week. And exactly seven days
later, Dean was dead.[1]

An actor at the Royal Academy of Dramatic Art lay on his
back, eyes closed. But while he remained motionless, his spirit,
soul, 'astral' self journeyed out of his body, left the building and
roamed the streets of London, describing events around him as
if he were seeing them directly.

And Shirley MacLaine, incarnating characters in film roles,
senses deeply within her that these are not just imaginary
people, mere playthings for our entertainment. Far from it.
They are the spiritual essence of people who have lived and
died, reborn to be among us.[2]

These remarkable experiences hint at mysteries of human
nature as yet unfathomed by science. But what they have in
common has a more particular significance. For they are
introductions to the way of the actor as a path to personal
knowledge and power.

Many actors have described powerful experiences which
seem to tap extended dimensions of life, though the paranormal
is not the only criterion of profundity. Glenda Jackson has
stepped onto the stage fearing that she is risking life and death;
that her soul may be snatched away leaving her to wither and
die. To act is to risk, and takes courage. Charlton Heston has

pushed himself to the limits in tackling on stage some of the
great Shakespearian roles; challenges which feel to him like
that of a hunter trekking ever higher up the slopes of a
mountain in search of unknown prey. Antony Sher's roles enter
his life like someone he loves, another person always present,
always close. And yet at the core of his performances lies his
own being, constantly probed, explored, expressed.

And Liv Ullmann, in performance, encounters and reveals
her inner self, experiencing the film camera as photographing
her thoughts, emotions, fears. And yet these are not her own
thoughts, emotions and fears, for in performance she is filled by
another presence, a character possessing her, a spirit shared by
the actor and audience.

There is a particular significance to all of these experiences,
for they unlock secrets within actors, and ourselves, which we
only barely understand. And yet in times past this knowledge
was accessible to us. For in traditional societies around the
world, actors were *expected* to foretell future events. To travel
beyond the boundaries of their bodies. To incarnate spirits of
the mysteries. To risk life and death in performance, to hunt
the unknown, to love and reveal inner spirit which communicates with others at the deepest levels.[3]

For thousands of years actors were regarded as the guardians
of wisdom. And the way of the actor was a path to personal
knowledge and power.

I believe it still is.

Insights yielded by the actor's path were known to all
traditional societies, but have in recent centuries been trampled underfoot in the pursuit of the rational. And yet this
intuitive psychology thrives today, unrecognized in our midst,
in the work of the actor. It is knowledge that needs to be
rediscovered, looked at afresh. Old knowledge seen anew.
And that is why the way of the actor is a *new* path to personal
knowledge and power.

Actors as Shamans
Film director John Boorman journeyed deep in the rain forests
of Brazil, researching for *The Emerald Forest*, his film about a
white American boy who is captured by and grows up with a
native South American Indian tribe. Boorman was flown into

tribal lands, trekked through the jungle to a meeting with Takuma, a famed shaman. When they finally met, Takuma asked Boorman to explain his work: 'It is not easy to describe a movie to a man who has never seen one or watched television. I struggled and he listened intently. I told him how one scene would stop and another begin, in a different place and time as it does in a dream. He lit up, grasping that. I told him of some of the tricks and wonders we got up to. Finally he was satisfied. "You make visions, magic. You are a *paje* like me." '[4]

All so-called 'primitive' societies have at their head important people with special powers. These people have the ability to transform themselves in public performance from their normal personality into somebody or something else: a god or animal, ancient ancestor or representation of a spirit. Their crucial role in society is to transcend the boundaries of their own identity, follow a path to personal knowledge, and in dramatic performance, to lead their audiences into ritual journeys into their own psyches. They are mystics, magical seers and creators of visions. These people, commonly called shamans, sorcerers or medicine men, were the first actors.[5]

Today the 'creation of visions' is the responsibility of others besides actors; directors like John Boorman, writers, producers, cameramen, technicians, stage-hands, and so on. But at the centre of it all is the actor. Pre-eminently on the stage, of course. Yet even in films where the director's special effects create powerful images, the actor provides the path, the key, the identifiable character who unlocks the visions for us.

Actors occupy a very special status in traditional societies. They are people chosen for their abilities to communicate directly with the 'spirit world'; the powers and forces of life that we know to exist but cannot see, visions of truth that lie beyond our normal senses. Actor shamans manifest the 'spirit' in dramatic performance, in which they are believed to 'fly' to the spirit world, or be possessed by and become the spirits themselves. This view of actors as people with extraordinary abilities is still widespread in Oriental cultures, and in South America and Africa.[6] But in times past, hundreds of years ago, actors in western societies also performed the role of visionary, healer and sage. Actors were essentially performing mystics.

Many western, present-day actors describe profound

experiences which directly parallel those of the 'performing mystics'. Shirley MacLaine reports sensations of travelling out of her body, and 'seeing herself' from some disembodied state: an experience accompanied by ecstatic emotions and visions. This description is very like the traditional actor's practice of 'flying' to the spirit world to discover the secrets of life.

Shirley MacLaine also talks about her work directly in terms of self-discovery: 'I needed to reach inside me and touch me if I was going to understand the world and be any good in my work.' But for the actor this inner understanding is not gained through a process of self-absorption: 'I loved to be involved with concerns outside myself because, to be honest, I believed that was actually my path to understanding myself.'[7]

There is a hidden power in acting. It is that energy in performance that is directed outwards, away from the self. The work has an external target. The experiences of the actor, revealing and exciting though they are, are not themselves the objects of contemplation and examination, as they would be in therapy. Just as in Zen in the art of archery, in which the archer's concentration on oneness with the target releases hidden powers, so the actor becomes whole with the character, role, performance, play. The way of the actor is a Zen-like path to self-discovery.

Primitive actors work with a vision of the psychic unity of life which gives purpose and guidance to their work. Liv Ullmann articulates a similar image when she describes actors as seeking intimate contact with their own emotions so that they may be closer to other people. . . . It doesn't make you become a great conversationalist, or a great beauty, or a great mind, but it does make you feel very much a part of the living process. You are in closer touch with people because you are in touch with yourself.'[3]

Sometimes the actor's knowledge of self explodes in a cathartic release of emotion. This is a concentrated form of self-discovery which can alter a life in dramatic fashion. Marlon Brando, for example, talked about the effect on him of his earlier work: 'Acting has done as much as anything . . . to make me realise my violence and get rid of it. And when I finished *The Wild Ones* I think it was gone forever.'[9]

When a dramatic role demands that a highly-charged aspect

of oneself, an aspect hidden or even repressed, needs to be released, then the result can be very powerful. But the work of the actor is unlike most systems of psychotherapy, in which energy is directed inwards to focus on past experiences, bring them into the consciousness and subject them to detailed analysis. The actor connects with, and apprehends past experiences in an intuitive way, but the inner material is employed in breathing life into a character or role. Inner emotion remains inner emotion, but expressed through a different form – that of the character. Strong emotional forces within the actor are reintegrated creatively, without the loss of power that sometimes accompanies the conscious, rational analysis of inner experience. Marlon Brando has talked of the emotional turmoil which powers his performances, and his accounts match those of 'primitive' actors who enter states of mind we would label pathological, but yet they emerge unscathed and with lessons for life in the world of the sane. It is a kind of healing madness which Brando shares with the performing mystics of traditional societies.

Ben Kingsley won an Academy Award for his remarkable film performance as *Gandhi*. Ten years earlier he had played *Hamlet* at the Royal Shakespeare Company. Looking back on that experience, he says, 'It allowed me to explore myself so profoundly that I believe the experience changed and restructured my whole life. From *Hamlet* onwards I allowed myself to surprise myself, and I did that by becoming more and more still.'

For an actor outer action unconnected to inner stillness appears frantic. Finding a personal centre, a point of power, and linking it strongly with external action is the basis of an actor's presence; the capacity to hold the attention and command the concentration of the audience. It is a presence which goes beyond the mere physical and, as we shall see, edges into that 'twilight zone' of science we label 'paranormal'.

Clearly we do not need to travel across the world to other cultures, or back in time to societies of the past to rediscover the way of the actor, although these perspectives help to fill out the details. All we need to do is to explore the life of the actor with fresh eyes. Not as theatre or film critics, or television reviewers, proponents of a method of actor training, academic theorists of dramatic literature, or analysts of popular culture. Rather, we need to enter into the *experience* of being an actor. And an examination of this inner world of the actor reveals what we have to learn about ourselves and about life, by exploring the way of the actor, a *renewed* path to personal knowledge and power. In fact, the evidence afforded by the experiences of today's actors reveals that far from being an anthropological or historical curiosity, the way of the actor is very much alive as a path to personal knowledge and power.

Actors as Neurotics

Of course, our opinion of actors has changed. Today we seem deeply ambivalent about their abilities and qualities. Some actors become cultural heroes, public figures of international repute, accorded tremendous prestige and power. Dustin Hoffman, Jane Fonda, Marlon Brando and Meryl Streep are paid millions of dollars for a few weeks, or even days of work. And recent stage performances by Antony Sher, Liv Ullmann, Charlton Heston and Glenda Jackson have filled theatres with 'hot ticket' shows. Clearly, judging from our treatment of 'stars', actors are considered to be of major significance.

And yet they are often depicted as insecure people, in need of constant attention and applause. Or they are thought to be neurotically seeking refuge from themselves in the different personas of their roles. Alternatively they are accused of harbouring overblown egos, indulged by a career of professional 'showing off'. While we may enjoy, even admire their talent and skills, we do not think to turn to actors for lessons about life.

In contrast with the traditional societies of present and past, we have consigned the practitioners of the imaginal world to the frivolous category of 'entertainment'. They are given the task of amusing us in our idle hours, of being objects of recreation for adult playtime. We now look instead to scientists for instruction in the conduct of our lives.

I believe we are making a tragic mistake. For the actor's journey is identical to the path we tread through life, but an actor travels much further along it. By exploring other characters, actors explore themselves. And by sharing the experiences of actors, we can understand our own experiences.

We are all actors

We are all actors. Every day we play a number of roles with varying degrees of skill and commitment. Our stage moves from home to car and train, work place, restaurants, shops, parties and public settings of all kinds. Some of these 'productions' are pedestrian, and our roles in them minor. We reveal parts of ourselves and conceal others to fit the demands of the situation.

Many actors have recognized and commented on the performance requirements of everyday affairs and the ways in which the art of the actor is integrated with the very pattern of life. Rip Torn points to the little dramatic performances that punctuate much of our social conversation: 'I think we all know people who, especially when they start gossiping, will do imitations of different people.'

And for all of us there are some scenes of high drama, settings in which we feel the need to appear different from our 'normal' self – usually more effective, attractive, powerful. In these scenes we play 'in character'. As Rip Torn remarks, 'We're all experts at the preparation of characters. What do you do when you gird yourself up to go ask the boss for a raise? You've already played the scene out in your head, right?'[11]

And Marlon Brando emphasizes the all pervasive nature of the performance demands of daily life: 'Acting is something that most people think they're incapable of but they do it from morning to night.'

We may practise aspects of the other performing arts in our lives from time to time. Most of us have danced for fun or fitness, painted for pleasure, sung in choirs or in the shower, played musical instruments. These are common leisure activities. But we are actors all the time. We develop our own performances, and cast of characters, each becoming a familiar and well-rehearsed version of ourselves to be performed in appropriate settings.

Indeed it is because we all 'know' how to act, what it is like to talk in front of a group of people, to strive to behave in particular ways to create certain impressions – it is because we are so familiar with these activities that we are bound so intimately to the actor's way of knowledge. Almost everything that actors do can be identified with things we do in less dramatic form, in everyday life. But in order to express the concentrated truths which are the life-stuff of drama, and to project convincing performances before large audiences, and the piercing eye of the film and television camera, the actor must develop depths of self-knowledge and powers of expression far beyond those with which most of us are familiar.

Director Peter Brook suggests the essential difference. 'Acting begins with a tiny movement so slight that it is almost completely invisible. . . . I make a proposition to an actor's imagination such as "She is leaving you". At this moment deep in him a subtle movement occurs in anyone, but in most non-actors the movement is too slight to manifest itself in any way; the actor is a more sensitive instrument and in him the tremor is detected.'[12]

There are differences like this in other areas of an actor's responsivity, imagination, psychological and physical resources, and means of expression. And the ways in which actors achieve this state of advanced responsivity, and awareness of personal powers, forms the background to this book. For while we may not wish to acquire all the actor's technical skills, I believe that there is a rich world of intuitive knowledge and human insights in actor performance, rehearsal, training, and life experience.

Personal Knowledge and Power

These ways of the actor are not simply a system of self-improvement, by which we attempt to develop ourselves towards some ideal goal. Nor is it psychotherapy, in which we delve within us to 'sort out the mess'. Rather, it is a way of apprehending, getting in touch with, and using our inner resources for a balanced life. The way of the actor does employ specific techniques, some of which are described in this book. But more importantly, it concerns a *way of living*, which transcends some of the limitations engendered by the assumptions about human nature, so deeply embedded in contemporary society.

Of course, all this is not to claim that actors are a species of superhuman beings. The acting profession has its full share of people who exhibit the foibles of human nature. And while the world of the actor reveals a practical path to personal knowledge, it does not necessarily mean that what is discovered is easily absorbed, digested, integrated. There are plenty of actors who know a lot about themselves and do not like what they see. The way of the actor is not a sanitized, secure and safe child's path. But there are actors, many actors, who have learned from their work and have *integrated* the knowledge in an understanding: themselves and others.

Personal knowledge leads to power. But it is not a power to dominate and control others, which stems from personal insecurities. Rather, it is the power to direct one's own destiny in the face of pressures to lead a life defined by the well-rutted channels. While the supposed aims of scientific psychology are to 'predict and control human behaviour', the way of the actor aims at self-understanding, which may render the person *less* predictable and controllable by outside forces.

This book reveals, through the experiences of today's actors, what it is that actors have to teach us about ourselves. Finding our inner identity. Changing ourselves. Realizing and integrating our life experience. Seeing life freshly and with insight into others. Becoming aware of the powers of our mind. Risking and commitment. Learning how to concentrate our lives into the present, and the secrets of presence and charisma. Extending our sense of who we are, and achieving liberation from restricted concepts of what a person is. Getting in touch with our psychic powers, and communicating with others in that realm.

The Book

I first encountered the world of the actor about ten years ago, when I was invited to teach psychology at The Royal Academy of Dramatic Art. The Academy, usually known by its initials, RADA, is one of the world's leading centres for actor training, and numbers among its graduates many of the leading international stage and film actors.

I started with seminars, covering subjects I believed to be relevant to actors. But actors like action. Discussions about the psychology of madness were punctuated by demands to be allowed to 'get up and try it, act it, see how it feels'. I loved it. Acting workshops followed, then acting projects based on the personal experiences of the actors, then devised stage productions, and eventually I was writing and directing my own plays.

All of this was very far from the original intention: that I should offer psychology to the actors. For I soon realised that actors *are* intuitive, creative psychologists.

I do not believe that psychology, the science which sets out to understand people, should take place only in laboratories and mental health clinics. Psychologists should be wherever human nature can be explored. And being with actors in workshops, tutorials, master classes, counselling sessions, interviews, rehearsals and performances has taught me about a way of self-understanding that is both new and perennial. Of course, psychology is relevant to the way of the actor. But this book is not about how psychology would 'understand' acting. Rather, it is an exploration of how actors understand human nature.

My research and writing concerns shamanism, and other traditional paths to personal knowledge. It did not take long for me to realize that the actor is a living example of the approach of the shaman. Not every actor, of course. Some would find such a notion preposterous and pretentious. But most actors I have worked with have welcomed this framework. It helps them to understand what it is that they know and do. And researching the shamanic background of the actor made clear what it is that actors do for *us*.

The inspiration and background for this book is my work with hundreds of actors, over the years, at the Royal Academy of Dramatic Art. A selection of my encounters with these actors are described in the chapters that follow. But in choosing to express most of the ideas through the experiences of actors, both to check the validity of the concepts and to ground the book in direct experience, I was very fortunate to have the time, support and advice of four remarkable actors: Glenda Jackson, Charlton Heston, Liv Ullmann and Antony Sher. I recorded interviews with each of them, and their ideas are incorporated throughout *The Way of the Actor*. And when these actors are quoted without reference to the bibliography, then the quote is taken directly from the transcript of my taped interviews. Talking with each of them confirmed my belief that the way of the actor is a path to personal knowledge and power. For not only are they remarkable actors, they are also stimulating, challenging, and inspiring people.

But the common conception of actors is the opposite. And

before exploring the actor's way of knowledge, we need to consider how the actor's tradition of knowledge was lost and to deal with three misleading subjects of debate about actors: what techniques do they use, is it a creative or interpretive art and are not actors neurotic and insecure people seeking approval and applause? These questions contribute to confused and derogatory stereotypes of actors. They need to be considered because they are obstacles to our understanding of the way of the actor.

William Hurt, talking about his Academy Award winning performance in the film *Kiss of the Spider Woman*, described his work as that of a 'psychic explorer'. Which captures perfectly the theme of the second part of this book: the way of the actor as a path to personal knowledge and power.

PART ONE

ACTORS

CHAPTER 1

The Lost Tradition

WHEN MERYL STREEP flew into London to promote the film *Kramer vs Kramer*, the media went crazy. For three days solid, journalists jammed the corridors outside her hotel room, being admitted one by one to the inner sanctum for interviews. One journalist, perhaps kept waiting in the corridor too long, is contemptuous of such spectacular press attention, 'In the London hotel they came and went, journalists from Italy, Holland, Belgium, Spain, Germany, Scandinavia and South Africa. They came to hear a young woman, aged 33, whose job it is to pretend to be other people talk about herself.'[1]

Presumably the media circus would have been forgiveable had the celebrity been a politician. Or even a scientist. After all, these people are concerned with important matters. But an actress? A person whose job it is to 'pretend to be other people'? Surely adulation of someone so frivolous is childish and shameful.

On the other hand, another writer, after interviewing Al Pacino, admitted, 'Of course, we expect too much of our actors. We interview them, even put them on covers of magazines, and repeat their words as if they were God-given on tablets of stone, but their craft is one which does not admit of rational analysis. . . .'[2]

But what really defies rational analysis is our confused attitude towards actors. We admire them and detest them. We deify them and sneer at them. We watch in our millions when they appear on television interview shows, but then we require them to talk about the most trivial aspects of their lives. And while a few actors are rewarded with knighthoods, others are served up for breakfast as titbits of notoriety beneath the cheap headlines of the popular press. Even more puzzling, these contrasting treatments are sometimes directed at one and the same actor. Almost all well-known film and television actors have suffered adulation and assassination in the columns of the press. And even in England, where stage actors are accorded a degree of respectability, Ian McKellan has protested at the popular assumption that the world of the actor is all about ' . . .dressing up, booming voices, and shrieking exhibitionism'.[3]

Why are we so confused? Why do we have such a schizophrenic view of the actor? There cannot be many professions which provoke reactions ranging right across the spectrum from star worship to contempt.

Discovering the reasons for this requires a journey back in time to the source of the actor's power.

A Lost Purpose

'It does seem sometimes that acting is hardly the occupation for an adult. False noses, lots of make-up and gum on my face. I can't stand it any more.'[4] In 1970, on the English National Theatre's first visit to the United States, Laurence Olivier surprised the American press with this statement, shocking from someone so widely identified as being at the pinnacle of the acting profession. Ashamed of his life as an actor, Olivier's views were nevertheless tempered by a strange obsession with the work, 'I hope I'll never do another West End play . . . But without it I would die, I suppose.'

Stripped of understanding, purpose and significance, the work of the actor can seem facile and rather silly. Actors continue to 'do it', and we continue to 'watch it', and we all get something out of it. But we seem to have forgotten exactly what it is all for.

Even actors wonder why they do it.

Richard Burton, at various times during the 1970s, distanced himself from his own work. 'I am totally alienated from the craft that I employ so superficially and successfully', he grumbled. And then, more vehemently, 'It seems to me the most ludicrous, undignified job in the world to sit down and learn tedious lines written by some tedious man.' And finally, echoing Olivier's lament, 'Acting is somehow shameful for a man to do. It isn't natural to put on make-up and wear costumes on stage and say someone else's lines. So you drink to overcome the shame.' Yet, like Olivier, Burton also confessed his deep attraction to the work, '. . . It's very difficult to know exactly what the actor does. He's a very odd being and I watch him with fascination.'[5]

Feeling 'silly'. Doing something 'shameful'. These are sentiments running through the comments of many actors. For example, Gene Hackman was 'looping', re-recording his dialogue in scenes from a film called *Eureka*. 'I found myself in the looping room all by myself', he says, '. . . and I see my image go up – this is a sequence where I discover gold in Canada. And I'm yelling and jumping up and down, laughing and screaming and hollering. So, I'm fifty-two years old and I'm jumping up and down like a clown. What a way to make a living!' But like the others Hackman adds, 'It does seem silly at times, but I do love the acting part of it.'[6]

Perhaps the most extreme statements about the worth of the actor have come from Marlon Brando. It is widely known that at times Brando has been alienated from the world of the actor, denigrating it as 'A bum's life in that it leads to perfect self-indulgence. You get paid for doing nothing, and it all adds up to nothing.'[7] But then later he admitted, 'I've always tried to run acting down . . . I don't know why. It's not a bad thing to do in life at all. . . .'[8]

These actors find their work fun, fascinating, even addictive. Yet they also feel that their work is sometimes shameful and silly. It seems as if some actors share the confused view expressed by the media: the simultaneous delight and denigration of acting.

Helen Mirren has been interviewed frequently during her lively and widely admired career. Her reflections on the attention she has received tackle 'silliness' head-on. 'I always find it so curious that people want to talk to actors', she says. 'You don't have the media interviewing engineers with the same regularity. And it's no longer the glamour aspect really. It's something to do with it being such a silly thing to do.'[9]

This observation is important. It turns neatly on its head the assumption that actors ought to be vaguely ashamed of their 'silly' way of earning a living. Or that journalists should feel silly waiting in line to interview such frivolous subjects as 'star actors'. What Helen Mirren is suggesting is that it is the very 'silliness' of the actor's work which so fascinates us. The pretending to be other people, the costumes and make-up, the 'jumping up and down like a clown'. And when the 'silliness factor' is investigated closely, it proves to be an important step on the way to understanding the actor's tradition of knowledge.

Because people who 'act silly' are outsiders.

Outsiders

When Charlton Heston directed and starred in a recent production of *The Caine Mutiny Court Martial*, his arrival in London's West End caused a traffic jam, 'He was surrounded on a pedestrian island in the middle of Shaftesbury Avenue by microphones and flashing camera bulbs. He stood tall, head and shoulders erect above the jostling throng of his admirers'. Eventually, Heston managed to reach the setting for his press conference, 'His current popularity can be gauged by the fantastic turn-out of press, photographers, radio, TV and other members of the media who assembled to pay homage at his London press conference held in the bar of the Queen's Theatre.'[10]

Charlton Heston has coped with public attention for many years. But he told me about a very different side of the actor's life. One of Heston's first professional engagements was as leading man in a small-town theatre in Pennsylvania Dutch country, an area of conservative farmers. When Heston arrived, the Director sent for him to have a quiet chat and explained that, 'The local townspeople like the theatre, they like to come to it, and they don't want you mingling with their children or their wives. There's a street in the town that marks the spot beyond which the company is not allowed to go. If that upsets you, you'd better tell me now.'

Heston had been made, literally and figuratively, an outsider. And while this conservative community is an extreme example, it is nevertheless illustrative of a common attitude towards actors. Charlton Heston accepted the restrictions then, and has accepted them ever since. For even though he has long been one of the biggest 'star' names in the acting world, with personal access to powerful and privileged circles in politics, business and royalty, he is still by virtue of being an actor, an outsider. 'Actors are still socially suspect,' he explains. 'As far as I know, to this day an actor cannot register at the Ritz in Madrid, which is one of the great hotels in the world. Directors, yes. Writers, yes. Perfectly respectable. But actors, known or unknown . . . no.'

Heston emphasizes that, more crucially, actors are discriminated against in the conduct of their day-to-day affairs. In America, actors find it difficult to get telephones installed in their homes, 'If the telephone companies know that the applicant is an actor, they will resist giving him one, even though the telephone is a crucially important tool for a freelance actor. But because they are regarded as fiscally unreliable and emotionally unstable, actors find it hard to get a telephone.' This discrimination is so firmly established that Charlton Heston raised the issue with the telephone companies during his term of office as President of the Screen Actors' Guild. It is still unresolved.

So what is it about actors that leads society to resist giving them telephones, refuse them rooms in the best hotels and to isolate them on one side of town? Why do we treat them as outsiders?

With a mischievous twinkle, Heston puts his finger on the stereotypes which fuel suspicion of actors, 'Actors – they'll seduce your daughter and possibly your wife. And what's more they don't pay their bills, everybody knows that. And they don't wash very often, and they swear terribly in public. They scratch their balls, and they drink a great deal.' We both laughed at this litany of decadence. Indeed there are actors who *do* commit these sins, but what makes it so funny is that it is such an accurate summary of the popular prejudice against actors.

Of course, acting *is* an insecure profession in that steady employment cannot be guaranteed. So there may be some justification in society's jaundiced view of the actor as a reliable payer of bills. But where do the other defamatory notions come from: the image of actors as unwashed, lecherous, uncouth, swearing inebriates?

Heston circles closer to the source of these stereotypes,

'People tend to regard acting with some scepticism as a serious undertaking, because what do actors do? They pretend to be other people. They are not considered to be trustworthy and straightforward because they can persuasively become people that they are not. And we don't like people who can fool us.' Even worse, 'Anyone who can become another person must be lacking a proper "self"; there can't be much of him there.'

Untrustworthy. Dishonest. Lacking a proper self. These are strong indictments – much more damning than the view that actors are merely 'silly'. And the evidence shows that actors in western cultures have been considered in such terms for a very long time.

In 1895 Henry Irving became the first actor to receive a knighthood from a British monarch. In the same year George Bernard Shaw wrote that, 'Numbers of respectable English people still regard a visit to the theatre as a sin', even though many of the privileged had now 'become accustomed to meeting even rank-and-file actors and actresses in society where thirty years ago they would have as soon expected to meet an acrobat. . . .'[11]

Actors were still suspect, but were apparently making some inroads into respectability. For the first half of the twentieth century, until John Osborne's *Look Back in Anger* and the rise of 'working class movies' opened the door to a wide variety of aspiring actors, English stage acting became an almost respectable occupation for the middle-classes.

But we need to go much further back in time to glimpse the beginnings of official discrimination against actors. The year 1372 saw an Act of Parliament passed which designated as 'Roges, Vagabondes and Sturdye Beggars all Fencers, Bearewardes and Common players in Enterludes and Minstrels'.[12] Anticipating Charlton Heston's summary of stereotypes by 600 years, the Act went on to categorize all the activities of actors as 'lewd' and liable to punishment.

And half a century later an anonymous author published a staggering catalogue of the attributes of the professional actor, 'Players are discredited in the very subject of their profession, which is only scratching the itching humours of scabbed minds with pleasing content and profane jests; and how can he be well

reputed that employs all his time in vanity and lies, counter-
feiting and practising nothing else. . . .'13

This is uncompromising stuff. The outlawing of actors was
clearly well established early on. But why all this opposition,
even to the point of government laws being passed against
actors. And why were they considered to be 'lewd sinners' –
moral and spiritual degenerates?

The answers to these questions reveal the original power of
the actor's tradition. And we can see why, even after centuries
of official 'bad press', we are still fascinated not only by the
work of actors, but also by actors themselves. For, if we go back
in time a further 600 years, before the advent of Christianity in
the west, actors were not treated as outlaws. They were not
even, as today, thought of as 'frivolous but interesting'.

Actors were considered to be sacred.

Sacred Actors

'A spasm of shivering works through the diviner, then another,
and his head begins to shake from side to side. The head
movements continue with increasing velocity until it seems as if
no human vertebrae could stand the strain . . . a strangled sob
bursts forth from him – the first articulation of the god speaking
through his chosen medium. With jerky, strangled utterance,
the diviner's voice serves as the mouthpiece of the deity.'14

This account from South India is like an inspired improvisation. But there is something extra. It is beyond acting. For in
traditional societies, the actor's performance gives access to
secrets, mysteries, visions, and voices from the spirit-world.

All traditional societies had, and in some cases still have,
extraordinary people called 'shamans' or closely associated
practitioners of the sacred called medicine men, sorcerers or
diviners. Shamans are people who have special abilities to
change their states of mind and body, and to ascend to the sky
or descend to the underworld where lie the worlds of spirits and
gods – the agents of perennial truth and knowledge. In our
terms, the shaman's journey is undertaken in the imagination,
although in many traditional societies there is not the sharp
distinction we draw between what is 'real' and what is 'imaginary'.

Anthropologist Weston La Barre, who has made a

comprehensive study of shamans, describes their abilities and functions as '. . . The original artist, dancer, musician, singer, dramatist, intellectual, poet, bard, ambassador, advisor of chiefs and kings, entertainer, actor and clown, curer, stage magician, juggler, jongleur, folksinger, weatherman, artisan, culture hero and trickster-transformer.'[15] In other words, shamans were mystic performers, purveyors of wisdom. Sacred actors.

'Primitive actors' perform for a range of purposes, none of them simple 'entertainment'. They enter extraordinary states of mind in which they are believed to be able to divine future events, preside over sacred festivals, serve as keepers of myths and legends, passed on in public storytelling performances. Some of the 'performances' also take the form of public healing rituals, in which the actor induces trance states within himself which enable him to see the nature and causes of illnesses. He then heals in a manner very like highly intensive drama therapy. The actor in traditional societies fulfils a wide variety of very important functions and central to all these functions – the core of the actor's powers – is his connection with the 'spirit world'. Traditional societies today, as were western societies before the first millenium, are crowded with spirits.[16] These pervasive beings co-exist with the material world and are a manifestation of the forces of life and death. They give identity and form to many phenomena for which we have only general terms because they fall outside the understanding of science: deep psychological needs, spiritual energies, healing powers, archetypal fears, prophetic dreams, forces of nature, and the souls of the dead. The spirits represent wisdom; knowledge from 'the other world'.

These spirits are invisible. Invisible, that is, until the actor incarnates them, is possessed by them, and brings them into the presence of the public through his performance as a human medium. Shamanic actors were believed to be able to *see* spirits and deal directly with them. In some rituals the shaman-actor enters a trance during which his soul is believed to leave his body and ascend to the sky or descend to the underworld. These journeys are often presented very dramatically in front of an audience. The actor 'mimes the ascent or descent to the other world which his soul is at that moment making and the performance is supported by costumes, properties, music, even primitive lighting effects and scene changes. The costumes range from animal suits to stylised representations of the human skeleton, and often display elaborate color symbolism.'[17] Many performances take place in candle and firelight, with conscious use made of the lighting effects thus available. Primitive actors impersonate the forces they experience; they are excellent ventriloquists, and can imitate the cries of birds and animals. They are expert conjurers and can produce powerful stage effects – such as shaking the huts in which they hold their seances as if by an unseen agency, and making footsteps sound around the walls.[18]

The shamanic actor in performance becomes not another person, but another class of being. And the being is not a fictitious character, but a spirit. The spirit, through the actor, gives access to visions, voices, mysteries and deep truths. The actor in performance dips into the timeless ocean of human concerns, and intervenes in the conduct of life by incarnating the spirits and their wisdom. The actors and audience know why they are there. They are witnessing, participating in, a sacred ritual.

So what happened to sacred actors? Religion. A rival religion.

The world of spirits belonged to pre-Christian spirituality and fell outside the jurisdiction of the Christian Church. Spirits were agents of folk religion, attacked by the Church as 'paganism'. And actors, as spirits made manifest in performance, were therefore enemies of the new orthodoxy. In its missionary capacity, the Church had to remove actors from the religious 'stage' in order to convince the heathen populace of Europe that the spiritual forces of life were expressed not by actors but rather through the intercession of ministers of the Church.[19]

The Christian missionary campaign in Europe was quickly allied to the political and military authorities, and repressive measures instituted against actors. Performances were restricted and banned. Actors were declared from the pulpit as outcasts. They were described as being possessed not by 'spirits', but by 'devils and demons'. Actors tumbled from their position as high status 'performing mystics', interpreting the knowledge and power of the spirit world.

Eventually actors were allowed to perform comic characters,

giving rise over the centuries to the Commedia dell' Arte in Italy, and similar traditions all over Europe. And they were permitted to perform in Christian festivals, where they led the largely amateur 'productions' of mystery plays celebrating the life of Christ. Pre-Christian features continued to play a large part in the popular productions, but gradually the work of the actor became re-defined as merely 'entertainment'. While the general public still flocked to see their productions, the establishment increasingly legislated against actors, forcing them further to the fringes of society, classing them as rogues, vagabonds and outsiders.

Because of the work they do actors have retained, throughout the centuries, elements of personal knowledge and power which can be seen in the lives of actors today. But gradually the original significance of the actor was forced 'underground', and became a lost tradition, frivolous entertainment cut off from its source of inspiration.

But not entirely. If we compare the traditional role of actors as spirit mediums with their function today, the spirits can still be discerned incarnating themselves just below our levels of awareness.

The Return of the Spirits

There are eighty thousand Shinto shrines scattered over the islands of Japan. Each village has its own god and assembles several times a year to invoke his favour with dances and plays. 'In the open air before the temple the players form a sacred act, a magic rite, in which they perform mythical tales in which gods and men are linked by fate.'[20]

This ancient tradition is one of the surviving examples of rituals which parallel closely those practised in the west a thousand years ago. Traditional actors in Japan have survived the onslaught of religious, cultural and scientific revolutions. While now largely a tourist attraction, their traditional theatre is still vibrant and alive.

In Japanese Noh theatre, the stylized and more formal extension and development of village traditions, the actors wear masks. The spirits and other supernatural beings appear in the masks. Some eighty masks have been created over the centuries to represent all the characters that populate Noh plays, stock characters who are considered timeless.[21]

Masks, in traditional societies, are surrounded by rituals that reinforce their power. For example, there is a Tibetan mask which is taken out of its shrine once a year and set up overnight in a locked chapel. Two novice monks sit up all night chanting prayers to prevent the spirit of the mask from breaking loose. For miles around the villagers bar their doors at sunset and no one ventures out. Next day the mask is covered over the head of the dancer who is to incarnate the spirit at the centre of a great ceremony. As Keith Johnstone suggests, 'What must it feel like to be that dancer, when the terrifying face becomes his own?'[22]

The gods and spirits of the 'primitive' actors' masks are a way of making tangible what we, in modern western society, leave unsaid, sometimes unrecognized, often not understood: the repressed and hidden forces of life. An anthropologist encapsulated something of this when he described practices in Haiti, 'Haitian voodoo ceremonies are quite clearly theatres, in which problems and conflicts relating to the life situations of the participants are dramatically enacted with great symbolic force . . . Repressed urges and desires, the idiosyncratic as well as the socially conditioned, are given full public reign.'[23]

Of course, actors today rarely use literal masks. More often they use make-up, the source of embarrassment to Olivier and Burton. But the original mask, as we have seen, was an object of great power, because it represented or incarnated the mighty forces of life. Today the entire performance of the actor is the mask, because we see the forces of life through the medium not of spirits, but of people. Contemporary cosmology views the world through the prism of human experience. The world is acted upon from a centre within us. We no longer materialize our hopes, joys, concerns, problems and issues through the 'external' agencies of spirits.

But actors nevertheless still represent, incarnate, fictional beings who, in our dramas, live heightened, dramatized lives. The great forces of life: birth, death, love, conflict are commonly represented by actors in character in films and plays, just as they were and are in traditional societies by actors in masks.

By recent analysis, *Dallas* draws 250 million viewers in more than 80 countries. It has been suggested by Esther Shapiro, creator of *Dynasty*, that the popularity of this show and *Dallas* lies in the fact that they '. . . are essentially fantasies about power, money and sex. Both are about the rich, about people who live beyond the rules. Both contain people with problems that many of our audience have. They can feel comforted that these extraordinary people have the same difficulties in life.'[24]

This makes it sound as if the characters and plots of these programmes reflect everyday human problems, except on a larger scale. But can this aspect alone account for such popularity? Perhaps a little closer to the truth is the suggestion that popular dramas such as *Dallas* and *Dynasty* confront in a non-threatening way the moral structures of contemporary society. If the Ten Commandments are taken as key conflicts in the plot lines, for example, there are many clear parallels. Thou shalt do no murder; thou shalt not steal; thou shalt not commit adultery; thou shalt not covet; thou shalt not bear false witness, and so on: the character 'J.R.' from *Dallas* probably violates every one of these strictures in each episode. But the character is a *safe* personification of the devil. Audiences love to hate him. Simple notions of identifying with dramatic characters do not apply here – very few people would wish to use the character J.R. as a role model. Like the devil in the York Mystery Plays, J.R. is popularly evil. And Larry Hagman's great skill in acting this highly stylized role is to make J.R. appear human and therefore watchable.

These fictional characters occupy an important place in our hearts and minds. They seem to provide an extended family of 'people' with whom we can identify, and who sometimes begin to occupy a place in our lives as important as some of the 'real' people we know. When the character J.R. was shot in the final episode of a *Dallas* series several years ago, the event was reported on national news programmes in many western countries.

It is fashionable in some circles to deride this fascination with the 'lives' of fictional characters. It is considered a symptom of lives devoid of sufficient real human contact, and to be a negative, regrettable aspect of modern, media-dominated life. This seems to me to be moralistic and short-sighted. Rather than decrying our needs like repressed Victorians, trying to believe that we do not really behave as we do, it makes more sense to try to understand exactly what it is we *do* need, and why. What is it that these fictional characters do for us? *Why* are they so popular?

It is easy to dimiss 'popular entertainment' as frivolous, even decadent. But when films like Sylvester Stallone's *Rambo* fill cinemas around the world, to the dismay of many because of the violence depicted in them, then we need to ask searching questions about what these dramas represent for us psychologically. Traditional cultures see the spirits of violence and death manifested by their actors, but they are aware of the significance and power of what they are watching. We pretend that the spirits incarnated by our actors are merely for entertainment, and are then alarmed when people respond to some of them with almost fanatical enthusiasm.

Could it be that they represent the 'spirits', those emanations from our unconscious which are expressed and encountered as 'external beings' in traditional societies through the mediating presence of actors? These fictional characters are not inspired messages from a tradition of knowledge, but they are written, directed and acted to stir deep feelings of recognition within us. Rambo, the characters in *Dallas* and similar television dramas, 'capture' in their personality, appearance and behaviour the problems, hopes, joys and fears of people through stock characters and plots. Like the spirits in traditional societies.

Actors as Spirits

Traditional actors in Bali today believe that when they enter trance states, spiritual beings are able to descend to earth and live through the actor's body for the duration of the performance. People watching the actors see them as spirits. The spiritual beings portrayed by the actors have particular personalities and are like stock characters. The behaviour of the actor-as-spirit corresponds to the expected behaviour of that particular deity.[25] The pantheon of deities comes to be looked upon as a kind of repertoire of dramatic roles. Particular spirits are assigned to individual actors, either on a permanent basis or on the occasion of each ceremony.

In the West we are accustomed to actors playing a wide

variety of roles. But the incarnation of spirits by actors can be seen most clearly and simply in 'personality' movie actors. The earlier years of Hollywood saw personality actors become enormously popular figures: James Cagney, Gary Cooper, Humphrey Bogart, James Dean, Marilyn Monroe, Mae West, Jean Harlow. Today, there are actors like Clint Eastwood and Sylvester Stallone who, regardless of their private personality, always embody a particular screen character. The roles may change, but the audience always knows what sort of character Eastwood or Stallone will portray.

As in traditional Balinese theatre, these actors incarnate a particular, well-known spirit who behaves in a predictable and expected way.

Some actors are trapped by the spirit they represent. Robert Redford, for example, is known more for his screen personality than for the individual roles he plays – though he plays them with great skill. Bruce Dern says of Redford, 'Fine actor though he is, he is probably to be included in a group of internationally famed actors who are not only personality actors but who seem to represent a similar collective spirit.'[25]

Personality actors often attract a tremendous personal following of 'fans', and the significance of these actors is clear from the very word 'fan'. It comes from the Latin *fanaticus*, meaning 'someone inspired to frenzy by devotion to a deity'. The actor-in-performance is still seen, by fans, as incarnating a deity or spirit.[27]

The spirits of traditional societies make manifest, and therefore observable, the forces with which we deal in life. The purpose of transformation of the early actor was to represent these 'spirits' – a dramatic mirror in which the audience could see life reflected. We no longer recognize spirits, but we still have the same inner selves, relations with others, fears, dreams, passions, personal dramas, and issues of life and death which we somehow need to contain in our lives. Perhaps we *do* still need spirits of a kind, manifestations of the forces in and around us.

We see these matters now in secular, psychological rather than spiritual terms, but this does not lessen their significance and impact on our lives. I believe that deep down we still recognize the importance of the actor's representation of characters. Our endless fascination with actors betrays the ritual function of their art and the hold it retains over us, still surviving under the candy-floss disguise of entertainment.

The way of the actor is still a path to knowledge and power. And that is surely reason enough for the world's press to interview Meryl Streep.

CHAPTER 2

Actors, Not Acting

MARLON BRANDO WAS still asleep when Francis Ford Coppola arrived. The actor had been experimenting with make-up for the character of Don Corleone, the title role in the film *The Godfather*. Coppola had come to discover how the make-up looked on film.

Coppola, and three technicians with 16mm cameras, waited until Brando finally awoke, appeared in a robe, and began talking about approaches to the character of Don Corleone. One of Brando's biographers described the work session.[1] 'Coppola suggested a thin moustache such as his Uncle Louie used to wear. Brando pencilled in the moustache and began blackening his blond hair. He added some dark make-up under the eyes, and stuffed tissue in his cheeks to give himself a jowly look. Gradually he began to take on the aspect of Don Corleone'.

Coppola produced a plate of apples and cheese, and poured a demi-tasse of espresso to serve as props for Brando to use. 'Marlon put on a frayed shirt, a well-worn tie, a faded jacket. He spent two or three minutes adjusting the shirt collar so that it extended outside the jacket. He lit a bent Italian cigar. The transmogrification continued without a word being spoken. The Brando shoulders began to sag, the belly extended. The face seemed to take on a waxen appearance. He breathed more measuredly, the exhalations coming as enormous sighs.'

At that point the telephone rang, 'Don Corleone lifted the instrument and placed it slowly to his ear. He listened, nodded slowly and patiently, then replaced the telephone without a word. Whoever was on the other end heard nothing but the

heavy breathing of an aged man.' Marlon Brando had transformed into Don Corleone.

This account of Brando's early preparation of the role is
remarkable. It is light years away from the stereotype of the
Method Actor, playing every role 'as himself'. In fact, the
description of Brando building himself into the role through the
make-up sounds very like the approach to acting of Laurence
Olivier, who says, 'It's primarily a visual thing with me. A man
I see . . . might give me an idea; as often as not it's my make-up
which determines how a certain character should be played.'[2]

No doubt Brando has worked himself emotionally and intuitively into the role of Don Corleone prior to the experimental
make-up session. But Olivier also draws on the intuitive. And
while he realizes that his approach differs in emphasis from that
of Method Actors, he insists that they are not that far apart.
Olivier believes, for example, that it is an over-simplification to
stress how an actor like Brando essentially works from the
inside out. 'Don't believe Marlon', Olivier said, 'Don't tell me
he searches inside himself for everything. He looks out, too.
He's peripheral, just as any character is peripheral. You have
to be.'[3]

An overlap between Brando and Olivier? Common ground
in the way they approach their work? Surely this cannot be
right. We all know that there are distinct techniques of acting,
'Method' and 'English', embodied by Brando and Olivier.
Books on acting have been telling us this for years. Unfortunately, most books on acting bear about as much relation to
what actors actually do as painting-by-numbers does to the
great works of modern art. This is not really the fault of the
authors, some of whom have developed interesting insights into
actor training. But can you imagine a book on 'How to train
your voice to sing opera'? Or 'Twenty easy lessons in ballet
dancing'? Books on acting have placed the emphasis on techniques, rather than the experience of actors with a most
unfortunate result. The impression has been firmly established
that actors use exclusively one or other approach to their work.
Actors do differ, of course, in the detailed way in which they
work, but slightly divergent paths leading to the same destina-
tion are talked about as if they existed on separate planets.

In particular, the differences between 'Method' and

'English' acting have been exaggerated to mythological propor-
tions. It is a myth which needs to be examined because it
effectively camouflages the true way of the actor.

Method Acting

The Method, sometimes caricatured as an 'inside-out'
approach in which the actor bases performances on his own
emotional experiences, and by identifying the role with himself,
was founded in America by Lee Strasberg. While the Method is
increasingly criticized these days as an approach to acting, any
discussion of its value must take account of the astonishing
catalogue of American actors who have trained in Lee Strasberg's Method Studio, or one of his associate's similarly structured training academies. Some of the better known names
include: Marlon Brando, James Dean, Geraldine Page, Shelley
Winters, Eli Wallach, Anne Jackson, Paul Newman, Joanne
Woodward, Karl Malden, Jane Fonda, Anne Bancroft, Caroll
Baker, Dustin Hoffman, Robert de Niro, Faye Dunaway, Al
Pacino and Sally Field. And, of course, Marilyn Monroe.

Since the 1930s, many of the principal doctrines of acting
theory have been derived from the writings and work of Konstantin Stanislavsky; most notably from three works published
after his death – *An Actor Prepares*, *Building a Character* and
Creating a Role.[4]

In 1923, Richard Boleslavsky, an early member of the Mos-
cow Arts went to America and founded the American Lab
Theatre. Among its earliest students were Lee Strasberg and
Stella Adler, who were destined to become architects of the
Method, the Americanized version of Stanislavsky's basic
teaching. Theatre director Charles Marowitz points out that it
was Boleslavsky who developed 'Emotional Memory', the
principal focus of the Method approach.[5] The idea of this
technique is for the actor to decide the emotion appropriate for
a particular part of his role. The actor then attempts to discover
in his 'affective memory' a recollection similar to that particular emotion. Then, by a series of exercises using his memory
and imagination, the actor prepares himself to arouse that
emotion when he needs it in the performance.

Some Method-trained actors feel that this and related techniques help in specific ways. Bruce Dern feels that 'Method

acting enables you to find the things which will relax you, unlock you, and let all of that private emotion come out. It has to do with being able to recall the emotions and sensations of a particular incident, but it takes about five years of total concentration to learn how to do it.' Dern also feels that the Method gives an actor a spontaneity that adds to the performance: 'The two films in which I worked with people who were trained the way I was trained were two of the most spontaneous movies that I've been in – *The King of Marvin Gardens* and *Coming Home*. Those were all Method-trained actors – Jon Voight, Jane Fonda, Jack Nicholson, Ellen Burstyn and myself.'[6]

The basis for developing a character in Method is for the actor to employ his own characteristics, personality and style. In the Method, 'It is *your* vacillation that feeds Hamlet, your ambition that permeates Macbeth.'[7] And Geraldine Page describes the Method as allowing the actor to discover 'less obvious connections between yourself and your character'. She suggests that while an actor automatically and unconsciously brings personal connections to the part, the Method actor, who has acquired skills and a knowledge of what is in his unconscious, can *consciously* bring material from within the self. 'You can then add more of your own colours to the tapestry of your character.'[8]

There are many books detailing versions of the Method, and also many theatre writers who criticize it as an approach – mostly, on the grounds that it leads to actors playing 'only themselves' or that it is so lacking in expressive technique that method actors simply 'emote' on stage, and need the intimacy of a film camera to be able to project anything.

The criticisms clearly cannot apply to some of the finer exponents of Method acting. Dustin Hoffman, for example, has played a very wide variety of roles since his film debut in *The Graduate*, including Ratso in *Midnight Cowboy*, the 'woman' Dorothy in *Tootsie*, and recently Willie Loman in the Broadway production of *Death of a Salesman*. But when one considers Hoffman's acting closely, it is clear that he does not conform to the stereotyped image of the classic Method: brooding and introverted performances based on the troubled areas of the actor's internal emotional life. Perhaps Hoffman uses the Method, rather than allowing it to use him.

Liv Ullmann is renowned for film and stage performances that are unparalleled for 'reality, honesty, truth'. In particular, the roles she has created with Swedish director Ingmar Bergman reveal clear windows to the characters' innermost emotions. She sounds like the ideal Method actor.

But Liv Ullmann scorns the Method, 'I think it's bullshit. I don't believe in it. I've worked with some Method actors, and they're very difficult to work with because you never know who's coming in on the stage. Every day somebody new comes in.' She also objects to the sometimes distracting effects of the Method preparations for a scene, 'They have been behind stage concentrating so much that they're spaced out when they come in. Or else they've suddenly got themselves into "It was such a cold day outside", so instead of doing what should happen between the two people, they are doing a big thing about a person who is getting warm after having been out during a cold day. And that's very interesting, you know, but it's not what the play is about.'[9]

This is probably more a criticism of *bad* Method acting than the Method itself. Good actors are aware of the pitfalls of an approach charged with immediate and personal emotion. Simon Callow was trained at London's *Drama Centre*, which uses Stanislavsky techniques akin to American Method. He feels that experience led to a fine tuning of his technique, 'At the beginning you spend hours working up to the state required of you for a part. Eventually you discover that it is neither necessary nor valuable. It leads, in fact, to bad acting, because the "state" up to which you work yourself then permeates every scene you play, leading to generalization. The important point is not to feel a lot, but to feel accurately.'[10]

But, significantly, Liv Ullmann feels that the most effective actors use an organically developed approach which suits them, not ones that subscribe rigidly to one school or another. She played opposite Sam Waterston on Broadway in *A Doll's House*. She felt that his supposedly Method approach to work would be as at home in Europe as in America, 'Most good actors actually do the same . . . Sam Waterston, for example, could just as well be acting in Norway. And Marlon Brando is a Method actor, but he is also a great actor. I don't think any method will ruin a good actor, because a good actor will always use what he needs. It's for the bad actors that the Method can be dangerous, because they don't know what to take and what to leave.'[11]

In other words, the Method can help a good actor and hinder a less talented one. It can be a powerful technique in talented hands, but is extremely limiting when used by actors who are seduced by its invitations to emotional self-indulgence.

English Acting

The Method approach is often contrasted with the 'English' 'outside-in' approach, in which the actors are believed to create illusion by acquiring sophisticated technical skills in voice, movement, costume and make-up. And the list of 'graduates' is equally glittering: Laurence Olivier, Alec Guinness, Paul Scofield, Glenda Jackson, Jeremy Irons, Ian McKellan, Ben Kingsley, Alan Bates, Peter O'Toole, Vanessa Redgrave, Albert Finney, John Gielgud, John Mills, Maggie Smith, Ralph Richardson.

But what is the relationship between 'English' and 'Method'? How do they really differ? Bruce Dern subscribes to the stereotyped image of 'English' trained actors. He claims that the elements distinguishing between the Method and the English approach are '. . .reality, honesty, truth. You're saying real things to each other. You may be portraying another person, but the lines you're speaking have meaning for yourself as well. There are a lot of actors who just act *per se*. English actors, for instance, are trained in a totally different way: they work on a character from the outside-in, and it's much more mechanical.'[12]

The 'English' style of acting is often caricatured as working from the 'outside-in'. Laurence Olivier ostensibly works in such a fashion, 'I usually collect a lot of details, a lot of characteristics, and find a creature swimming about somewhere in the middle of them.' Olivier finds a physical model that inspires and guides his creation of a character, 'I ask myself, "Who do I know like that?". It might be me, but it might be a dozen other people as well.'[13]

While it is probably true that most English acting schools train actors to a sophisticated degree in stage skills of movement, voice and so on, it is a caricature to believe that this is all or most of what they do. At the Royal Academy of Dramatic Art, for example, intensive technical training is complemented by a range of challenging workshops aimed at connecting the actor with his own emotional resources. Charles Marowitz, the American theatre director who founded the Open Space Theatre in London which he ran successfully for many years, knows both 'American' and 'English' acting well. Working with actors in London convinces him it is time to ' . . .explode the fallacy that the British actor is some kind of living advertisement for speech-training and physical deportment with none of the resources usually associated with the Stanislavsky-trained actor.'[14]

Perhaps the best-documented preparation of a major role is that of Antony Sher's *Richard III*. This production, mounted by the Royal Shakespeare Company in 1984/85 was especially notable for Sher's playing of Richard, compared favourably with Oliver's legendary performance of decades ago Sher kept a diary of the rehearsals, ideas, setbacks, dreams and practicalities involved in his preparation of the role.[15] It established a vivid picture of an actor working simultaneously from the 'inside-out' and the 'outside-in'. He began his preparation for the role by seeking images of Richard's appearance. Sher sketched pieces of landscape, animals, murderers, finally himself. The same pattern was followed in creating the character of Richard: research into historical personages and famous criminals, led finally to Sher's own psyche. His triumphant performance of Richard III was informed by a considerable amount of research, but acted powerfully from within his own physical and emotional being. And when I talked with Sher about his performance, he said that Richard was based on himself, his own psychological and physical presence, but was nevertheless also a 'character' performance.

When we look at the experiences of actors, it perhaps becomes clear that there is no uniform, homogenous 'English' approach to a role. Many actors tend to approach different parts in different ways. Antony Sher told me that his approach 'depends on the requirements of the part. I think that's what's exciting about acting. For example, the Peter Barnes play I did – *Red Noses* – at the Barbican Theatre. I wanted to use myself as a basis for the role. So in order to tap one's own imaginings and feelings, it was important not to characterize the part too much.'

Is this 'English' acting? Or a combination of English and Method-style inner searching? Or something else? Maybe African acting? Clearly, Antony Sher cannot be dumped into a bin labelled 'English', nor a bin labelled 'Method'. His approach to acting is much too complex, flexible and interesting for such stereotyped categories.

It seems very difficult to identity with any precision what, exactly, 'English' acting is because, in contrast with 'Method', it is not a consciously constructed system. Instead, we are left with the conclusion that non-Method actors are just that. They do not adhere to *any* rigid technique. Roger Rees, for example, has at a young age already established a distinguished record with the Royal Shakespeare Company. He says that his approach to each role is different and follows no set pattern, 'I just let each part hit me. Some seem to demand that I do a lot of work beforehand. Others seem to instruct me that I must keep my options open until as late as possible. It's a process, different each time . . . it's not a system.'[16]

There are, of course, actors who are English by birth or residence. But there is considerable doubt as to the existence of 'English' acting. And since Marlon Brando, Dustin Hoffman and Sam Waterston do not seem to be classically 'Method' actors, where does this leave us?

Actors, Not Acting

Charlton Heston assured me that when he was a drama student at Northwestern University, he knew what acting was all about. But as he grew older and more experienced, he became aware of all the potential difficulties in performance. 'In a certain sense my whole career has been a process of finding out more and more about which I know less and less. I first played Macbeth when I was 19 and I was far more sure about it then than I am now. I've played it four or five times, and each time has become more and more complex. Each production has revealed to me aspects I hadn't seen before.'

Fixed ideas about technique became less and less appropriate. 'As those experiences scar and bruise you, you retreat to a position of simple dogmatism: acting is what works. It doesn't matter whether you use a sense memory of the days your son was almost hit by a car to give you the feeling of sudden horror and danger, or whether you use some more immediate technique. It's all too easy to clutter it up with a lot of bullshit.'

Glenda Jackson agrees. She feels that over-awareness of the way one works, whether it is 'Method', 'English' or anything else, can lead to a situation in which, 'A technique for discovery can take the place of discovery. At one time improvisation in rehearsal was a help, but then actors began to be just very good at improvisation – and it didn't necessarily connect with the performance. The truth is that anything and everything is grist to an actor's mill, and it doesn't matter where it comes from or how it's discovered. If it's valid and it's truthful then you use it.'

While recognizing the value and insights of Method acting, the evidence seems to suggest that many effective actors develop techniques and approaches which suit them as individuals. As Glenda Jackson says, 'There are as many approaches to acting as there are actors.'

If most actors develop their own individual approaches, then it makes little sense to pursue the way of the actor through theories of acting. Theories have their uses and can help in training actors, but in considering the experience of the actor there seems no point in separating *acting* from the actor. Sam Waterston says, 'You can't really talk about acting because acting is a person. There is no such thing, maybe, as acting: there are only actors, and they all devise techniques that they hope will make it easier for them to get God's gift out.'[17]

CHAPTER 3

But Is It Art?

Is ACTING AN interpretive or a creative art? Is it an art or a craft? Do you care?

I must confess that I did not until I began to write this book. I soon discovered that plenty of people *do* care greatly, and the artistic status of the actor is debated by actors and others as though it were crucial to the life of the profession. And in some ways it is relevant to a serious consideration of the way of the actor, because many people assume that 'There isn't much to acting'. Doubts about the creative and artistic status of actors are widespread. 'After all,' I was told by someone dismayed that I should be writing a *whole* book just about actors, 'Anyone can learn a few lines and repeat them in front of others – we all did it at school.'

Of course, acting can be discussed at almost any level. John Hurt, on being asked about his performances in such films as *Midnight Express*, *The Elephant Man* and *1984* undercuts much of the talk with a delightful quote, '. . .Acting is simpler than some make it out to be. Dame Edith Evans was asked how she went about giving a performance and she said, "I pretend, dear boy, I pretend".'[1] At its most basic acting *is* just pretending and it is refreshing to be reminded of this sublime simplicity at its heart.

At the other extreme, theatre directors such as Antonin Artaud and Jerzy Grotowski have claimed the work of the actor as a ritual testing of the soul, a stretching of the limits of human communication.[2] It is an ambitious, esoteric deeply philosophical view of the actor, which has inspired experimental theatre from creative risk-takers like Peter Brook, who asks the theatrical equivalent of a Zen Koan: what is the true source of spontaneity and sincerity?[3]

Both views of the actor – basic and esoteric – are valid. The work of the actor is at one and the same time nothing and everything. There are simple and practical things, as there are philosophical, even spiritual things, to be said about the actor. But in exploring the way of the actor, it seems to me important to ground the ideas in the *experiences of actors*.

So what do actors say about their art? Or craft. Or whatever.

Writers and Directors

'. . . You are dealing with someone else's creation', says Estelle Parsons. '. . .You may create a character out of somebody else's created play, but I am very aware that if I tried to write a play, a novel, or music, I would have to have something to say, and as an actor, I only have to agree or disagree.'

The writer is of course, by definition, an essential part of scripted theatre. When acting is talked of as an 'interpretive art', it is usually in relation to the writer who is the 'creative artist'. So actors are thought to be merely expressing the ideas of the writer. Estelle Parsons again, 'I am only putting forward what the playwright has to say.'[4]

But this is sometimes more difficult than it sounds. For the number of 'creative artist' writers who are truly creative is rather small. Marlon Brando underlines the scarcity of good writers as he praises a superb one, 'Tennessee Williams is really an actor's writer. His use of conjunctions, syntax and colour is brilliant and flawless. What's more, his plays have psychological progress. You're building all the time. Most writers write haphazardly. The actor is fighting unjustified words all the time.'[5]

Of course, it is not the writer but the director who has, especially in the past couple of decades, gradually taken control of productions. And films have always been heavily biased towards the vision of the director who edits the performances of the actors in the cutting room. This greatly annoys some actors.

Simon Callow complains that a theatre dominated by directors is a mistake, because, 'A play is not a score, with specific notes which have to be played as they're written, needing one man to coordinate and discipline a group of players.' He emphasizes the actor's contribution in bringing a script to life, 'A play needs to be discovered, *un*covered one might almost say, liberated. Every single actor has a personal responsibility in this matter; every scene, every part needs to be implied from the bare text. This is an active undertaking, not a passive one.'[6]

Bruce Dern agrees, and applies a different connotation to the idea of 'interpretive art' from that suggested by Estelle Parsons. Dern considers that when an actor 'interprets' the writer's script, he is judging and distancing himself from it, 'I'm not interpreting. I'm creating – a life. My feeling is that when it becomes interpretive, you're not really doing it. Then you're doing what the word says, you're "interpreting" what you feel about something, and you're a step removed.'

He describes acting as a creative art because, 'The character of Robert Hyde in *Coming Home* is a creation. He's nothing until he's brought to life by me – or by whoever plays him. So isn't that creation, when something is non-existent and then suddenly it's alive? Moving?'[7] Dern's comments focus on the creation of a role, the building of a believable character.

Liv Ullmann described the process of collaboration with writer/director Ingmar Bergman, in which she was creating a character called Jenny, 'The part I am now playing is written for me. We both feel that I can identify with Jenny. That I can transform Jenny into Liv. Build on my own experience, on that of others – on everything I have heard and seen in thirty-six years. The day Ingmar gives me the manuscript he also gives me the right to feel that henceforward *I* understand the part best. She becomes *my* reality as much as she is Ingmar's.'[8]

This is a clear picture of the way in which the work of collaboration can take place, the director and actor each breathing life into the creation of a fictional character. And it is interesting to hear the comment of film director John Boorman, 'Talking about the characters with actors is a process of discovery. Even if you have invented the characters yourself, how well can you know them? Indeed, on the page there can be little more than indications. Until an actor occupies the role, it really has no existence.'[9]

The problem with this sort of debate – whether acting is an interpretive or creative art – seems to me to be like that other mythical dichotomy, Method versus English acting: it has no foundation. The question of whether acting is *creative* is an aesthetic judgement rather than an intellectual category of analysis. And if creativity refers to the qualities of originality and disciplined imagination in an actor's performance, it is often impossible to judge without knowing how the part was developed from the script, and the respective contributions of the actor and director.

'Acting' is seductive as a subject for discussion because we imagine that we all know what it is. But when the discussion gets under way, it becomes clear that we are dealing with an 'umbrella' word which covers a vast array of activities. To decide whether 'acting' is creative or interpretive art would require a highly sophisticated breakdown of all the various kinds of acting, and the myriad ways in which 'acting' is produced. The result would be so complex and abstract that it would be of academic interest only, too far removed from the world of actors to provide any practical understanding of 'acting'.

I believe that a shift from abstract discussion of 'acting' to a more focused consideration of the *actor* promises greater insight and less hot air.

Actors, not acting.

Stage and Screen

It is conceivable that stage actors could be taken seriously as creative artists. But film actors? A common assumption, fuelled by publicity agents and the popular press, is that they are feather-brained, self-indulgent, over-sexed and neurotic 'pretty faces', who photograph well and can stand on the right floor markers at the right time. There may be actors who fit this description perfectly but they are a tiny minority of the thousands of actors who perform in films every year.

Movies are expensive to make. Enormous profits and, apparently, even more enormous losses are there for the taking. There is little room for mistakes and therefore little room for experimentation. Most films are pitched at the 'lowest common denominator' in an effort to attract the largest audiences possible. And because lots of people see films, and they are often purely escapist entertainment, they are stamped with the label 'popular culture'. As a result critics who think, talk and write about 'high culture' tend to write about theatre, while people who are concerned with 'popular culture' write about films.

But this is absurd. Many theatrical productions in the West End, on Broadway and elsewhere, are 'popular' escapist comedies or musicals. They do not make pretensions to be 'high art'. And although many films are, to put it mildly, less than challenging opportunities for actors, there are nevertheless some every year which feature towering performances from actors. I have seen recent film performances by William Hurt, Jack Nicholson and Geraldine Page which rival, for creative power and energy, anything to be seen on the stage. It should also be remembered that many film actors work also on the stage. The way of the actor is an equally exciting path whether Ben Kingsley is playing *Othello* at Stratford or *Gandhi* on film.

Mind you, film actors have got problems.

'Film is not something that feeds an actor. The people who claim it does are liars,' claims John Malkovich. 'You can say a lot about film – that there are certain stories told in that medium, that more people attend film than theatre or that the finished product may surpass theatre – but I can't believe it when an actor says he gets a lot out of it besides money. I know why I do it and it's not for my growth as an actor.'

John Malkovich is a young American actor who has already completed an impressive body of work on stage, notably with Chicago's *Steppenwolf* theatre company, and recently on Broadway as Biff, son to Dustin Hoffman's Willie Loman in *Death of a Salesman*. He has also achieved recognition for his film work, included *The Killing Fields* and an Academy Award nomination for his performance in *Places in the Heart*. But he is adamantly in favour of theatre work, 'With films you're exhibiting things you've learned, whereas in theatre, you're learning them.' Malkovich clearly does not enjoy the experience of film acting, 'It's real difficult to get used to films and what they entail, and how long they drag on', he complains. 'It's too technical a medium and it's unfair to actors.'

He explains how a film crew will spend four or five hours setting up lights, yet the director would not dream of rehearsing a scene for four or five hours, or shooting for four or five hours once the scene is perfectly lit and the camera movements are marked out. 'The acting part which people watch is given the least attention. I find that infuriating.'

In addition to the subjugation of the actor to the technical demands of the film set, Malkovich feels that the very process of recording an actor's performance on film means that the actor's best work cannot be captured, 'Half-way through the fifth take you suddenly realize you shouldn't be doing the scene that way. It's completely wrong. The thing is you've just spent the whole day doing it the other way and on film scenes have to match. So, unless the director's insane and the producer's dead you're not going to go back and reshoot it the right way.'[10]

Indictments of film acting on technical grounds are common. So it is easy to imagine an actor's frustration in waiting around for hours while a set is lit, and for the time to be spent on, essentially, rehearsals for technicians rather than actors.

Some actors have seen the mastery of technical 'obstacles' as part of the actor's challenge in films. We are aware of the technical skills in stage acting: movement, voice projection and so on. But we are much more ignorant of the technical requirements of film acting. Why are they any less important?

Marlon Brando counters denigration of film acting by pointing to some of the technical requirements, 'No stage actor's training can be considered complete until he has first made a picture', he says. 'It is the toughest form of acting, and anyone who can come through it successfully can call himself an actor for the first time. When you have to portray a shattering emotion while realizing at the back of your mind that if you move your head an inch too much you'll be out of focus and out of frame, that's acting.'[11]

Certainly, the concentration needed for film acting is considerable because the environment of film-making is not supportive. Technical arrangements take a long time to set up, and the actor usually has to be ready to perform when the technicians are ready, rather than the other way around. Also, the technical hubbub of a film studio can militate against the actor's concentration, as Al Pacino says, 'It's not easy, frankly, trying to hold on to your character, while all the circus of film-making is going on around you, and you have to wait hours for your next take. . . .'[12]

Simon Callow, describing the filming of *A Room With a View*, says that while one scene took over eight hours to shoot, the actors spent about ten minutes out of those eight hours in front of camera, popping in and out for short takes. 'The work is concentrated and not usually very sustained', says Callow. 'It is, in fact, not unlike very bad sex: it's all over in 30 seconds, and it's an hour before you can do it again.'

Quite what this makes a stage performance lasting a continuous 2½ hours I am not sure, but it is clear that the requirements of film and stage acting differ considerably. Callow says that, 'On stage you project. In film, it's different: instead of offering yourself, you admit the camera into your aura. This is a little like being X-rayed. . . . You can feel absolutely transparent, as if the camera had passed through your veins and organs. Very exhilerating.'[13]

Bruce Dern, who punctuates his very successful film career with occasional stage work, says that the theatre makes a film actor aware of his physical instrument, especially things like voice projection. But he runs counter to John Malkovich when he says that on stage '. . . an actor just has to go on living the life of his character straight through; he isn't able to cut and say, "Let's do it again, I did that wrong".' In other words, Dern finds film acting gives him *more* freedom, of a kind, to produce the performance he wants.

He also stresses the technical differences in the *style* of acting, 'For a stage actor adjusting to film, it's learning the intricacies of letting the small things stand for themselves. In other words, having the confidence to do something on a small level and let it be seen by the camera. I think you can get away with things in the theatre that you can't in the movies. You can cover up certain deficiencies with a kind of theatricality, you can be flamboyant, you can take off in different directions, you can hide certain faults, and yet you can't do that in film because the camera picks up *everything*.'[14]

Television tends to encourage an easily accessible style of acting. When John Boorman was casting for his feature film *The Emerald Forest*, he scanned videos of all actors playing lead parts in American television drama series. Boorman formed the opinion that they were all acting in the same way, 'They have rugged good looks and they set out to charm and seduce rather than enter a role and act it out . . . They develop tricks for getting through the scenes. What else can they do, the way American TV is made? Many of them are capable of much more, I am sure, unless the bad habits have spoiled them forever.'

Boorman was reminded of Burt Reynolds' acting, when he cast him in the film *Deliverance*. Reynolds had just finished three consecutive television series before beginning work on this movie. Boorman says, 'He was full of tricks. . . . What is treacherous about an actor who is clever but shallow is that he will impress you moment to moment. Only when you put the film together do you see the lack of substance.'[15] Boorman was impressed with Reynolds' acting, but points out how he needed to adjust his style to perform in the film.

Another actor working with Boorman, Jon Voigt, draws an interesting parallel which, for him, forms common ground between stage and film acting. When he was filming *Deliverance*, John Boorman wanted to 'loop' the film, that is, have the actors record their performances in the studio after filming, dubbing onto the film, so that the quality of sound is better. Boorman describes the dilemma, 'When I came to this stage in making *Deliverance*, Jon Voigt was strongly opposed to looping on the grounds that the actor gives something at the time, an immediacy, a spontaneity, a truth, that cannot be recaptured. "But surely," I argued, "on stage you are obliged to reproduce it every night." "No," he contended. "On stage you are giving an original performance each time out." '[16]

For Voigt the search for a fresh and original performance is there in both stage and film, even though the working circumstances diverge so markedly.

Despite the difficulties of film acting, there is at least one aspect of a film set that can make things easier for an actor. Charlton Heston recalled the filming of a scene in which he played the Spanish warlord *El Cid*, 'I rode on a white stud, wearing armour, through the gates of one of the last walled cities in Spain, got off the horse and climbed up a winding flight of one hundred steps to the top of the wall, and turned and looked at 3,000 people shouting, "Cid! Cid! Cid!". You don't have to act that! The exterior circumstances of the place, the people, what you're wearing, the feel of the horse, all these things give such an authenticity to what you are doing that you just go with it, but control it.'

But it has to be admitted that there are many aspects of film work which make it a less enjoyable experience than the stage for many actors. The technical requirements of film means that the actor's performance has to be 'on tap', turned on whenever the set, the lights, the external circumstances are ready. Usually, the actor has to shoot the scenes of a film out of sequence, a practice designed to make the most economical use of sets and shooting time. It means that an actor is robbed of the chance to develop a character and plot his progression through the story. Also, the film actor lacks the stimulus of a live audience, and the sense of occasion which a theatre production engenders.

Charlton Heston, who in addition to his phenomenally successful film career has performed often and with distinction on stage, describes the theatre as 'actors' country', whereas film is a director's medium. On stage, 'You have to do it all yourself six nights a week, twice on Wednesday and Saturday, and you have to go on. . . . In the theatre acting means the whole performance. There are no rolls of film hanging on racks in the cutting room where the director and editor are there to help you. There is nobody but you up there on the stage.'[17]

Very few actors would argue that film work is more creatively satisfying than theatre. But this does not mean that it is less significant, or that there are not film performances as challenging and exciting as theatre performances.

It is also important to remember that a film or television performance may be seen by audiences numbering tens, twenties, even hundreds of millions, worldwide. It seems to me that media which can project an actor's performance into a global theatre deserve serious consideration. Different media set different challenges and problems for actors, but also different audiences and opportunities. And behind it all, there lie many aspects of the actor's work which vary little from one medium to another.

The way of the actor is about actors' experiences on stage *and* screen. Empty arguments about 'art', 'high and low culture' and the like are, I believe, transcended by the power of those experiences, as we explore the actor's path to knowledge.

CHAPTER 4

And Aren't They All Mad?

'DUSTY, DUSTY, DUSTY!'

Dustin Hoffman was scared. Six years old, he stared into the chrome toaster on the kitchen counter at his home, chanting his name, trying to make a connection with the face he saw reflected. Sometimes he failed. He could not identify with his face and it made him afraid.'[1]

Recalling his childhood experiences, Hoffman explained to one of his biographers, that he was six and a half years younger than the Hoffmans' only other child. His older brother, now an economist for the US Treasury, was an excellent student, captain of his high school baseball team, and a member of the American football team. Dustin grew up tiny and skinny, and he wore corrective braces on his teeth for eight years. The family moved to six different houses in the Los Angeles area during Dustin's first twelve years. This combination of factors led Dustin Hoffman to feel second-best at home, unable to match his brother's prowess, and he often found himself being 'the new boy' at Los Angeles schools and neighbourhoods. The result was a loss of contact with his self-identity – and the panic-stricken sessions staring at his reflection in the toaster.[2]

He recalls that as a child, the only way he could gain contact with people was through humour. When his father became angry with him, he remembers trying to defuse the situation by imitating his father's rage. If his father saw the funny side of this, Hoffman was saved.

He also remembers having to cope with taunts from other children about his physical appearance. They told him that his big nose and darting eyes made him look like a rat. So Hoffman adopted the role of a clown at school and with his friends. He says that being laughed at was better than being ignored.[3]

Is this how Dustin Hoffman became an actor? Is his work a legacy of his coping with childhood problems? Certainly a popular stereotype of actors, as people who do not know who they really are, would support such a view.

Of course, most of us have early memories, perhaps long buried, which we find painful. Sometimes they are repressed so that, while they affect our personalities and lives from the unconscious, we are no longer consciously aware of them. Even if we do remember painful incidents it is rare that we talk about them to others, except in the most intimate settings.

Are these experiences any different for the actor? Were Hoffman's insecurities and fears greater, or less, than the average childhood traumas? It is impossible to generalize, of course, and experiences that sound similar can have markedly contrasting effects on different people. Nevertheless, it is interesting to consider a few more examples of actors' early experiences.

Meryl Streep grew up in the leafy and comfortable suburbs of New Jersey on the American East Coast; her father was a pharmaceutical company executive and her mother a graphic artist who did most of her work at home. But Streep had a difficult time because she was rejected by her peers as a physical outsider. 'I didn't have what you'd call a happy childhood', she remembered. 'For one thing, I thought no-one liked me . . . actually, I'd say I had pretty good evidence. The kids would chase me up into a tree and hit my legs with sticks until they bled. Besides that, I was ugly. With my glasses and permanented hair, I looked like a mini-adult. I had the same face I have today, and let me tell you the effect wasn't cute or endearing.'[4] So she turned to acting in school productions. Was she driven to acting in desperation, attempting to find a setting in which she could be accepted by other children?

William Hurt remembers his childhood as one in which a sudden and dramatic change in his home environment plunged him into an alien world. For, when he was ten years old, his mother remarried and the young Hurt found he had Henry Luce III, founder of Time Inc, for a stepfather. The change in his life was tremendous, 'I was a punk kid and suddenly I was in an Eastern establishment-type school. It was a big transition at that time in my life.'[5] He claims that the sense of being a person 'in the wrong place' has dogged him all his life.

These remembered childhoods have in common the experience of being an 'outsider'. Different. Struggling to belong. And while it would be facile to accept them as representative accounts of the actors' childhoods, it is striking that they have such a similar theme.

Other actors depict themselves as 'outsiders' when they were children, but the outsider role was instigated from within, rather than being the result of victimization. Marlon Brando seemed to stay determinedly out of the mainstream and defied authority from an early age. 'Throughout his school life he rebelled against the authority of the teachers and consequently was not the most popular pupil.' Eventually, Marlon's father decided that his son needed some military discipline, and Marlon, aged 15, was sent to the Shattuck Academy in Minnesota. 'I hated it every day I was there.' he said later. 'The authorities annoyed me. I had to show respect to those for whom I had no respect.'[6] Brando was expelled from the Academy a few weeks before graduating.

One of Jack Nicholson's biographers describes similar rebellion. A good student academically, Nicholson 'was decidedly prone to "deportment problems".' He was suspended three times, once for smoking, once for swearing and once for what is nowadays known as vandalism. Another school's basketball team employed tactics which Jack found unacceptable, so he comprehensively sabotaged their new electric scoreboard by way of revenge.'[7]

Of course, these may be extreme examples. There are many actors who would not describe themselves as 'outsiders' in their childhood. But it *is* common to hear actors talking of themselves, in milder terms, as being 'different'. Roger Rees, who appropriately was to achieve fame in the West End and on Broadway as *Nicholas Nickleby*, went to a fairly tough secondary school in Balham, London. There he says that he 'felt myself to be something of an endangered species, since I was very sensitive, and so retreated into the art room.'[8] Rees went on to Camberwell Art School and then the prestigious Slade School of Art in London, where he trained as an artist and lithographer, before eventually going into acting.

We have all felt ourselves to be outsiders at some time, somewhere in our lives. But perhaps this is a more important dimension of the actor's experience. For, in traditional societies, being an outsider was not only a common experience for the future actor. It was obligatory.

The shamanic actors of Siberia had a particularly thriving tradition until early this century.[9] People who became shamanic actors had one thing in common. They invariably had a difficult time growing up; and troubled childhood and adolescence. Sometimes the problems were psychological, caused by the loss of a parent through death or abandonment; or the future mystic would exhibit, as a child or adolescent, strange alienating behaviour, vivid dreams and visions.

Principally, the children destined to become shamanic performers exuded a sense of 'otherness'. Something about them marked them out from the norm, especially when considered from the 'inside', from the perspective of experience. The 'otherness', or outsider status, was considered to be the necessary prerequisite which opened the way for the young person to be connected with the spirit-world.

The primitive actor is viewed as someone who has suffered emotionally in some way in childhood, and that his manner of healing himself is to become a magical actor.[10] It is a way of using and expressing the deep connections with one's inner nature which stem from living as an outsider.

Perhaps some western actors have a similar pattern governing their lives. Acting may be a way of healing. Traditionally this was seen as a positive process, a creative balancing, an harmonious integration of lonely childhood with inner strength, to achieve re-integration with the audience. It was not to be sneered at as a neurosis publicly exhibited. Rather, it was a gift, shared.

We all want our hurts healed. The way of the actor serves this function for some actors, and vicariously for us, too. But today, when we are out of touch with the original inspiration of the way of the actor, we more often view with suspicion the choice of acting as a profession. We think that people who want to follow such a difficult path must be crazy. Literally.

Ego

In the absence of educational support and a massive unemployment rate in the profession, why do people still want to be actors? After all, there are many more obvious and accessible ways of earning a living. In fact, it appears to many to be such a perverse choice of profession that we look for negative, even neurotic reasons for people becoming actors.

Sam Waterston thinks the answer lies in '. . .The basic motivation to become an actor – for me and maybe for others – is partly a love of fantasy worlds, and partly a kind of ego reinforcement that you don't find elsewhere . . . I think the impulse to act alternates between those two things, and one is more respectable, I suppose, than the other.'[11]

I do not know many people who would avoid praise, or even applause when they can get it. But actors are sometimes thought to require 'chronic' support and approval. Sometimes they are depicted as having 'neurotic egos'.

'I have no respect for acting. Acting by and large is an expression of a neurotic impulse. . . . I've never in my life met an actor who was not neurotic. . . . I think the truth is that actors are actors because it gives them sustenance for their narcissism. Acting enables them to experience a false sense of love and attention, the same kind of attention given any exhibition. . . . Acting is a bum's life in that it leads to perfect self-indulgence.'

This stunning dismissal of the actor's sanity is an extreme form of a common stereotype: that actors are neurotics. But the views expressed are not those of an irate film producer, theatre director, or newspaper arts critic. They are Marlon Brando's disillusioned comments, when the frustrations of directing the western *One-Eyed Jacks* led him to despair of acting.

'All egos need a certain amount of pampering', says one of Jane Fonda's biographers. 'Actors' egos demand an extraordinary quantity, and successful actors surround themselves with a small army of sycophants, some on their payroll, some not.' Actors are often accused of harbouring grossly overblown 'egos', by which people generally mean that actors appear egocentric, overly self-conscious and narcissistic. They are self-absorbed, love talking about themselves and are, in a word, obnoxious.

Some of this is exaggeration, principally because the public's perception of actors-as-people is formed by television and the press. When actors are interviewed, they are asked endless question about *themselves*, their opinions, ambitions, hopes and fears, their love lives and sexual proclivities, and in general are asked to reveal as much about themselves as possible. Not surprisingly, viewing or reading these interviews tends to give one the impression that actors are self-regarding, interested only in talking about themselves.

Actors could, of course, refuse to give interviews. Many of them do, but because television and the press do not run lists of people who have refused interviews, the public does not hear about it. And of course media exposure is sometimes important for an actor who wants to publicize the production in which he is appearing.

However, this is not to attempt to explain away the impression people have that actors 'are big egos'. Rather, it appears that the popular use of the term 'ego' does not fully express the behaviour people observe. For in psychological terms, the wish to constantly be the centre of attention suggests just the opposite: an inadequately formed ego.

The 'ego' is a theoretical construct which refers to that aspect of our minds which is at the centre of consciousness, and filters our experience of the world outside and the world inside. But the popular use of the term 'ego' implies that a person is egocentric, or *self-centred*. The idea of the 'self' includes the totality of who we are, including material both from our conscious and unconscious minds.

Actors are themselves the medium of their work, and need to be in touch with their inner worlds in order to be able to create characters from their personal resources. For some people the actor's high degree of 'self'-awareness seems narcissistic. Wrong. Taboo. But I believe that what most people are really seeing in actors is something rather different. And this hinges on another 'depth psychology' concept popularly applied to actors: 'extrovert'.

Introverts and Extroverts

Actors are often assumed to be extroverts, because they professionally 'show off' and respond to an audience. But when we look more closely at the psychological meaning of the popular terms 'introvert' and 'extrovert', a different picture begins to emerge.

In the original theory of C.G. Jung, from which these terms are derived, introvert and extrovert are tendencies of the personality which are present within all of us. No one is purely introvert or extrovert. We are all a mixture of the two and while each person tends towards being one or the other, most of us avoid giving full rein to the expression of either tendency, and stay safely in the middle.[14]

Jungian analyst, June Singer, has described *extreme* introvert/extrovert tendencies so that they can be compared.[15] Looking at this description, most of us would find our personalities fitting a little more into one or the other. But consider these factors from the viewpoint of the actor.

The introverted nature perceives life in symbolic forms, while the extroverted nature is practical and grounded. The introvert is directed primarily to understanding the world around him, while the extrovert is more concerned with finding ways and opportunities for self-expression and communication. In the introvert, the person's own self is the centre of interest and outside events are judged according to how they affect the person. In the extrovert, the outside world is the focus of and largely determines the person's interests. The introvert is concerned with personal development, the extrovert with social involvement. And finally, the introvert places high value on subjective psychological processes, while the extrovert seeks the recognition of others as a predominant value.

These characteristics represent *extreme* examples of introvert/extrovert tendencies. While most of us would see ourselves as a modest mixture of the two, the actor needs to be, at one and the same time, extremely introverted and extremely extroverted. Actors are required to be absorbed in self-understanding and simultaneously, yet paradoxically, oriented towards the outer world, social stimulation, audiences, both to a greater degree than almost any other group of people.

Of course, no one is altogether an extrovert or introvert, and it is doubtful whether anyone could survive living simultaneously at both ends of the spectrum. They would be emotionally torn apart. But whereas most people settle towards one side or other near the middle of the continuum, for the actor it is different. An actor who would normally tend to introversion, towards internal analysis, self-discovery, a rich interior life, is required professionally to behave in an extremely extroverted manner: performing before large groups of people, engaging their attention and approval – a psychologically stretching, and demanding, process.

Similarly, an extrovert-tending actor is faced professionally with the necessity for internal exploration, an attention to self, a finding of inner connections and emotions. It may be that film acting is more slanted towards the introvert's world, with the film camera 'coming in to get the performance' from close up, stealing it away; and that stage acting is more extrovert, more concerned with the need to connect with the viewing public, the 'live' audience. But, again, both of these are extremes. The basic requirement for all actors is to operate in both spheres. And while many of us work in settings which reflect, express or complement our natural psychological tendency, be it extrovert or introvert, the actor has to function effectively in both modes.

This is a prerequisite of self-discovery. And it is a major step on the actor's path to personal knowledge.

There are dangers, of course. Stretching oneself to such extremes of emotional style can, not surprisingly, result in instability. The classic actor Franchot Tone observed, 'Actors are in a unique position. They are both introspective and exhibitionist. You have to be an introvert before you can find within yourself the symbols of extroversion that are required to put the performance across. It is a paradox. . . . Actors suffer from being half narcissistic and half self-critical. . . . It is easy to see why actors are insecure in regard to their own personalities. If you're used to building a personality around the work of someone else, you don't get much time to be yourself.'[16]

A Neurotic Profession

I asked Glenda Jackson for her reactions to the image of actors as neurotics. She protested vehemently, 'As some of our basic material happens to be some of the greatest writing in the world', she said, 'and as great writers invariably and inevitably tackle the perennial and even beautiful problems of "What are we? Why are we?", it seems to me that acting is an entirely reasonable occupation for reasonable minded people. I don't see it as a permanent outpatients' clinic for the emotionally wounded.'

Lynn Redgrave also feels that the stereotyped view of actors as people who are unstable is a myth. The truth is, she says, that to be an effective actor you need to be strong and stable emotionally, but the difficult, uncertain nature of simply getting work in the acting profession can be emotionally undermining. 'It is a very unstable profession because the employment patterns are so peculiar.' she points out. 'You never know when you're going to be constantly employed. Many actors have a very hard time just making a living. So from that point of view it's very up and down. Unless you happen to be in a bit show and get a year's contract, you don't know where you're going to be three months from now.'[17]

While relatively small numbers of actors are elevated to superstardom and superwealth, up to ninety per cent of professional actors are out of work at any one time. And insecurity about employment can affect even the most established actors. Rip Torn tells the story about his performing in *The Father* at Yale. The critics hailed it as one of the finest productions they had seen at the theatre, and on the opening night Rip Torn received a tremendous ovation. Someone said to him, 'This must be one of the happiest moments of your life; you're like a god.' He replied, 'No, all I can think about is that in a couple of months I'll be looking for another job.'[18]

For most of us, our work provides a security blanket, a guarantee of basic protection from the vicissitudes of life. Income for food and shelter, companionship and structure, a sense of being valued. Research on unemployment has demonstrated the damaging psychological effects, and it is no different for actors. Corroboration of this comes from a surprising source: an actor now constantly in demand. Over the past several years Antony Sher has produced a series of acclaimed performances which have elevated him to 'star' status in the British theatre. I asked how this had affected him.

'I think I've found my personality changing over the last year because of a change in my status within the profession', he says. Then he adds thoughtfully, 'But one sees that even more clearly in reverse with actors who are out of work for a long time, as their self-image drops because they have a sense of being rejected all the time. You see them start to change as people.'

Sudden and frequent unemployment is endemic to the actor: a chronic pain tugging at the confidence and security of people who are trying to take creative risks when they *are* working. Any consideration of possible emotional instability in actors must take account of the instability of the profession.

As Marlon Brando observed before he banished all actors to the depths of neurosis, 'If you're successful, acting is about as soft a job as anybody could ever wish for. But if you're unsuccessful, it's worse than having a skin disease.'[19]

When actors *do* go to work, to audition or be interviewed for a role, it is a more stressful experience that most job applications because the work is so indivisible from the person. 'It's insecure because you're selling yourself all the time', explains Laurence Luckinbill. 'Just what is it you're selling? You open your sample case some days and there's nothing in there. And most of the time, you open it and they ain't buying. . . .' Even when actors are successful in auditions, Luckinbill points out, there is some ambivalence about why they have been offered a part, 'Therefore you fix up your case to have all the shiny wares on top, and underneath you put the bugs – your good, true stuff. If they buy the shiny layer, you feel slightly violated. If they don't buy the shiny layer and you can't show them the other stuff, then you don't know what to do. You feel totally rejected. That makes you insecure.'[20]

'Why did it take me twenty-three years while it took Warren Beatty a year and a half?' Bruce Dern, now an established actor, says that the arbitrary nature of success is something that actors often find difficult to accept. Obtaining work and being rewarded for it has much more to do with being in the right place, at the right time, with the right contacts, than it does with talent. 'Everyone talks about the training of an actor, but no one talks about the marketing of one, and it's a fascinating area: why some make it, why some don't: how some make it, how some don't. We all know that people who are extremely talented often don't get the opportunities that people who aren't as talented do get. Why?'[21]

The combination of insecurity of employment and the seemingly random nature of obtaining employment, leave many actors feeling a lack of control over their lives. Despair sets in as months go by with no opportunity to practise their chosen profession. The extremely high risk, freelance nature of the work is something few people could survive happily. That actors *do* survive it at all, and manage to remain in the profession, is a sign of great commitment and emotional stability in the face of debilitating circumstances.

For actors with high standards of professional conduct, the demands and contradictory expectations of even the most respected directors can seem capricious. Liv Ullmann describes a conversation in which the famed film director Ingmar Bergman colluded with an American film director in the attitude to actors as talented but emotional amateurs. The American director interviewed Bergman. Ullmann sat beside them, listening. Bergman began talking about the romantic aura which surrounds certain actors. 'Filled with enthusiasm, he sings the praises of some he has heard about who come late to work', says Ullmann, 'but who have so much charm; who don't learn their lines, but have fantastic charisma; who bring their love life to the studio, but about whom that is understandable, given their sensitive natures. . . . "One cannot make the same demands on them as on other professions," he says.'

Liv Ullmann was furious. She points out that on the film set Bergman demanded absolute professionalism from his actors and would not for one moment permit the behaviour he was blithely condoning in the interview, 'Does he really know how it feels to go to bed at seven o'clock every night in order to be up before sunrise the next morning, learn a role, and be on time for make-up, appear before the camera, and look rested under his scrutiny? Does Ingmar understand why I boil when he speaks about amateurs with understanding, while from his own co-workers he demands total support?'[22]

Reviewers are another potential hazard to the sanity of actors. Bruce Dern says that all he has learned from reviewers is to 'have my heart broken again and again because I take them very personally. . . . Not only are they saying "no" to you personally in bad reviews, but they're also saying "no" to you in the market place, and that's much tougher because it affects your ability to get that next job.'

As an example, Dern describes playing a scene in the movie *Coming Home* in which he picked up a gun and pointed it at a character played by Jane Fonda. He had played a similar scene, with very different motivation, in his previous film *Black Sunday*, and several reviewers who saw both films wrote to the effect 'Oh, there's Dern doing his thing again'. Dern says, 'It wasn't at all the same thing and that scene would not have worked if I hadn't done that. . . . Nobody in this world can tell me that they aren't affected by criticism, negative and positive. I used to save reviews a few years ago, and I'd save the good ones with the bad ones. . . . Now I don't save either. I guess that means I've matured.'[23]

Reviews can be even more destructive at the beginning of a theatre run. In New York this is a matter of commercial viability, because New York audiences tend to allow reviewers to influence them strongly in their judgement of whether a production is or is not worth seeing. But reviews can be disturbing even when they are ecstatic. Antony Sher explains that 'Both good and bad reviews distort one's own image of what one's doing, and you have to try not to be too distracted by them. Reviews usually come when a production has just opened, and you really have to hang on to those decisions that were made in rehearsals. It is hard enough reproducing something night after night, and actors want as little outside interference as possible. Good reviews can throw you off by praising "wonderful moments" in the production, and every time you come to that moment you become overly aware of it, especially if you didn't intend it to happen the way the reviewers saw it.'

Something of the impact of reviews can be sensed if you imagine that on the first day of a new job, an inspection team was sent in to assess your performance, and their reports published in the press. In small ways most of us present our work, from time to time, to other people, but applause or rejection from hundreds of people, and published reviews from others create an intensity of judgement far beyond that of most occupations.

There are, of course, actors who are 'neurotic' and probably would be regardless of their chosen profession. And there are undoubtedly people who choose to be actors because the work allows some 'acting out' of their problems – though just about any profession must have its share of such people. But it is most emphatically true that actors work in a highly stressful, competitive, tough environment. If actors sometimes seem nervous, tense, hyperactive, eager to make a fast impression, those seem to me to be sane responses to an insane working environment.

A Method in the Madness
Marlon Brando recalls that his first meeting with James Dean, 'was at a party. Where he was throwing himself around, acting the madman. So I spoke to him. I took him aside and asked him didn't he know he was sick? That he needed help. . . . He listened to me. He knew he was sick. I gave him the name of an analyst, and he went.'

James Dean idolized Marlon Brando. He admired Brando's powerful presence, and the inner strength he seemed to exude in defying normal social conventions of acceptable behaviour. Often this meant nothing more than behaving outrageously at public gatherings and being rude to influential and 'important' people. But in the 1950s, a period in which young people were beginning to feel a 'youth' identity, the press and media were casting Marlon Brando and James Dean in the same anti-establishment roles. The film studios provided appropriate vehicles for this image: Brando (*The Wild Ones*) and Dean (*Rebel Without a Cause*) were required to embody personally their film personas. But while Dean and Brando represented, for the public, an anti-establishment persona which merged their artistic and personal lives in an apparent seamless identity, Brando controlled it, Dean did not. A director who knew them both noted, 'The major difference between Brando's behavior and Dean's was that Brando's was very often a put-on. If people didn't realize that, Marlon always did. But Dean was self-destructive. Masochistic. It was no act with him – he was sick.'[25]

At first glance this appears to be an encore of the 'neurosis' argument, with Marlon Brando once again opening the discussion. But there is an important difference. The work actors do makes them appear, at times, to be mad.

Lynn Redgrave considers that the view of an actor as 'sick' is a myth that '. . . has come from the people who have fallen apart in a celebrated way. And of course, you're more likely to hear about the actors who have trouble than about your top executive who has fallen apart from the strain. You don't hear about the others because it's only the actors who are well followed by the press.'[26]

But William Hurt, one of today's most acclaimed young actors, blames the Method school of acting for encouraging actors to exhibit their neuroses, 'There is a big difference between acting and acting out. One's crazy and the other isn't. We're not schizophrenics. You are not there to cathart your personal angst in front of somebody else. It's not a therapy session for you.' Hurt believes that the Method school is responsible for debasing the art of acting, '. . . What happens is that we have a system in which underdeveloped actors are allowed to indulge themselves. . . . So irresponsibility is sanctioned.'[27]

Geraldine Page, a distinguished actress and advocate of the Method admits that the Method *misused* is potentially dangerous, 'I have seen actors who were so busy making conscious connections to their characters that they swamped the material; instead of enriching it, they smothered it.' She feels that the Method can seduce people into depths of self-centredness that can miss the point. 'People get so enamoured with these techniques of exploring parts of themselves, that they forget what the object is. As an actor, you must do the fullest, best, most interesting interpretation of the *character*, and not the fullest, most wonderful exposition of your own discoveries of yourself.'[28]

If we look closer at what actors actually do, the picture becomes clearer. Bruce Dern characterizes the self-exposure aspect of acting as being crucially important, '. . . To be succinct and to be publicly private – those are the keys to acting.

You have to be able to look in the mirror in front of a thousand people and tell them exactly what you see: what your fears are, what your hopes are, your joys, your disappointments.'[29]

And the Director of the National Theatre, Sir Peter Hall, corroborates this view. He says that 'Acting is not imitation, it is revelation. Actors in performance reveal their inner selves.'[30]

The extent to which actors who do dig deeply into their own experience can suffer for it is illustrated by returning to Marlon Brando. The film producer Sam Spiegel, who was responsible for Brando's film *On the Waterfront*, says, 'Marlon was a tortured man in the early days and he was great on screen. When he ceased being tortured he had to pseudo-torture himself in order to function.'

Brando has corroborated this theory, 'You have to upset yourself. Unless you do, you cannot act. And there comes a time in one's life when you don't want to do it any more. You know a scene is coming where you'll have to cry and scream and all those things, and it's always bothering you, always eating away at you . . . and you can't just walk through it . . . it would be really disrespectful not to try to do your best.'[31]

In modern theatre and film, original life experiences are transmuted into art by the writer. The actor takes the script and breathes life into it. But sometimes the actor does much more. Marlon Brando travelled through both phases himself when he built his remarkable performance in Bernardo Bertolucci's film *Last Tango in Paris*. One of Brando's biographers[32] describes the preparation, 'When Marlon arrived on the set for the first day's shooting, he wore his usual make-up, which Bertolucci described as three centimetres thick.' The cameraman wiped away most of the make-up while the director explained that he would be filming with only a minimum of lighting. 'Marlon wiped away the remaining traces with his hands. "That okay?" he asked. Director and cameraman agreed.' The first layer of protection had been stripped away. One layer more vulnerable. One degree more naked.

Bertolucci was asking Brando to do something he had never attempted, 'Instead of entering the character, I asked him to superimpose himself on it. I didn't ask him to become anything but himself. It wasn't like doing a film. It was a kind of psychoanalytic adventure.'[33] Brando approved of the Italian director's method of working. 'I treat actors all the same: they are my co-authors', Bertolucci said. 'I'm interested in people, and fiction is my way to create the kind of atmosphere within which you can perform a deep kind of probing.'[34]

The discovery of rich inner material in a performance to be seen by millions was only possible because Brando could live at the extremes of introversion and extroversion. Bertolucci described him as, 'On one side he needs to be loved by all; on another he is a machine incessantly producing charm', in characteristic extrovert fashion. But also, '. . . On still another he has the wisdom of an Indian sage.' This introverted depth of self-knowledge could be expressed, Bertolucci thought, because Brando '. . . is like one of those figures of the painter Francis Bacon who show on their faces all that is happening in their guts – he has the same devastating plasticity.'[35]

Marlon Brando entered into a period of work which involved revealing his innermost self. In one scene, Brando's character Paul begins to disclose his real identity to his girlfriend, Jeanne. The scene was ad libbed by Brando and filmed in one take. He began by describing his past; he had been a boxer, an actor, a bongo player, a revolutionary, a journalist, a resident in Tahiti. All the things Brando himself had been, or had wanted to be. The character talked about his childhood, 'My father was a drunk, a screwed-up bar fighter. My mother was also a drunk. My memories as a kid are of her being arrested. We lived in a small town, a farming community. I used to have to milk a cow every morning and every night, and I liked that. But I remember one time I was all dressed up to take this girl to a basketball game. My father said, "You have to milk the cow", and I said, "Would you please milk it for me?" He said, "No, get your ass out of there." I was in a hurry, and I didn't have time to change my shoes, and I had cowshit all over my shoes. Later on, it smelled in the car. I can't remember many good things.'[36] One of Brando's biographers, after reporting the above scene, points out that much of this monologue was based on Brando's own experience.

The ten weeks of filming for *Last Tango in Paris* required Marlon Brando to draw from himself memories and emotions which had been forgotten, rejected, even repressed. And before each scene, Bertolucci waited until Brando had connected with his own experience. Then the actor nodded to the director that he was ready to begin.

When the filming was over, Brando said to Bertolucci, 'Never again will I make a film like this one. For the first time, I have felt a violation of my innermost self.'[37]

The sort of emotional pressure Brando experienced is expressed clearly by the British actor Simon Callow, 'Acting promotes such insecurity and uncertainty that one can easily lose one's bearings altogether. It's so hard to be sure because one is inside oneself. One is one's own instrument, and inside the complex maze of one's own personality, one can go sadly astray.' In playing a highly charged, emotional role in the play *Mary Barnes*, he says, 'It was necessary to protect oneself against what one went through with complete commitment every night. The more experience one has, the more one learns to husband energy, to use exactly as much as is needed and no more and above all, to use it on the stage and nowhere else.'[38]

There is probably a cut off point for all actors who dip appreciably into their own emotional reservoir in preparing a role. If the character is wracked with strong emotion, it is difficult to give a truthful performance without suffering some of the backlash.

Estelle Parsons indicates how different this highly emotional state can be from our natural, daily quotient, 'I'm never involved in a role after the moment is over. I don't think you could be really. It's not a pleasant experience to be very deeply, emotionally involved; it goes against the reflexes of the human instrument. . . . And as an actress, it's tiring and painful to do, so you really don't want to continue it for any longer than you have to.'[39]

Rip Torn puts it more directly, when asked his view concerning the fact that actors are often seen as being unstable, 'Adults are supposed to be controlled; they're supposed to repress their emotions: that's our Puritanical background. But an actor must go through the emotions in a night that some people only go through two or three times in their life – at weddings, funerals, and by the side of death beds.'[40]

So are actors mad?

Perry describes schizophrenia as follows, 'Because of the

activation of the unconscious and a collapse of the ego, consciousness is overwhelmed by the deepest levels of the psyche, and the individual finds himself living in a psychic modality quite different from his surroundings.'[41] But the actor purposely enters the 'deepest levels of the psyche', and encourages past experiences and emotions into consciousness for performance. Actors therefore need a strong ego to withstand this sort of material, and to maintain their equilibrium.

Psychic material which most of us would not care to recall, let alone confront and express in public performance, is the material from which actors fashion their characters. Whether it is done in a conscious way as in Method acting, or less directly in other approaches, it is a confrontation with parts of the self that we might consider 'problems'.

Interestingly, Brando, in his denunciation of acting as a neurotic activity, added a caveat, '. . . Not that it's bad to be neurotic . . . the fact is the actor is released from the confinement of neurotic inhibitions by being, so to speak, the part he *plays*.'[42]

But it is a matter of what we call 'neurotic'. Laurence Olivier, for example, values madness in his work, 'It is one of his privately expressed theories that you have to be "a little mad" to touch certain histrionic heights.' Further Olivier admits that he might have really gone mad if he had not become an actor and so found an outlet for his emotional energies.[43]

Of course, madness is something everyone fears. The thought of getting lost in repressed emotional experiences, and losing control over one's own psychological processes is a chilling prospect. And since one person out of every ten is, at some time in their life, under treatment for psychiatric difficulties, the danger seems too close for comfort. And yet if insanity is classed as being overwhelmed by inner anxieties, memories and images from our past, bizarre perceptual experiences, most of us experience states of mind that could be classified as 'insane'. But they happen in private, or in dreams, or in fantasy life, or under sanctioned conditions both legal and illegal (such as drink and drugs).

Keith Johnstone has suggested that for most of us sanity is a pretence, a way we *learn* to behave because we do not want to be rejected by other people. 'Most people I meet are secretly convinced that they're a little crazier than the average person', he says. 'People understand the energy necessary to maintain their own shields, but not the energy expended by other people. They understand their own sanity is a performance, but when confronted by other people they confuse the person with the role.'[44]

Geraldine Page, asked whether acting made James Dean and Marilyn Monroe into tortured souls, said 'No, they were that way before they got there . . . but that canker inside them had nothing to do with acting. On the contrary, the fact that they did turn out to be actors probably relieved some of their innate grief, because acting *is* a release; it is a way of taking anguish and making something beautiful out of it.'[45] In other words, actors recover, and use, those experiences which most of us never confront. We are aware of them within us, but are afraid to admit to them. Afraid of what others might think of us, or what reliving the experiences might do to us. Actors transmute the experiences into art, and run the risk of being labelled 'neurotic'.

But when an actor is able to contain such powerful emotional experiences, extraordinarily strong relations are developed between the personal unconscious and the conscious mind. The inner life is sensitized to one's own depths, but also clear channels are developed for expressing this material. For most of us fragments of unconscious images struggle into our dreams, to be quickly forgotten. For many actors there is a tremendous stream of imagery and emotional experience which bubbles up and surfaces to enrich the sombre outlines of life with rich and vital colours.

Inevitably, actors allow more of themselves into their conscious lives – negative as well as positive aspects. I find this refreshing. And while the discussion has necessarily concerned 'actors-in-general', I have found the many individual actors that I know to be far from the 'neurotic' stereotype. Actors I have met, from drama students to international 'stars', tend on the whole to be open, integrated, lively, balanced and stimulating people.

It was these qualities which I saw in actors which inspired me to explore the way of the actor. And to write this book.

PART TWO

THE WAY

CHAPTER 5

Possession: Finding Inner Selves

Actors Possessed

'I started to walk slowly round and round the room emptying myself of myself, thinking pain and loneliness, bewilderment and age, fear and the terror of dying in solitude. Willing von Aschenbach himself to come towards me and slip into the vacuum which I was creating for his reception.'[1]

Dirk Bogarde was being possessed by the character of von Aschenbach, his acclaimed role in Visconti's film *Death in Venice*. The takeover of Bogarde by his fictional character sounds almost sinister, '. . . He came, not all at once, but in little whispers . . . bringing with him the weight of his years, the irritability of his loneliness, the tiredness of his sick body. . . . Arrogance slid in like a vapour.'

Bogarde had become a receptacle, a shell, for a presence he had trained his mind and body to accept, 'I had absolutely no doubt that I was him, and the exterior shell of my normal body was only the vessel which contained his spirit.'

The rest of the cast and film crew left Bogarde alone. They knew that he wished to maintain a sense of concentration, 'in order to contain this spirit which was so completely alien to myself.' Bogarde admits that throughout the months of filming, when he left the set each day and went home, 'I still retained his walk and mannerisms . . . as a man possessed without consciousness of the present world.'

For most of us, the sensation of being taken over by an alien being, having our body possessed by an outside 'personality', would be terrifying. We would fear that we were going mad. But for some actors possession is not only what they experience, it is what they *seek* to experience.

Bruce Dern, for example, says that, 'To be a pure actor in a play, one hundred per cent of the time, you have to do two-and-a-half hours of absolute moment-to-moment behaviour. . . . You are really the character, you are really the person.'[2]

Klaus Kinski has been possessed many times. Especially in the films he has made with German director Werner Herzog, such as *Fitzcarraldo* and *Aguirre, Wrath of God*. Kinski describes the state as long-lasting, like Bogarde's incarnation as von Aschenbach, '. . . For the entire period of filming you become completely what you have to be for the role. It continues inside you, whether you are in front of the cameras or not.'[3]

Kinski has found his possession by the character he is playing to be so overwhelming that he rejects the term 'acting' as inadequate. For Kinski it is more a matter of 'being', 'You can try to exist outside the character while you are waiting for the next shot . . . you think you step out of it, and make your coffee and eat and so on. But actually all that is mechanical. Much more than anything else you continue to be this character that you have to incarnate.' Kinski describes a state of suspended animation, 'You're not able in your normal life to do the same things any more. Somebody has to come to you and tell you that it is time to eat: you're not interested in that. . . . It is as if you are paralysed. You don't do anything else. You give all of yourself to being what you have to be in the character.' Kinski's experience of possession extends even to feeling a physical presence, 'You are taken by this personality, inside of you, even physically, so that there's no space for you, and you're breathless.'

Bogarde, Dern and Kinski are experiencing the takeover, even subjugation of their selves by outside 'characters'. They are possessed. But today possession is taboo.

Possession

Possession was a powerful experience which lay at the centre of the actor's way in traditional societies. The actor became possessed by the spirits, gods, deities of the 'other world', manifestations of eternal and universal forces incarnated in performance as 'spirit personalities'.

Today, we associate possession with superstitions, primitive cultures, and modern medical opinion casts possession states into the bin labelled 'madness'.

There are many reasons for our aversion to a state of mind which was once held in great reverence. Initially, possession by spirits was denied by the early Church which, in its opposition to 'pagan' actors, claimed that the possessing beings were demons and devils. When on occasion a person's state of mind led to an involuntary possession, people became afraid that it was the devil taking control of innocent victims; a diabolical external agency for which the treatment was exorcism.[4]

Psychiatrists, dealing today with people distressed by involuntary possession (now called hysteria or dissociation), and seeing possession in an exclusively clinical environment, have reinforced the taboo nature of the state in Western societies. And psychiatric jargon, supposedly providing an objective, scientific language for discussing mental states, represents the behaviour of a possessed person as '. . . gross non-reality ideation, abnormal perceptual experiences, (and) profound emotional upheavals' which constitute a 'schizoid' state – regarded as a serious pathological condition.[5] Stripped of its unscientific bias, this is saying that possession is a mental state involving highly imaginative ideas, unusual perceptual experiences and strong emotion – which is what actors experience in almost every performance.

Of course, our image of possession is of a person totally out of control, dominated by some psychic force more powerful than himself. But the common image of a zombie-like body, inhabited and controlled by an external agency, is misleading. While we often assume that the possessing force completely obliterates consciousness and will, even in traditional societies when actors 'become' the spirits and are 'possessed' by them, they do not lose contact with the requirements of the performance they are giving.

For example, one traditional shamanic actor says of a possession experience, 'I was obliged almost without ceasing to utter cries, weep, sing, dance and roll upon the ground where I went into horrible contortions; I was forced to jerk my head and feet in all directions, howl like a bear . . . (but) I am never absent, I always know what I am doing or saying.'[6]

The traditional actor's state of possession is a powerful

phenomenon, which alters the actor's behaviour and experience to that of the 'spirit'; but it is nevertheless a *performance*. It is a controlled possession. The traditional actor has a double consciousness; one part is possessed, the other observes and controls.

Theatre director Charles Marowitz points out how, for modern actors, the process of creating a part leads to a trance state very like that of possession, 'The actor . . . learns his lines through repetition. This repetition becomes the main preoccupation for several weeks' time. The actor continually repeats lines, moods, emotions, situations'. This is spread out over a period of weeks, rather than being concentrated into consecutive hours or days as with traditional actors. Nevertheless, 'The actor in effect, hypnotises himself by repetitions into his role. The fact that he is still conscious, still aware of everything going on around him on the stage and in the auditorium, does not alter the fact that his "performance" is the result of these hypnotic repetitions.'[7]

Indeed, for many actors, entering this state of mind and body involves a simple ritual. Even the time spent putting on stage make-up can take on such a function. Antony Sher recently played the drag queen in the London production of *Torch Song Trilogy*. We were sitting in his dressing room at the Albany Theatre before an evening performance. 'I come in here and I sit for an hour,' he said, 'during which time I'll put on the drag and get into the dress and everything. I've left behind my life and I've gone through this ritual. Then just before I go on, I go through that door to spend five minutes waiting backstage. It's a ritual that removes you from yourself, so that by the time you're on stage you are in a kind of different state.'

This 'different state' would traditionally have been part of the possession experience, but today actors rarely talk about 'possession' experiences. More often they think in terms of 'getting into' the character; stepping into an imagined external person, rather than letting the character into them.

Indeed some actors today deny ever 'being' or 'becoming' the characters they play. Rip Torn, for example, says, 'I never believe that I *am* the character. . . . When I was doing Whitman, they'd call me at the desk in Baltimore and say, "Time for you to wake up, Mr Whitman" and I'd say, "He ain't here." '[8]

But even Rip Torn admits to a fleeting identification, a momentary merging of self with the role: 'I might believe it for a moment in the scene because I'm concentrating as the character would be. . . .'

Most actors today do not think of themselves as being possessed by the characters they are playing. The vivid examples provided by Dirk Bogarde, Bruce Dern and Klaus Kinski are unusual in their intensity and they parallel the experience of actors in traditional cultures who are possessed by spiritual beings. But more often, Western actors talk about 'building a character' using themselves as a base. Or they 'get into' the character, putting themselves into a conceptual model or mental image of what the fictional 'person' is like.

Nevertheless, it is clear that elements of 'possession' are commonly present in many working actors' experience. Meryl Streep, for example, declares that on the whole, she does not live with the role after the day's filming, 'I am very good at stepping out of the character at the end of the day – I think I'd die if I didn't with some of the work I've done.'9 And yet her desire to avoid the disturbing effect of possession by difficult roles does not prevent them from sometimes insinuating themselves into her life, claiming a part of her.

When she recently played the title role in the film *Silkwood*, about an anti-nuclear protester who was killed in a mysterious car accident in 1974, her preparation for the role included immersion in the literature on the nuclear controversy, and especially seeking a deep understanding of the protesters' argument. While Meryl Streep was in natural sympathy with this viewpoint, she nevertheless entered the subject to a much greater depth than she intended. 'The movie was very absorbing', she said afterwards. 'In the end, I began to feel I was so involved, it was driving me nuts. I thought I've got to get away from this stuff when I'm not on the set.' She began to read a book about the Middle Ages. But then she realized it was really the same thing all over again, 'There was a society facing total annihilation. The plagues moved about like an invisible enemy, like radiation, travelling from city to city. . . . It's still all a bit too real for me, the movie.'10

Sometimes, the emotional atmosphere of a film leads the character to be an insidious invader of the actor's consciousness.

John Hurt was filming *1984*, based on George Orwell's nightmare vision of society. He admitted, 'I usually maintain that I never take parts home with me. This one is difficult to leave behind. When you create a whole fantasy world like this you can lose your self in it.'[11]

Frequently, actors form a very strong attachment to the character being portrayed, and find it difficult to leave when the role is over. Lynn Redgrave discusses this haunting form of possession, '. . . The more successful you are at submerging yourself in someone else, the more schizophrenic it can make you feel. Depending on the nature of the character you're portraying, it can have a very strong and strange effect on you.' The portrayal of an emotionally disturbed character affects her a great deal, 'After you play a very neurotic person, if you've played the role for a long time and played it very successfully, you can have withdrawal symptoms. I found that when I did Saint Joan; I played her for six months. . . . When it ended, I was terribly sad . . . but my depression was out of all proportion.'[12]

In contrast with the traditional actor's experience, these partial 'possessions' no longer involve spirits or deities, but rather dramatic characters, imaginery people. And the character somehow asserts a presence which the actor finds difficult to exclude from his own life. Of course, most of us have been involved at some time with tasks or projects that have stayed with us, occupied our thoughts even while we are not working on them, 'haunted' us. But for the actor, when the project is an imaginary person who is occupying mental, emotional and physical space within him, the presence offers intriguing glimpses into the construction of the self. Especially when the character takes over in performance, briefly but decisively.

Possession in performance

Charlton Heston had an attack of panic on stage in London. But who panicked? Heston or the character?

He was playing the role of Commander Queeg in his London production of *The Caine Mutiny Court Martial*. The play concerns the court martial of Queeg, who is accused of bad captaincy and also of pilfering from his ship's supplies. He, on the other hand, alleges mutiny, because subordinate officers took over the command of his ship when they felt that he was heading it for destruction in a storm. The proceedings lead to Queeg's breakdown in court; a performance for which Charlton Heston won critical acclaim from London theatre reviewers.

There is an intense moment in the cross-examination when the lawyer (played by Ben Cross), defending the subordinate officer, traps Commander Queeg in a lie. Queeg, with a darting movement of Heston's eyes, *shows* that he is trapped. Panic. And the emotion of the scene surprised Heston.

He explained to me what happened, 'Ben Cross and I had been using more and more that moment when he looks at me and says, "Commander, there are many points of dissimilarity between you and the testimony of other witnesses. If you like I'll ask for a five minute recess so that you can put your thoughts as best as you can." He's using more and more a moment of real sympathy, because he does hate the fact that he is going to have to destroy Queeg's career to defend his client.'

Heston entered this moment in the play carrying with him the feelings of Commander Queeg. He explained that as Queeg he didn't feel sorry for himself. He felt persecuted. He also felt just in his cause; he was one man against a whole ship of mutineers. He did his best. He served for years without making one single mistake and he could prove it. His reputation had been spotless until then, and he would not have it besmirched by lies and distortions. But Heston points to the breaking point in Commander Queeg's emotional armour, 'It's all mixed with fear, because somewhere deep down he knows it isn't true.'

Allowing the character of Queeg to possess him, Charlton Heston lost control, 'That moment when Ben gives Queeg a chance to escape, the emotion builds up, and the last night it frightened me, as Queeg. To the point where there was, in my judgement, too much emotion. I couldn't control it.' At the crucial moment in the scene the character took full possession and Heston realized that it was *his own emotion* being expressed.

'It's a scene in which it is very easy to generate real emotions because the emotions are very strong ones.' Heston continues, 'But I have come to believe that real emotion in a scene – in a performance – while very exciting, is nevertheless also very dangerous and seductive. You can't control it.' In other words, he feels that the best acting comes when the actor allows himself to be only partially possessed by a character. 'I think real emotion in a scene is a necessary ingredient like salt in a stew – it must be used judiciously. After all, when I'm playing Macbeth, if I lose control in the dagger speech then I'm going to stab some poor stagehand.'

Charlton Heston continually returned to the 'loss of control' when 'real' emotion took over from the acted emotion. When an actor 'puts himself' into the character or, to express it in terms of possession, allows the character to 'enter into himself', he feels the emotions *of that character*. How can this happen?

The actor uses his imagination to construct a vivid picture of what the situation would be like – and then reacts as if he were the character. He registers the emotions, and how they can be expressed to the audience, during rehearsal, and then practises it until the emotion becomes automatic rather than a charge. It is distanced a little from the actor's own primary experiences of emotion, and becomes the emotions of the character.

Of course, in performance the actor must invest the character's emotion with spontaneity and vitality. He must prevent the 'fixing of emotion' in rehearsal from becoming too mechanical. The emotions of the character need to be fuelled by the juices of the actor's own emotion. Even with the actor's inner self observing and controlling, it is hardly surprising that there exists the risk of confusion. 'Fixed' emotion can suddenly merge with that of the actor, and the actor experiences emotion *as himself*. In other words, it was not Commander Queeg who was panicked. It was Charlton Heston. And for one surprising and disturbing moment, Charlton Heston was suddenly and totally possessed by Commander Queeg.

But while it is possible to conceive of the actor's own emotion becoming fused with that of the character, we are still left with an unclear picture of where the character's emotion comes from. For although actors might *act* emotion, we have all witnessed performances in which the quality of that emotion was undeniably real.

In the film *Face to Face* Liv Ullmann depicts a psychiatrist breaking down. In one six-minute scene the character loses and gains and loses control of her emotions. Of her control, as the actress, over the emotional energy of this long, demanding and extremely intense scene, Liv Ullmann says, 'I like to think

I'm in control all the time, that it's not the character doing it. But it's a mixture.' She explains that, 'There are two ways of crying: one is that you allow your character to cry; but the other is that you get so moved by yourself that you cry. And then you are in deep trouble because then you are into self-involvement.' She fights this temptation, 'That's a danger for a lot of actors – their work becomes too much feeling – they cry their own tears and that isn't art. I think I'm aware of that. I'm trying on stage not to cry my own tears and shiver my own shivers.'[13] This view sounds like that of Charlton Heston: the actor is in control of the character's emotions, though occasionally the actor's own emotion becomes involved with the character's and a fusion, or possession, takes place.

A further dimension is revealed when she reflects on a particular stage role. Acting in the play *The Chalk Circle*, Liv Ullmann is playing a character called Grusha. Revolution has come to village where she lives in poverty. Everyone has fled the murder and fire that followed in the wake of war. While she herself was running away she found an infant abandoned by its mother. In playing this scene, Liv Ullmann describes an unexpected experience, 'Grusha is sitting beside the baby whose mother has abandoned it, and as she bends down to pick it up, a tear comes into her eye and rolls down her cheek. Suddenly the tear is there and it is a wonderful feeling. And I am surprised because I hadn't known she would weep at that moment. But it is no longer myself caught in an emotion, not *I* that weep.'

Liv Ullmann explains that her approach to the scene was to be open, so that what happened to the character Grusha would happen *through* Ullmann, 'I was open to her fears and her emotions.' She goes on, 'Actually the fun of acting is to use your openness in such a way that the character can come through you. And if the character needs to cry, it's the character and not you feeling all over the place. It's a kind of openness that allows you to stand beside and watch, like having an instrument so tuned that whatever you choose to play on it will come out right. The moment you feel too much private anger or private anguish you aren't in tune any more.'[14]

So how can we understand this process of containing a character's emotions? It sounds as if an 'alien being', in the form of a dramatic character, is literally using the body and mind of the actor in order to exist. Of this process Ullmann says, 'I see myself as a sieve. Everyone's feelings flow through me, but I am never able to retain them. In the evening I am put aside empty – only to be inundated the next day with new emotions.'[15]

The opening and maintenance of these emotional 'streams' are like an exercising of one's psychic being. But although Liv Ullmann describes herself as a kind of empty vessel through which the emotions flow, she nevertheless recognizes something crucially important for our understanding of the way in which 'possession' works, namely that the character and herself are one and the same person. The emotions of the character, contained within her, keep Liv Ullmann open to depths of her own emotion, 'What happens to a role is a kind of life, and now as I sit talking with my colleagues, Jenny is living inside me. So that in a way I am she; and what are her tears and fear and anger keep open in me that which I shall use to portray her.'

The character within Liv Ullmann is experiencing its own emotions, but they are derived from Liv's own emotional 'reservoir'. Of the parts written for her by Ingmar Bergman she says, 'His women, whom I always see as real, become a natural part of me. Without my believing that they are created in my likeness. Even if he gives me a role that seems unfamiliar to me, I know that while he was writing, he knew I could understand the character – that I have a backlog of experience which can be utilized when her experiences are to be unfolded.'[16]

The possessing character, personality, being, is allowed a stream or channel of space into the 'backlog' of the actor's experience, going right through the layers from deep unconscious to surface persona. Sometimes, Liv does not know where the emotions come from; sometimes, the possessing character surprises her.

But the observations of Liv Ullmann and other actors make clear that when the possessing character becomes too powerful, it dips into other areas of the actor's psyche, and begins to take over control.

Possession reconsidered

Who are the dramatic characters, the beings that possess

modern actors like succubi, using parts of their emotions, and yet leading an independent existence as the 'Mask' seen by the audience? To answer this question we need to look afresh at the nature of possession.

Psychotherapist Rollo May advocates a redefinition of 'demonic possession'.[17] He suggests that the 'demon' be defined as any natural function in the individual that has the power of taking over the whole person. 'Demonic possession' is, then, the takeover of part or all of the personality by one of these powerful functions. He maintains that we all have 'demons' within us, aspects of ourselves that we have not allowed freedom, and that have remained lost, ignored, or hidden and there are lessons to be drawn from Rollo May's suggestion, because we are 'possessed' every day of our lives.

Everyday possession

Most of us are aware that significant portions of each day are spent in 'daydreams', fantasies, and a kind of reverie in which we talk to ourselves. This inner talk is essentially identical to the way we might talk to someone else, except that the words are not spoken aloud. This self-talk even has the structure of an inner conversation, evidenced by the curious mixture of pronouns, names and modes of address employed. Often an inner voice says 'I' ('I'd better hurry up'), but also from time to time says 'You' (as in 'You're going to be late again'). Sometimes one part of the inner self even offers a statement, directive or question, and another aspect responds with an 'answer'.[18]

Of course, it can be argued that this internal dialogue is simply the way we voice ideas in our minds, and that it differs from the 'split self' experienced by the possessed person who, while perhaps aware of what is happening, is nevertheless in a trance. But the basic characteristic of a trance state is that the mind is fully, or almost fully engaged by an activity that excludes it from awareness of 'external reality' as we usually conceive of it. In other words, a person in a trance has lost their mind, but only in the sense that the mind has been relieved of moment-to-moment checks against the social environment that is the hallmark of the state we would recognize as 'normal waking consciousness'.

Actor and teacher Keith Johnstone points out that while

people in a trance will sit quite motionless for long periods of time, so do theatre and cinema audiences, 'entranced' by what they are watching. Until, that is, the scene ends and the 'spell' is broken.[19]

Individuals, alone in a room, or driving a car, or doing anything that isolates them from social intercourse enter a state akin to trance, in which they float away on a sea of internal reverie. When someone knocks on the door, we 'come back to ourselves'; to social reality. In fact, it is clear that significant portions of our waking lives are spent in mild trance states, in which we carry on an internal dialogue with a presence which resides inside us. But the 'character' possessing us does it in private and silently, while the character played by the actor possesses in public, and is expressed externally.

Inner Selves

Shirley Maclaine started wondering about her personal identity from an early age, 'It intrigued me that there might be more to me than what I was aware of in my conscious mind. Perhaps there were other identities buried deep in my subconscious that I only needed to search for and find.'[20]

This appears to be a common experience for actors. Sybil Thorndike remarked that 'When you're an actor . . . you're a person with all the other persons inside you.' And another great classical actress, Edith Evans, said, '. . . I seem to have an awful lot of people inside me.'[21]

It is sometimes suggested that actors do not know 'who they are', and that they become confused by adopting the identities of the characters they play. But the evidence suggests that the reverse is true. By playing many parts, actors develop a strong sense of self, of who they are. And there is of course an important sense in which we *do* have a consistent self which remains *us* no matter what roles we may be playing. But the work of the actor leads to the recognition of something else of equal importance. The notion that we have a single 'personality', coherent, integrated and stable, is one of the most limiting myths of everyday life. While we each have a personal essence, an essential self, we also have within us a wide variety of subselves, aspects of ourselves that normally remain hidden, locked away, even repressed.

In a sense, to be influenced by hidden, unknown aspects of ourselves *is* a sort of possession. The ghosts of our life experiences lead us this way and that without our conscious knowledge. For most of us, who do not enter into depth psychotherapy, the deep waters of our unconscious run undisturbed by even a dipping toe of consciousness. Our only clues to the hidden parts of ourselves are the fragmented images of dreams, and the frequently inexplicable nature of the strength of our emotional responses to everyday events.

For the actor it is different. The actor seeks to 'encourage those of his inner impulses which are relevant to the role to emerge as dominant; and to encourage the domination of the whole personality by one part is to invite possession.' This is why in amateur acting we are often stunned by the transformation of a person in performance: the 'tough guy' who reveals surprisingly vulnerable aspects; the shy girl who is totally convincing as a whore. The role provides opportunities for repressed aspects of the personality to burst free of their bonds. We all have 'parts' of ourselves which we repress, or at least neglect, and which do not find expression in our daily lives. But the way of the actor releases these elements.

Actors create imaginary characters within themselves and deal with them in the same way we deal with the imaginary self that lives inside us. But we often forget that our inner self, with which we converse and argue, is an imaginary construction, a trick of the mind which allows us to negotiate with our life experience in the form of an inner character.

The actor constructs a new inner character; the imaginary person he is to play. And in so doing, he calls upon the various depths of his inner experience in new ways. Whether the actor tries to work from within that experience to build a character, or creates first an idea of the character and allows his emotional resources to respond to it, either way the actor is activating his inner experience around a new focus. Creating characters keeps life experience moving, flowing, and flexible.

'When I was working on the role of Torvald, the male-chauvinist husband in *A Doll's House*, I completely figured the guy out. But it took an audience to tell me that I didn't like him and that I was standing away from him and saying . . . "I am not at all like this".'[22]

Sam Waterston, who won an Oscar for his superb film performance in *The Killing Fields*, is talking here about how an intellectual analysis of a role can destroy a performance by distancing the actor from the role, and how, in 'live theatre', the audience can help the actor to open up to the character, to allow himself to be possessed by an alien personality. 'I walked on the stage in Philadelphia, and the audience saw that I thought Torvald was a figure of fun, and they made fun of him. Then within five or ten minutes, they began to wonder what the hell they were doing in the theatre. If he was so ridiculous, why did Nora marry him in the first place?'

The audience response forced Waterston to open himself more to the character, to begin to admit that the character was not so totally alien that he could not be penetrated by him. Waterston described the effect, 'I inched closer: I made him like people in my family. Finally I had to say: I am he, he is me. . . . It's satisfying to an audience to see (a play) clearly structured, but what they really want to know is *you*. All they really want to see is *you*. Because you and they are all people and they want to see people.'[23]

Waterston is suggesting that by allowing the character to live through him, he is revealing himself, opening himself up, showing his inner life as if it belonged to the possessing personality. And to be possessed by a character is to reveal your self.

Antony Sher, in his book *Year of the King*[24] chronicles his preparation of the role of Richard III, and one reviewer summed up vividly the picture he paints, 'Sher must himself become the freaks or fiends he imagines, permitting them house-room inside him. . . . Though he begins to assemble the character authologically, from mimicry of others and from trying on a battery of prosthetic disguises, as he goes on he sheds the assumed personae, the false noses and lank wigs, admitting that Richard is himself: he uses his own voice, his own hair, his own body, his own personality. For the coronation, he appeared naked: what is acting, after all, but self-denudation?'[25]

It is interesting that possession is expressed as self-denudation. The allowing of creatures within oneself is the same process as revealing oneself. The theatre director Peter

Brook says that 'Actors are mediumistic: the ideas suddenly envelop the whole in an act of possession . . . the actors are "penetrated": penetrated by themselves.'[26] So actors possess themselves.

When an actor is partially 'possessed', either by a character that takes over during performance, or maintains a presence in the mind afterwards, he is essentially experiencing, confronting, digesting aspects of his own self. Aspects that might never be realized if the only inner self available through which experience could be expressed was the usual inner self with which we converse silently.

Creating a character which calls upon so much of the hidden, repressed, inner experience of the actor that the character possesses the actor, is less common but not unusual. Dirk Bogarde and Klaus Kinski tapped something of themselves in their performances which led them to feel possessed. That 'something' was once held in awe by members of traditional societies. It is the level of human experience which is deeply embedded in all of us.

It is often assumed that actors are people who like to 'escape' from themselves into being 'other people'. But when we look more closely at the way actors work, the necessary intensity suggests a very strong orientation towards 'other people', or characters. Lawrence Luckinbill expresses the paradox of the actor as wanting to be someone else – but as a way of expressing himself, 'I have inside myself an unchanging, undying need to be somebody else – that's being born to be an actor and maybe that's being born to be an artist in general. That, however, is paradoxically coupled with the unchanging desire to express *myself*. So while I want to be somebody else, I also want to give voice to who I am. . . .' Luckinbill explains that while he is himself, he is also other people, and '. . . somewhere in the dim relation between those statements is my understanding of others and capacity to understand them.'[27] There is a suggestion here that we share with other people hidden identities, such that if circumstances had been different we could have 'been them', and they us.

As Marlon Brando says, we each contain within us the seeds of all the characters we will ever play. Actors do not play 'autobiography', they build from observation and imagination as well as personal experience. Individual life-patterns can be transcended, albeit temporarily, by actors, and in their place they can reach into the depths of themselves to produce new people – it is this 'Everyman' ability which in traditional societies bound person to person, and people to life.

It is the secret of self-possession.

CHAPTER 6

Transformation: Changing Our Selves

'YOU'VE GOT to make me look convincingly Chinese.'

Chalton Heston's make-up man considered Heston's distinctive features uneasily. Moses, Yes. Michaelangelo, El Cid, Abraham Lincoln, certainly. But Chinese?

'O.K.', he said, taking a chance.

'And I've got to be able to put it on myself', Heston continued. The make-up man's doubts grew. Although Heston was practised at applying his own make-up for stage roles, a Chinese make-up promised to be complicated.

'And I have to be able to put it on in no more than 12 minutes.'

This was going to be one of those Impossible Assignments. But perhaps, with careful preparation, it might just be feasible to design an ingenious make-up which Heston could apply in such a short space of time.

'Oh, and I have to be able to take it all off in about thirty seconds.'

'Forget it!'

Charlton Heston was preparing to play Sherlock Holmes in the play *Crucifer of Blood*. In one scene Holmes adopts a comprehensive and convincing disguise as a decrepit, aged Chinese man who runs an opium den. And it has to be well done, because the trick is to fool the audience, so that even *they* do not know that the Chinese gentleman is Sherlock Holmes. Not until, that is, he takes off his costume and make-up (in thirty seconds) to reveal his true identity.

Charlton Heston is a persuasive man. His make-up expert

agreed to the project. And with great relish, Heston described to me the details of the disguise that was designed for him, 'A full wig so that I could be bald with wisps of white hair coming down, and plaster pinning my eyes back into slits. Old hands and long fingernails. And a loose Mandarin robe, so that I could conceal my height by walking with bent knees.' Heston prepared himself to make the best use of the disguise, even working with a voice coach learning to move his voice up in range, and to speak English with a Chinese accent.

The show opened. Eventually it was time to play the China-man scene. And at the end of the scene Heston, as the Chinese opium dealer, walked across stage, crouched behind a piece of furniture, quickly removed the make-up, and then stood up as Sherlock Holmes. The audience reacted strangely. They seemed pleased to see Holmes, but did not applaud the clever transformation.

'Some people I knew came backstage after the show', Heston explained. 'And one of them said, "How did you get behind that piece of furniture in the scene with the Chinaman. Were you there all the time?"

"What do you mean?"

And the friend said, "When you came out from behind the furniture, the Chinese man disappears. Where did he go?"

I said, "That's me."

He said, "No, no I mean the changeover. How did you switch places with the Chinaman?"

I said, "Both of them are me for Chrissakes!".'

The transformation had been so effective that the audience did not realize that Heston had been acting the Chinese man as well as Holmes; they thought a Chinese actor had served as Holmes-in-disguise, and then exchanged places with Heston-as-Holmes. But at least the audience had thought it clever to change places so quickly!

The scene had to be adjusted so that the audience could *see* Charlton Heston taking the make-up off. But of course, they then enjoyed the fact that they had been fooled, for this is the classic transformation: an actor pretending to be another person, who is in turn pretending to be another person. And fooling the audience in the process.

And yet even the basic process of transformation can be disturbing. When an actor takes on a role, goes into character, becomes 'someone else', we normally contain what the actor does within the time and space confines of a three-hour theatrical performance, or a film set, where the actor as 'someone different' is recorded for transmission in the controlled settings of film theatres and television. However it needs to be contained within these bounds, because in principle, the idea of a person turning into someone else is very disturbing.

The actor-in-character is a person transformed into someone different. Looking, moving, behaving like someone other than themselves takes away the person who is the actor, and substitutes someone we do not know. It depersonalizes and in place of the person who was, there is now a fictitious person created and maintained by the skills and concentration of the actor coupled with the suspension of disbelief of the audience.

There is something about the actor's disguise, presence, reason for being that is threatening for the rest of us. As the theatre historian Richard Southern has said, an actor in his part has still an element of the horrifying, if you go too near, because the actor is strange, 'His mind is working on other than normal lines. . . . He is concentrating on another situation than reality; he is concentrating on a fiction He is not unlike a mad person; he is abnormal; he is a mask; the man himself can no longer be seen.'[1]

So we sanction the actor's transformation only under strictly controlled conditions. For in the space/time setting of a theatre or cinema, we give actors permission to 'fool' us. We even help them, by suspending our disbelief. To be fooled into thinking the actor is someone else is the point of the whole exercise.

But people are made uneasy by the idea that we 'act' in everyday life, for it implies insincerity. We like to think that when we are interacting with others we are 'being ourselves'; to act is to be false, manipulative, shallow.

'Because an actor can transform, apparently, into another person, he is believed to have magical ability', says Charlton Heston. 'Magical, and thus suspect. He can seem to be what he clearly is not. And if he can do it on stage or screen, surely he can do it in everyday life. Nobody wants to depend on such a person.'

Heston's use of the magical metaphor to refer to transformation echoes the actors of traditional society, where the actor-becoming-something-else took on sacred overtones of the unknown. In that setting the actor maintained his prestigious, magical aura even while not performing. But they were also feared for their power. Today it is also the case that an actor outside the confines of the theatre is potentially a liar. He can fool us because we cannot be sure who he is, and how he is manipulating us.

Of course, acting skills *are* used to manipulate us in everyday life. But not by actors. Training in exploitative acting is, rather, the province of the salesman, who often takes courses in self-presentation, lines of argument to use with potential customers, 'tricks of the trade'. Much of this is merely to improve presentation, and we expect it in people who are seeking to influence us in one way or another. But when someone uses 'acting' to persuade us to buy something that we do not really want, our apprehensions are confirmed. The techniques of the much-maligned used-car salesman is the stereotype of everyday manipulative acting.

'Would you buy a used car from this man?' The caption, under a huge poster of Richard Nixon, was meant to highlight the perceived unreliability, dishonesty, manipulative 'acting' of this politician.

'Politicians are performers in a literal sense', Heston says. 'You cannot lead effectively as a politician, you can't persuade, rally your following, unless you can act. Churchill rallied the Free World in World War II as much because of his skills as an actor as for his political skills. His judgement as a politician has been brought into question many times. But no one can challenge his capacity to lead or summon up the blood and stiffen the sinews, and that was his acting skill.'

Heston then identifies the locus of fear that surrounds people who are dealing with an actor outside the confines of a play or film, 'Today a politician is horrified by the very thought that he might be acting because the verb implies insincerity, posing, and unreliability rather than the truth. For the politician who is described as an actor, as is President Reagan, it is still a pejorative label.'

This seems to be the crucial point. For whatever one's views on President Reagan's policies, there is surely no logical reason why an actor should not hold high office. They are not necessarily less intelligent than lawyers – a more common professional stepping-stone into politics. Actors can surely know as much, if not more, about people than accountants. And many actors are probably as honest and trustworthy as businessmen. So why shouldn't they hold high political office? The answer seems to be our deep seated suspicion, and fear, of the power of transformation. The talent and skill to pull the wool over our eyes. To do something deeply disturbing and at the same time frivolous: to appear to be somebody they are not. And we are afraid that actors who become politicans, or politicans who try to act, have skills of presentation which will blind us to the truth. 'Only actors are at all comfortable with being told they acted well', Heston concludes.

I brought up the common assertion that Margaret Thatcher has taken voice lessons to improve her vocal delivery, but that this is never openly admitted by the Prime Minister or her advisers. For such an obvious asset to her public performances might be considered underhand, manipulative, dishonest. 'Her voice lessons are kept quiet,' I told Heston, 'because there is the uneasy suspicion when you hear her speaking, that it is not her "real voice".'

'Or the real Margaret Thatcher?' Heston chuckled.

Physical Transformation
'I wanted to be a female Alec Guinness. Fat chance!' Helen Mirren was grumbling about one of the central features of the actor's transformation: the ability to appear physically different from one role to another. 'I wanted to be able to take on amazingly subtle personalities and completely change my physical appearance by the flick of a finger and the twitch of an eye – just to be quite different. But I've found that the most difficult thing is to obliterate what you have, your arms and your legs and your nose and your breasts.'[2]

Helen Mirren is a talented, compelling and daring actress, with many successful performances in classical and modern stage roles, and films such as *White Nights* and *Cal*. The adventurous depths of her acting experience include a demanding and provocative tour of Africa with Peter Brook, testing the

limits of improvisational acting as basic communication trans-
cending the barriers of language. Her talent and skills are
widely praised. But Helen Mirren has a problem as an actress –
she is very beautiful and very sexy.

Television soap operas have accustomed us to thinking that
physical attractiveness is a prime requisite for an actress. And,
of course, there is no doubt that Helen Mirren's physical
attractiveness has been an asset to her career. But for an actress
wishing to test her capabilities as an artist of transformation, it
can also get in the way. Helen Mirren's reviews through the
years have admired her acting, and her looks. Audiences have
wanted to see her acting, her transformations into roles, but
seem to prefer to see them acted through Mirren's physical
persona. She says, ruefully, 'People prefer you to reveal yourself
on stage rather than conceal yourself. . . .'[3]

There are many actors who have such a powerful physical
presence that they find it difficult to transform their appearance. Or rather, they are not *allowed* to change appearance.
Audiences focus on the actor's physical presence, and want to
see a role played in relation to that, rather than changing from
one physical incarnation to another. And this is how it is for
most of us in everyday life, whether or not we are 'beautiful and
physically compelling'.

Because, of course, we are all actors. We know that in
different settings, different company, at different times, we
behave as different people. There are strong elements of
personality which remain relatively constant – someone who
knew us in one setting would probably recognize us in another.
But the 'performance requirements' of everyday life vary from
one stage to the next.

On the whole, we are expected to play in these various
settings with minimal changes in performance. A person who is
a chameleon, totally different on separate occasions, is considered 'shallow', weak, lacking a strong centre. And while
changes in costume are of course allowed between the office and
the party, and between home and the beach, there are rules
governing the degree of flexibility allowed. A relatively stable
appearance renders a person predictable, identifiable, 'safe'.

Over longer periods, some changes may be allowed. A
person can gain weight (usually frowned upon), lose weight

(approved up to a point), adopt a new hairstyle (sanctioned if not too radical). It is a sign of how important are these external markers that people often comment upon sudden or even gradual change in appearance. A new hairstyle will often attract reactions from friends and colleagues. For a man, the beginnings of a beard or moustache, or the shaving off of an established one will usually provoke remarks. At the very least these reactions indicate that other people *monitor our appearance* and take note of changes. And sometimes we welcome, and even seek positive reactions from our friends. Most comments are evaluative. The change in appearance is judged as enhancing or detracting: the new hairstyle 'suits you'; the new beard 'makes you look scruffy'. But occasionally reactions are even stronger, suggesting that the fact that we have altered our appearance is *threatening* in some way. It appears to indicate to others that we have somehow changed as a person, since physical appearance expresses psychological states. We have become an unknown quantity, a transformed individual, a 'new person'.

Robert De Niro has gained and lost weight dramatically to suit the requirements of his roles. Photographs of De Niro in his bloated condition for the role of the boxer Jake LaMotta, in *Raging Bull*, are stunningly different from, say, his recent appearance opposite Meryl Streep in the film *Lovers*. Actors often change appearance for stage or film roles in ways which alter their everyday physical presence. They look different during filming, rehearsals or the long run of a stage play. Most of us would find this degree of alteration in appearance very disturbing. Our typical appearance is an important recognition cue to ourselves that we are who we are. The regular and familiar appearance in the mirror does much to reassure ourselves about our identity. Anyone who effects a significant change in their appearance will know what a shock it can be to forget about the change and to encounter oneself suddenly reflected in a mirror or shop window. A physical transformation powerfully affects the way we experience ourselves, and the ways in which others respond to us.

'The transformation was total and shocking,' says writer John Howard Griffin, a white journalist who convincingly disguised himself as a black man. 'I had expected to see myself disguised, but this was something else. I was imprisoned in the flesh of an utter stranger. . . . All traces of the John Griffin I had been were wiped from experience.' Looking into the mirror, Griffin was shocked and frightened by the unfamiliarity, the utter strangeness. 'The completeness of the transformation appalled me. It was unlike anything I had imagined. I became two men, the observing one and the one who panicked, who felt Negroid even into the depths of his entrails.'[4]

The extent to which a change in our appearance challenges our view of who or what we are reveals just how close to the surface, and yet so deep, is the act of transformation. To enter into it can be an educational, even liberating act. But to enter the world in a transformed state, we do not necessarily need to change appearance. Just thinking as a different person can change a life.

Being a Character

Charlton Heston recounted another experience of transformation, but this time it was far removed from Sherlock Holmes and elaborate disguises. He was in the desert, playing a cavalryman in a film called *Major Dundee*, which was about a pursuit by cavalry in Mexico at the time of the American Civil War. One day filming was taking place in a very desolate area far into the desert, and when the day's shooting was over the director, Sam Pekinpah, said to Heston, 'Look Chuck, there's a village down about two miles. If you don't want to wait for the cars, you can all go down the trail on the horses while we wrap things up here.'

Heston takes up the story, 'So we all mounted up, maybe thirty or forty troopers in uniform – tattered, unshaven, sweaty. We rode down the trail and through a very old village. It was a village that had been in existence almost as far back as the Spanish Conquest and had been overrun by the warring military factions many times. As we rode down the main street of this little village, you could see people nervously looking out of their windows and quickly easing back into the shadows. And I suddenly was struck by the realization that they were thinking "Christ, here they come again!".'

Charlton Heston experienced a deep and powerful sense of himself as a cavalryman, legitimized in that role by a public who did not realize he was acting. Heston *became* a cavalryman.

Being 'out in the world' in character, rather than safely cocooned in rehearsal rooms or film studios, means that the actor is perceived, approached, dealt with as if he were someone other than himself. The 'character' becomes the person. It is both shocking and exhilarating. And therein lies an important lesson in being ourselves.

Some actors have found that 'going out' in character is useful preparation for the actor's work. Bruce Dern, for example, consciously tries to incorporate this aspect of acting into his daily life, 'I may take the part of a character and play him for two or three hours during a day, just out in my general life. I'll go to the store or drive my car in town as somebody else'.[5]

Actors at the Royal Academy of Dramatic Art experience this as part of their training: to venture into London in character is a superb test of concentration and commitment; travelling around, buying in shops and restaurants, talking with people, being someone else in the midst of constant stimulation from the environment. After a series of workshops in which each actor develops a character, including interior life, personal history and external appearance, the actors go out into London in pairs, each to support and keep the other alert. I travelled around London on a bus with Fiona Shaw. This superb actress was in character as a very insecure young person who, unfortunately, was prone to fits of claustrophobia, accompanied by panicked attempts to get out into the open. Fiona-in-character wanted to ride on the top of the London red double-decker bus, because 'It feels more open'. We went up the stairs and took our seats. She talked incessantly and nervously about the trivia of her (character's) life – the food she fed her cat, her relationship with her aged auntie and so on. Fiona's character had a piercing voice which disturbed and attracted the attention of many people on the bus. I had to concentrate on the exercise to prevent myself being frozen by embarrassment. In England, eccentric people are tolerated, but they do attract attention.

Suddenly my partner stopped talking. I looked at her. She was gulping for air like a fish. She lurched to her feet and scrabbled at a window to open it. The window was stuck. The character began to panic. 'I want to get off', she screamed, scrambling over me to get out of her seat. Smiling weakly at the people surrounding us I follòwed as fast as I could. She galloped down the steps and leapt off the bus as it slowed at the next stop. She was better after that. Calmed down to her normal piercing commentary, we went for a noisy tea.

This character was not overplayed. In a thumbnail sketch she sounds 'over the top', but Fiona's bus performance was totally and compellingly believable. What attention she attracted that afternoon was directed at a *person*, not a show.

From the *inside*, the experience of many of the actors who do this work is one of exhilaration and when I tried it, the effect was frighteningly liberating. Simply *walking* as someone else makes the world look and feel different. But to interact with others as a changed person – a character transformed – is an enlightening experience. It subtly but dramatically alters the thousands of ways the environment feeds back, supports, shapes and channels the signals we send out. How those signals are returned shapes our view of ourselves. A change in persona can change your life.

Persona

Ben Kingsley, who stunningly performed the title role in the film *Gandhi*, recently starred in *Melons*, a play about the cultural destruction of native American Indians. Kingsley played an aged Apache leader. One review, typical of many, said, 'Ben Kingsley's performance . . . is an amazing act of transformation. Hardly made up, apart from a snow white wig, he presents a figure at once as frail as a leaf and immovable as a rock; slowing down the surrounding dialogue to his own resonantly impassive delivery, and radiating ceremonious dignity even when accepting a cigarette.'[6]

It is clear that, while make-up and costume can help, the actor's presence *in character* alters his appearance considerably.

For the actor there are many ways of achieving transformation; making the physical, emotional, even spiritual journey from one's being to that of a character, a role: another person. Quite often it is, as with Heston's *Holmes*, a combination of disguise and performance. But to concentrate on the physical appearance only is to miss a fundamental aspect of the actor's art of transformation. An actor can *look* different from his usual self because he is different 'inside'. Entering into the psychological, mental, emotional world of a character can result in quite startling physical changes. Sometimes a physical transformation can be literally 'coloured' by inner concentration.

For example, Meryl Streep has described her approach to a role as to simply assume the life of whoever she is about to portray, 'To become part of the landscape, to see into a character's world and simply step right in.' In the film *The French Lieutenant's Woman*, Streep plays a Victorian governess who has been jilted by her French lover and who spends her life in morbid devotion to her tragic fate. For a long scene with Jeremy Irons, Streep envisaged her eyes, which usually seem a blue-grey, or hazel, to be green. She tried contact lenses in preparing for the role, but then decided to play the part without them. 'When I saw the first rushes, my eyes came up green without the lenses, so I didn't need them.'[7]

This ability to apparently alter physical appearance without the intervention of make-up and other aids is noted in a number of actors. Juliet Stevenson is a young actress who has already taken on with great success some of the leading roles in productions of the Royal Shakespeare Company. One commentator talked of her immediately obvious qualities of technical virtuosity and daring, a fresh and direct emotional strength, and intellectual rigour. He then went on to say, 'Not conventionally pretty she has a far greater gift, the actor's ability to transform herself physically before your eyes. She has features of great plasticity and can transmute at will and almost without the aid of make-up from, say, the darting, bare-footed eroticism of her Titania to the grave beauty of her Yelenia in *The White Guard*, to the gawky and dazzling warmth of her Russian peasant girl, Polya, in Stephen Poliakoff's *Breaking the Silence*'[8]

The actress Janet Suzman says of Glenda Jackson's approach to acting, 'Some actors go towards the parts and transform themselves into them, becoming the characters they play. Glenda draws the role towards her and it becomes her with her silhouette, her persona. But it is the character all the same.'[9]

The term 'persona' is often applied to actors, usually referring to the actor's physical style or presence. Janet Suzman is here suggesting that while some actors prefer to change themselves physically to embody a conception of a role, Glenda does not dramatically alter her appearance. Rather, she transforms the character into her own physical presence, and convincingly plays the role through her own 'physical persona'.

'Persona' originally referred to the masks that actors used in the classical period of Greek history. Implied in each mask was a complete separate personality, often of a deity, which possessed the actor who wore the mask. But today, 'persona' is a psychological term, and refers to the personal façade that one exhibits publicly. This outward face includes significant aspects of physical appearance, but particularly encompasses the personal style or presence that an individual presents to the world. And this includes a strong element of conformity, because the aspect of oneself which is being presented at any one time is meant to fit in with, and satisfy, the people with whom one is interacting. The persona is the outward face of our psyche, the face that the world sees. And as we all know, what we show the world does not necessarily correspond with our inner self.

The psychiatrist Carl Jung developed the concept of persona as a modern psychological concept. 'Fundamentally the persona is nothing real', he says. 'It is a compromise between individual and society as to what a man should appear to be. He takes a name, earns a title, represents an office, he is this or that.'[10]

Each of us has a persona, or number of personas, which we present to the world in the various settings we enter: work, home, social occasions and so on. We have an 'image' which we show, which may vary considerably from one setting to another.

Each persona is a character. Each image of 'ourself' that we present to people we deal with constitutes a performance. People read a whole 'personality' from the persona they see. We are often embarrassed when we meet someone from one part of our lives, who only knows one of our personas, in another setting because the different personas we present reveal different aspects of ourselves. Just like the characters actors play.

But the crucial danger of the persona is that of identifying oneself with the mask, the role. Our whole, true self is not the same as the self which fits a particular role. If this happens, the person loses contact with the deeper sources of their own being. Life itself becomes one continuing series of role-plays, behind which the person's true self is denied. While a mask, or rather a number of masks, are essential for easy mixing with different groups of people, the masks must be interchangeable, flexible.

The persona is not the individual person. It is merely that aspect of the person which needs to be presented as a cog in the wheel of society. It is, in a way, an aspect of society rather than the particular individual. And an audience takes an interest in a character in a play or film not because the audience wants to know detailed, intimate knowledge of that actor as an individual, but because the individual character as presented in performance represents all of us, and is therefore of interest to all of us. Through the adventures of fictional characters, who are simplified versions of what a 'real' person would be like, we encounter life in general, and are entertained and enlightened by that.

There are aspects of the persona which lie hidden. These are either never known, unrealized potential, or they are unacceptable, not to be acknowledged. These aspects of the self, called by Jung the 'shadow', gather psychic force by not being expressed. They influence our lives, but are not seen. Until, that is, conscious efforts are made to create new personas. Then the shadow material rushes out 'into the light'.

The character being played by Glenda Jackson using, as Janet Suzman points out, her own persona, is actually projecting a new *shadow*. Glenda Jackson does not change the persona to a great extent, but she has a brilliant ability to allow, through hard work and intuition, the small expressions of behaviour which reveal the shadow of a character. And it is the shadow, not the persona, which interests us. The millions who watch *Dallas* and *Dynasty* on television enjoy seeing the shadows, hidden aspects of the characters, ruling their lives, often in total contradiction to their smooth, success-filled personas.

To think about others' personas and to try them on for size is to gain a remarkable feeling for the way people present themselves, the minutae of voice inflection, dress, stance, walk, mannerisms and so on. The actor's skill is to allow the elements of the shadow to penetrate the persona presented. Actors are not just mimics – people with a talent for simply presenting the voice, appearance and manner of another. The actor is attempting to do more. The persona, whether close to one's own or a created one, is there *to reveal the shadow*. The mask is presented in order to reveal what is behind it.

We only have to think for a moment of the effect of replacing our own persona, in a controlled and appropriate environment and adopting that of another person to gauge the psychological effects. Just existing outside of one's own persona is revealing. Being sufficiently aware and conscious of the personas of others creates insight into human nature. And acting, moving, speaking 'inside' a created persona is a liberating, startling and, sometimes, deeply revealing experience both to oneself and to others.

Emotional Home Range

Antony Sher described the experience of realizing the character of the drag queen in Harvey Feinstein's play *Torch Song Trilogy*, 'The American persona of the character is something that I have to travel a big distance away from myself to get. And also his entire manner of behaving, arising from him being a drag queen, is different to my own; so there's a lot of journeying to be done there. Yet on the other hand, because the emotional half of the play is such, I have to still keep the character related to myself as much as possible, so that when the emotional bits come up I can play them as truthfully as possible.'

The emotional lives of humans are rather like the territorial behaviour of animals. Most species of animals inhabit a 'home range', which is the area of ground over which they usually travel, often along the same pathways, in search of food. They rarely stray beyond these familiar circuits. Associated with the home range are areas of territory which animals will defend; spaces where they feel safe, comfortable, secure.[11]

People have physical home ranges, of course, but it is interesting to observe how we also have for our emotional lives a kind of 'home range' – experiences within which we feel comfortable or safe. We soon know when we are out of it, when we are in company we are not suited to, not 'our sort of place or person'. We range through our familiar, repeated patterns of emotional experience and expression, usually for an adult lifetime with only small and very gradual adjustments. Changing our habitual patterns of life is considered dangerous.

Sometimes the home range of emotional sustenance runs out of supplies; relationships weaken and go wrong, habitual ways of seeing oneself become inappropriate; a personal or professional crisis leaves us needing a different set of emotional pathways. We switch to different paths, but only after long delays and repeated runs over the now barren paths. Like animals, we mark out the areas of our home range with our own emotional scents and markers, and we are very loathe to leave them, until we are forced to explore more widely.

The work of the actor requires him to forage widely, sniffing, observing, even running along the paths and home ranges of other people. At the very least this breaks for the actor the illusion that afflicts most of us – that the psychological range of our lives is the only one available to us. Many of us are threatened when we encounter people who are obviously foraging a home range very different from our own – people who look and sound different and act differently, subscribe to different values. We guard aggressively and jealously the boundaries of our territory – we designate these rival people, see them as *outsiders*. For actors this experience is often rather different. Actors have to explore alternative pathways while at the same time retaining contact with their own home range.

It is interesting that for introverts, the area of their emotional life that is guarded probably corresponds to the outer limits of their home range. In other words, introverted people fix the pathways of their lives and defend all of them. On the other hand, extroverts will range further afield than the areas they are willing to defend. Their outgoing emotional style takes them into fields beyond their territory. Actors need to do both – range far afield, but also have a very strong sense of their own emotional territory. They have to integrate being introverted and extroverted. The actor Franchot Tone put his finger on this when he said, 'Actors are in a unique position. They are both introspective and exhibitionist. You have to be an introvert before you can find within yourself the symbols of extroversion that are required to put the performance across. It is a paradox. . . .'[12]

The way of the actor is a creative, growing, healthy paradox, a way of living which moves from one mode to the other rather than becoming fixed into a rigid pattern. And playing roles which stretch outside one's own home range can open new vistas.

Lynn Redgrave describes how playing the part of *Saint Joan* affected her, 'It was difficult for me, an agnostic, to play someone of great faith. I came nearer to understanding religion, though, than I ever had before. I *had* to believe, and . . . I'm much more open to what religion can do to people now. I'd always looked on religion as a rather repressive thing . . . but I began to see it in a different light.'[13]

Liv Ullmann talks of transformation as an extension of her range of expression. She says that, 'There are days when, during a rehearsal or a performance, unknown secrets within myself come forward, sparked by the shaping of a role, a dialogue with a fictitious character. The elation of a tiny advance. Adding to one's instrument.'[14]

Transformation into a 'character' may result in significant changes outside *and* inside, whether on stage, film, or in daily life. Transformation is a path to personal knowledge.

CHAPTER 7

Rebirth: Reliving Life

'WE HAVE TO get drunk at night . . . we need to be there at the birth of a baby, or at a death. We need to experience life as widely and fully as possible. And then we can interpret any roles we may play more effectively.'[1]

Getting drunk at night? Births? Deaths? Roger Rees' recipe for the actor's life sounds strong on adventure but short on discipline. And yet Rees, long one of the Royal Shakespeare Company's leading members, is a mature and disciplined actor. Shouldn't he be 'in training' somehow, when not performing or rehearsing?

He has an answer for that, 'We are not like ballet dancers. We don't have to spend two hours at the bar each day before we can begin working.' Is Rees advocating late night hours of work at a different kind of bar? And if so, how do young and dedicated actors, at the beginning of their careers, feel about this?

Juliet Stevenson, just a few years out of RADA, and already a leading actress at the Royal Shakespeare Company, admits that she is constantly on the move, often in a hotel, or rented cottage in Stratford, 'talking too much. Staying up late. Eating after the show. Not being very ordered or disciplined at all'.[2] The actor's life sounds determinedly dissolute. Very different from, say, dancers who tend to be religious about early nights, proper eating, rigorous and regular daily exercises.

The apparent laxity of actors infuriated the Russian theatre director Konstantin Stanislasvski. He protested that they should be in constant training, and that they should work, as do other artists, to maintain their fitness for their art, 'Let someone explain to me why the violinist who plays in an orchestra on the tenth violin must daily perform hour long exercises or lose his power to play? Why does the dancer work daily over every muscle in his body? Why do the painter, the sculptor, the writer practise their art each day and count that day lost when they do not work?' Stanislavski bristles with indignation, 'And why may the dramatic artist do nothing, spend his day in coffee houses and hope for the gift of (inspiration) in the evening? Enough. Is this an art when its priests speak like amateurs?'[3]

But Stanislavski, who did more than anyone to identify life experience as the spring-board of creative acting, seems to have confused training with classroom exercises. Singers and dancers have physical apparatus specific to their art which can be developed and tested in practice. Actors can, and many do, keep their 'physical instrument' in tune. But how do you train to become other people? And how can 'experiencing life fully' help actors to interpret roles more effectively, as Roger Rees suggests?

Drama often depicts highly charged events. Love, hate, jealousy, death, sex and violence are common themes of popular films, television drama and theatre. Even in more sophisticated productions, it is rare to go through a performance without witnessing some extreme conflicts or dilemmas. They raise emotions that we do not experience strongly every day. But we sample them just often enough in life to be fascinated, perhaps fatally attracted like a moth around a flame, drawn to films and plays to experience these emotions vicariously.

An actor depicting these powerful emotions needs to experience them at some level. Rip Torn has declared that an actor must go through the emotions in a night that some people only go through two or three times in their life. These sound like the experiencing of life's boundaries suggested by Roger Rees. But Rees also points to the desirability of actors socializing, spending time with people, experiencing the 'normal' dimensions of existence.

Actors do this by drawing on their own experiences, and extrapolating them to meet the needs of the character. This usually means finding something of their own experience in the character.

Living Characters

'For a woman you're intoxicated by, or enchanted by, or in love with, you take risks that you wouldn't take for someone else. I would take risks, accept sacrifices, including financial sacrifices, to do *Macbeth*, or *Long Day's Journey into Night*. You fall in love with the role.'

Charlton Heston was explaining the personal connection he needs to feel with a role to draw the best from himself as an actor. 'I usually stick to characters to which I feel subjectively drawn,' he goes on. 'That's part of what makes an actor perform well.' I asked if this meant that he could see himself in the role. 'It's the sense of "I know this kind of part. I know this man and I can make him real". It's gut reaction. You don't say, "I am like this man", but you say, "Yeah, I *know* him". Empathy.'

Paul Scofield described a similar first connection with a role, 'It's always intuitive, my reaction. What bells does it strike? What form of recognition does it call up?'[5]

So what is the nature of this connection between the actor and the character? Some actors have talked about finding elements of their own experience expressed in the role.

Sheila Gish, recently prominent for her triumphant performance as Blanche in the London production of *A Streetcar Named Desire*, opened in 1985 as Cecilia in Schnitzler's *Intermezzo*. She explained that she felt a strong connection with the part, 'I wouldn't play a part I didn't feel I could understand. I always have to find something of myself in a character.' For playing Blanche in *Streetcar*, she described exactly what this means, 'You don't have to have the same griefs and fears. You use your own, which is why I wouldn't go to an analyst to be cleaned up. And you do keep bits. You give parts of yourself and you acquire some of theirs.'[6]

Roger Rees talks even more specifically about the way his own experience connects with that of the character. Interviewed recently about his role of *Hamlet* in a new Royal Shakespeare Company production, Rees said: 'I am very moved by Hamlet's relationship with his father. There was a lot, for example, that I wish I could have said to my father, who died when I was 21. There are other things – I, too, have been in a position where I was not offered something that I thought was duly mine.'[7]

For other actors, it is specific incidents from life which fuel the portrayal. Lynn Redgrave says, 'When I played Saint Joan, I wanted at times to regress to being a baby again. . . . I felt that that would be the way to play her.' Redgrave's aim was to return to a naive, trusting, open, vulnerable self of childhood, '. . . that basic self that we all have in us, the self we put layers over when we grow up.' She prepared for this experience each night, just prior to the big scene of the play, '. . . Before I went on stage for the trial, I used to go into a sort of mental trance, a meditation where I would try to remember, as clearly as I could, tiny flashes of incidents from my childhood.' During the ten minutes of intermission, she would '. . . regress into that long-ago world. . . . The more I did it, the better I got, and the more I thought that I had forgotten resurfaced in my mind.'[8]

For many actors, using personal experience to enter the world of the character means using the physical and emotional presence of a 'real' other person, often someone well-known to the actor. Dustin Hoffman frequently models the characters he plays on people he knows. *The Graduate* was based on his brother, Ratso in *Midnight Cowboy* on the superintendent of a building he lived in, whilst *Tootsie*, in which he plays a woman, was modelled on his mother.[9]

Recently, he played the part of Willy Loman in a Broadway production of Arthur Miller's classic play *Death of a Salesman*. From the very beginning, Hoffman's feeling for the character, his sense of who the person was, focused on physical presence and style. For Hoffman, the character of Loman was as a little man; and this physical smallness was the link between Loman's appearance and inner life. In fact, when Hoffman first discussed the possibility of playing the part with Arthur Miller, the playwright offered to restore to the play lines he had cut from the published version which refer to Willy's smallness. But the presentation of the character went further for Hoffman. He even had to be satisfied with his make-up for the character before he agreed to play the part. The first step was to feel comfortable in character as a man of 63. After he tried on a number of wigs, without success, he agreed to shave his head almost bald to allow for a thinning hairpiece.[10]

Of course, physical appearance is only a part of the visual presentation of character; voice, movement, personal style involves many other factors. Hoffman asked Miller to his home and read the role to him. Instinctively, Hoffman acted Willy in the voice of his own father, Harry Hoffman, who, before his retirement, had been a furniture salesman.

'My first anchor for Willy was my father', said the actor.[11] Dustin fuelled the character with his father's attitudes, values and prejudices. For example, Dustin's older brother, Ronnie, became a University academic, yet was still apparently a disappointment in his father's eyes because he did not succeed in the business world, a world which became important to the older Hoffman through his struggle in the Depression. Dustin says, 'Ronnie . . . took his straight A's and his degrees, and, rather than making all the money and being in business like my father had wanted him to, he went into universities and taught. So my father knew Ronnie had done well, but he wanted him to have done well in Depression terms. It was the same kind of thinking Arthur's family had.'[12]

When Hoffman's Loman walked onto the stage of the Kennedy Center, his older brother was in the audience. The two have discussed their father a lot over the years. Ronald Hoffman says, 'So as I watched the performance, I was brought closer to experiences I've had. It was exhausting. It gave me insights. It was disturbing emotionally. When I left my seat, I continued to be moved, and I still am. I got a view of some major problematical aspects of my life.'[13]

Sometimes actors draw upon tragic personal events from their lives to provide an emotional basis for a role. In the film *Tootsie*, Dustin Hoffman played in drag, but made an effort to enter into what it felt like to be a woman. He based the character of Dorothy on his mother whom he had talked to little in recent years but who, before *Tootsie* was filmed, had suffered a severe stroke, for which she was hospitalized. Hoffman spent time with her under the emergency circumstances. Talking about these conditions, and his desire to use his mother as a model for his portrayal of Dorothy, Hoffman said, 'I know this sounds terrible, but my mother's stroke was one of the best things that ever happened to me. Yes, I got Dorothy out of it, but also my mother and I became friends, real friends, and had talks all through her illness that we never had before.'[14]

Actors are expected to 'use' their most private experiences in developing challenging roles. It is assumed that all of life is available for the art. For example, Joseph Papp, director of New York's *Public Theatre*, talked of Meryl Streep's relationship with the man she lived with, John Cazale. Streep and Cazale last appeared together in *The Deer Hunter* and Cazale, aged 39, had developed bone cancer. After the film was finished, Cazale and Meryl Streep returned to New York. 'I was very close to her then', say Papp. 'She has a very fine character as a person, a tremendous sense of loyalty. This was the most harrowing experience. She spent weeks at the hospital while John wasted away. There's no way she can forget that experience ever, but it's part of her life now, part of her art.'[15]

Part of her art? It sounds rather callous that such a profound and devastating personal experience should be allocated to the art-enhancing category of life. But, just as we recognize that every experience changes us in life, so for the actor, who uses all of himself in his work, every experience changes his work.

Life is not easy. None of us float from one triumph to the next, oblivious to disappointment, frustration, fear, anger. We have all undergone unhappy experiences which have left their mark on our lives. We hope to cope with them, live with them, come to terms with them – and usually the passage of time heals the pain. But these experiences can become locked inside us. A weeping, grieving person often literally crumples; we hug ourselves, we feel the physical pain of anguish in our stomachs and our hearts. While the initial impact gradually lessens, the incident stays with us, stored in our emotional memory forever.

In psychotherapy it can be stunning to see the way in which personal sorrow can insinuate itself into a person's life and affect their everyday nature. Even where it appears that the individual has 'got over it', the release of very old memories in the safe haven of therapy reveals the power of bad experience locked within us.

Often, when asked to recall experiences of emotional importance, people reveal negative rather than positive events from their lives. I discussed this with Liv Ullmann. She suggests that people *learn* more from bad experiences because they involve work, 'Actually what I've found and I don't think it's a rationalization, is I've learned more on the sad journeys, the ones that have led me off the track, than I have with the happy moments, though they were wonderful and I wouldn't do without them. But you don't have to struggle with happy events. They fill you with joy, but in more negative experiences you have to struggle, overcome, fight. And that is positive. We need our everyday troubles and disappointments to grow.' She does not romanticize tragedy. She points out that life sometimes visits tragedies upon us which are perhaps very difficult to bear. But the more everyday sadnesses are those we wish to resolve, and that is why they stay with us.

The way of the actor recalls, recognizes and releases the dark side of life. Bad experiences are not chewed over in a morbid and negative manner, but are given space to be *expressed* in the work of creating a character. From the novice amateur actor to the most accomplished professional, performances provide glimpses of what it means to be human in ways with which we can identify, and that provides the actor with scope for externalizing the negative as well as the positive.

Nor does it reinforce melancholy emotion. Rather the opposite. Liv Ullmann, for example, is widely recognized as a supremely gifted actor of tragic roles. Yet she also plays comedy well, and time spent with her as a person is full of laughter and light.

In fact, the way of the actor helps to bring personal darkness into light.

Ordinary Emotion

In finding aspects of one's own experience to match with those being undergone by the character, actors illustrate an important point concerning the *scale* of emotion. Often we assume that powerful emotional experiences accompany extremely dramatic events – birth, death, and the extremes of adult relationships. Of course, it is rare that personal experience of such events takes place without powerful emotion, but although drama in film, television and on stage often depicts events of enormous magnitude, actors know nevertheless that there is not a simple correlation between scale of event and scale of emotion. Events seemingly small and insignificant can have devastating emotional impact.

In daily life people often berate themselves for 'getting upset over such a little thing' or being 'over-emotional', implying that their responses to events are out of scale with the 'emotional rating' of such an event. But there is no absolute scale of measurement which lays down rules for how emotional one should feel in the face of a particular event.

Geraldine Page played a highly emotional scene in the film *Eve*, in which she portrayed a woman suffering from multiple personality. She was asked whether she drew on any particular emotional experiences of her own, 'Oh, I'm sure, but not in a conscious way. We've all been someplace where we had to behave nicely even though people were driving us batty. We couldn't protest, we couldn't get up and leave, we had to sit and put up with it. I'm sure that a variety of those experiences merged together in my mind, rose up to that part of the script, and responded to it.' 'Ordinary' experience contributed here to a convincing performance of an extreme event, and Geraldine Page points out that acting is a constant reminder of 'the kind of outsized emotions we can have over a small incident. All an actor has to do is remember that. So you don't have to be the kind of woman that Eve is to have lived intensely through the same kinds of feelings.'[16]

Glenda Jackson emphasizes that it is the small details of everyday life which provide the basis of understanding, and which lead to truth in acting, 'Most people live grey lives. Most people do not lead lives of great extremes, and it's the pinpricks of life that are really the hardest I think, because they go on forever. Great crises – at either end of the emotional spectrum, be it up or down, can in a way be coped with more easily than the grey areas of life, because you gear up for them, adrenalin flows, and you know that they won't go on forever. Now if you lose that in your own life, then you lose touch with how people are really living.'

So, in addition to a hunger for powerful experience, for tasting the boundaries of life and encompassing drama and tragedy in the actor's own world, the actor sensitizes himself to the *ordinary*, the *everyday*. Liv Ullmann says, 'You can't just float through life and not look to right and left because what are you then portraying? My material is the life I'm living and the life I'm seeing, the life I'm reading or listening to.'[17]

The way of the actor teaches respect for the power of emotion in everyday life. An emotionally rich life is not necessarily one of never-ending adventures. Rather it is living fully in the 'small' events as well as the 'large' events.

Reliving Life

The setting is a coffee bar/restaurant in an American high school town. A group of about eight teenagers are sitting around having a good time with much animated conversation, laughter and flirtation. Vicky, sitting towards one end of the table, feels totally left out, ignored, not recognized, rejected. She makes attempts to get involved with the group, leaning in towards the main part of the table, nominating topics of conversation which are ignored, slipping her hand inside the arm of the youth sitting next to her who turns, smiles unconvincingly, and immediately turns away again to the people down the table. Vicky looks distressed. She starts to shrink.

And then something incredible begins to happen. Driven by desperation, she decides that she is not going to be ignored. She is going to be noticed and attended to. Her eyes begin to take on a new focus. She begins to formulate some new plan. Something dramatic. A breakthrough action. The kind of thing which is only possible when a person is desperate, against the wall. She is going to stand on the table and dance to the music playing from the disco machine.

Deliberately and carefully, Vicky stands up on the chair. She steps on the table. Others glance at her in puzzlement, and then continue with their conversation. Vicky begins to dance. Her skirt sways above the heads of the others at the table.

Conversation continues around her feet. She dances more furiously. Irritated, people try to move her legs away when they interrupt their vision of each other. Vicky is even more desperate, and with a face contorted by anguish, she begins to strip . . . slowly unbuttoning her blouse, and letting it drop onto the table in the middle of the conversation. This does it. People stop talking and look at Vicky. But they are not impressed. They are angry. She is making a real nuisance of herself with this display of exhibitionism. 'Get down', they snarl at her. She stops dancing. 'What is the matter with you?' they demand, not really wanting an answer.

In a complete daze, Vicky bends down and picks up her blouse. Carefully, she climbs down from the table. She puts the blouse back on. Conversation is swirling around the table again, still excluding her. Dressed again, she sits quietly, small, dead, defeated. A tear trickles down her cheek.

This is an incident that really happened. One of the actors at RADA related her anguish to the rest of us. We dramatized it in a rehearsal setting because it touches those experiences all of us have when we are rejected, an outsider. And to see an experience enacted removes it from the personal and transforms it to the universal. *Shared* experience is a healing vision.

The actress who performed the piece was not the same person as the one who described it to us and to whom it happened, because when I work with actors on building dramatic pieces from their own emotional experiences, I structure it so that the energy is directed into performance. Otherwise, it becomes psychodrama in which the focus of the work is on the self. Energy turned inward in this way can be cramping for an actor, and wrestling directly with one's own emotional resources does not always provide the insights expected.

Actors recall an emotionally charged event, then describe their experience to a partner, in detail. The partner takes on the described event *as his own*. We then begin to dramatize each of the events. The actor who took on the event as his own directs a production of it in the rehearsal theatre. Events from people's lives are cast and performed, but the person to whom the event really happened is only a spectator.

So, for each actor, memories are recalled, the seeds of recognition of the original emotional impact are sown and the actor is able to re-experience, reflect and observe the re-enactments in a way which externalizes. For acting is an *expressive* way to self-discovery. It is not therapy, in which the aim is usually to focus attention inward, in an attempt to facilitate a self-regarding mode of functioning.

Psychotherapy can of course be extremely illuminating. It is a process which rests upon the central assumption that conscious knowledge of previously unconscious material can help to liberate us from the grip of unseen and unknown forces. And bringing to conscious awareness, by talking about dreams, recalling childhood experiences and so on, is a process which can lead to understanding of the roots of experience which pattern our lives.

But therapy often involves a double translation. The unconscious works in images, not rational, logical patterns of linear thought, as evidenced by dream events which are far outside the parameters of everyday experience: people suddenly change identity, time and place follow no reasonable order. Translating personal experience which has been stored in the unconscious involves a transition from deep imagery to conscious thought. The hope is that by consciously sorting out the strands of previously unconscious material, that particular element of one's life will now be under conscious control, subject to will, or that the deep structure of the psyche will respond, store and use the new framework constructed around the experience by the machinations of conscious consideration, discussion and therapy.

What makes acting such a powerful path to personal knowledge for me is that the actor is working with deep structure in a consistently appropriate language. One's personal experiences are recalled, tapped, used intuitively, and fed into the development of a character which is constructed also in images. Rarely does the actor intellectually analyze a personal experience before employing it in a character. Often the experience is 'sensed' and translated into the character's 'psyche' without going through the rational, logical, judgemental filter of conscious consideration.

When I asked Glenda Jackson whether she uses her dreams in creating characters, she replied, 'Yes. But not consciously.' The actor activates personal experience and relives it creatively. It is an organic, expressive mode of working which maintains the language of imagery. The actor's way is to work with memories of the past as living, or re-living, aspects of life in the present.

Our memories are stored in constellations consisting of experiences and related fantasies, from different periods in the life of the person.[18] The memories clustered together have a similar basic theme and have attached to them a strong emotional charge. The intensity of the release of emotion associated with childhood memories often seems to be out of proportion to the severity and relevance of the events, because emotion builds up in response to similar experiences from different periods of life. Recreating and living out some of these events, whether done by oneself or by others, suggests that to re-encounter one's life experiences is to emotionally relive them, along with the emotional impact of similar incidents from life.

Many of the potential doors to self-understanding are screened from our vision by our everyday conception of time. We normally perceive time in a linear, one-way flow – so we have memories of events that happened to us long ago, more recently, events happening now, and events which have yet to affect us. Of course, we need to have a linear, sequential understanding of time merely to exist in interaction with a complex social world. The fact that an action sequence of reaching out a hand, grasping a door handle and turning it will result in the door being opened is fundamental to our physically negotiating the world around us.

Perhaps a better sense of time is the 'eternal present', for if our life's experiences do affect the way we behave in the present, then those events from the past *are* present. Now. All the time. But we fail to recognize them as fully as we should.

The way of the actor recreates life's events in an expressive way. Past experiences are brought fully, intuitively into life in building a role, and it is a way of condensing a life into the eternal present. This makes the eternal present *full*, rather than being merely a brief interchange point through which the future rushes into the past.

Actors in workshop have dramatized experiences from my life. The actor who takes on my experience as his own casts and directs the mini-production. The effect is like watching a piece of your past life recreated into the living present, as if seeing something for the first time. Because you are not involved directly with the re-enactment, the event you are watching takes on a life of its own. It has also happened to me and others many times that the re-enactment turns out to contain characters, events, emotions which were there in the original event but *had been forgotten*. Emotionally, the original event is recreated and accumulated feelings about the event are liberated. The personal impact is awesome. For the re-enactment is truly a rebirth of one's own experience. Or reliving a life.

CHAPTER 8

Seeing: Facing Reality

'I COULD SIT all day in the Optimo Cigar Store telephone booth on 42nd Street and just watch the people pass by', declares Marlon Brando. 'Human behaviour has always fascinated me. Actors have to know how much spit you've got in your mouth and where the weight of your elbows is.'[1]

I find the very thought of walking past a telephone booth and noticing Marlon Brando, nose pressed to the glass, observing what I am doing with my spit and elbows disconcerting to say the least. Especially since Brando believes that details of behaviour reveal significant clues to a person's inner secrets. He remarked to a woman friend, 'I can tell a lot about people by the way they use their hands . . . the way you finger your pearls, for example.'[2]

The suspicion that we are being watched makes many of us feel self-conscious. It induces an awareness of self to a degree that we find uncomfortable. Most people are at least generally aware of 'body language'; that we give away information about ourselves which we cannot control, and which may be evaluated, assessed, judged. And for this reason, people are often apprehensive about psychologists, whom they feel can 'read them' purely from observation. I only once made the mistake of admitting, at a party, that I am a psychologist – a space quickly cleared around me, and people behaved like nervous deer around a cheetah until I convinced them that psychologists do not know anything.

Not compared with actors, anyway. For, in my experience, it is actors who are the real observers. They are talented and skilled at maintaining an openness towards people, to their presence, states of mind, needs, reactions and mannerisms. Liv Ullmann regards observing other people as an essential path to 'becoming other people' more fully and truthfully, and she feels that our understanding of ourselves is enhanced by our knowledge of others, 'If we fail to know others, we fail to know ourselves'.

From the Royal Academy of Dramatic Art actors go out into London to watch, observe and learn. The telephone booths are usually occupied already, but there are plenty of other vantage points and the principle is the same as for Marlon Brando. Detailed observation. It is a remarkable experience to sit and watch people, or walk around observing and listening. Because we are made uncomfortable by being watched, we tend not to really look at other people, apart from the sort of peripheral vision and brief glances necessary to ensure smooth passage through the aisles of a supermarket. But, working with actors, we have found that people can easily be observed without offending them. It is mainly a matter of freeing one's own mind to concentrate on looking, instead of walking around half blindly, aware only of the stream of inner thoughts, fantasies and chatter. About half an hour in the streets of London is usually ample time for finding a walk, stance, style, even a voice which can be collected like a life crystal, an essence of a person which is then developed like a hologram into a full-colour portrait back in the rehearsal room.

Early attempts result in actors coming back with a room-full of eccentrics, wooden-legged Long John Silvers and other characters who stand out from the crowd. But Brando-style people-watching builds quickly to sophisticated observation of the detailed behaviour and quirks of 'normal' people. It is always a revelation to me, whenever I do this exercise, to see the richness of human nature that can be 'captured' and condensed by acute observation of personal modes and mannerisms, vivid giveaways of personalities transparent beneath the flimsy masks of the public persona.

Actors have been observers for centuries, for without this keen attention to others, performances are limited to the prison of one's own personal life. Body language and non-verbal communication are now recognized by scientific psychology and have quickly passed into the applied field of image management. The idea is that by reading body language, Personnel Managers can tell more about a person than they know themselves. The converse application is in the management of personal style, controlling one's output of signals to create a specific impression.

The attempt to make a manipulatory science from observations of people's personal style results in some dreadful performances, convincing only to those who do not observe and therefore cannot discriminate. To become an observer in the way of the actor is a powerful preparation for seeing through an insincere performance. I have never encountered a truly effective businessman who was much concerned with the conscious control of body language. But I have met businessmen who *were* astute observers of others, and who as a result gained deeper levels of understanding and contact with people.

The way of the actor uses observation skills not for exploitation of others or power games, but for creating mirrors in which we see ourselves reflected. And Marlon Brando, a consummate observer of human behaviour, warns actors away from watching themselves on film, and attempting conscious control of their body language. He emphasizes the importance of outer-directed observation, 'Actors who watch themselves tend to become mannered. The less you think about how effective you are, the more effective you are. You don't learn to be effective from film, but from life.'[3]

Observation of behaviour details does not need to be restricted to body language. Posture, movement, tension, shape and demeanour can communicate a lot, but often there is a single feature, aspect or quirk of appearance which provides a clue to a whole personality – because people sometimes concentrate important elements of their lives into a single facet or a few features of their appearance.

A vivid illustration 'in reverse' of how an observant actor may use this principle is provided by John Hurt. When he was preparing his role as the 'junkie' in *Midnight Express*, all he had to go on was the description in the script, 'Max is an international junkie who has fallen to bits'. So he built up the character himself, imagining a seedy Oxford-educated drop-out who wears a pair of glasses with the left lens broken. Billy Hayes, the author of *Midnight Express*, knew the person upon whom the character was based. When Hayes saw John Hurt on the film set, he could not believe that the actor had not met the original Max. From the description, and Max's lines in the script, Hurt had developed an 'appearance exactly matching that of the real-life character. The original Max had even worn glasses with the left lens broken.'[4]

Observation is an active process. We are not passive recorders of the world around us. We select when we look – necessarily as humans, culturally as members of particular societies and personally as individuals. But the actor consciously develops open eyes. He still selects, of course; what he sees is governed by his personality and needs, or by the role he is preparing. But he *observes*. And for observing, in the way of the actor, out in the streets is as good a place as any to begin.

Or even a telephone booth. . . .

Facing Reality

'I love close-ups. To me they are a challenge. The closer a camera comes, the more eager I am to show a completely naked face, show what is behind the skin, the eyes; inside the head. Show the thoughts that are forming.'[5] Liv Ullman points out that film acting brings the performer *closer* to the audience than in any other medium. The close-up reaction of a face, even eyes, blown-up onto an enormous cinema screen gives an intimacy between actor and audience equivalent to the most close and intimate proximity between two people in real life. Our normal boundaries of personal space are psychologically violated in such close-ups – the character is inside our intimate, personal space, and our reactions are commensurate with the brains registering of this. This gives the actor the astonishing power to deliver an act of communication that can feel tremendously individual, as if aimed at each member of the audience alone.

And the camera reveals, through the close-up of facial expression, an intimate impression of the actor, 'Even when I tell myself that I am expressing a role, I can never completely hide who *I* am, what *I* am. The audience, at the moment of identification, meets a person, not a role, not an actress. . . .'[6]

Charlton Heston agrees, 'You are followed not only by the lengthening shadow of all the performances people remember you for, but also what your life has done to you – what kind of person it has made you.' On screen, in close-up, this experience is revealed. As an example, Heston points to a performance of Spencer Tracy, 'Tracy won an Academy Award doing a part in *Gentlemen of Nuremberg* in which he really said very little – sat there with his earphones on, listening. But his face said so much; it had to do with more than just acting.'

Glenda Jackson loves China. One of the things that impressed her, on a recent visit, were Chinese faces. She was struck by the fact that the colourless uniformity of their dress revealed their faces in startling relief and detail, unencumbered by distractions of costume and artifice. Glenda considers that people's faces mirror their whole inner being and provide the key to deep contact and communication between people. She wishes that in the West we were a little more like the Chinese, showing our faces more honestly and clearly, instead of overpowering them with showy, gaudy clothes. And as she told me this, over dinner, I began to wish that I had worn a less brightly-coloured jacket. . . .

Actors are aware of faces. Their features are enhanced, disguised, changed and channelled by make-up. The lines, bumps, shapes and wrinkles of their own faces, as revealing as a map of their lives' terrain, are studied in brightly-lit make-up mirrors. Bone structure and skin texture are known, understood and used. This is not vanity, but a necessary aspect of the profession. Individual actors do have vanities, of course, and when they have to alter their appearance to portray someone ten years older, or less attractive it is not easy. But it is non-actors who are vain.

People are vulnerable creatures. We often find it hard to live with ourselves as we are. Self-improvement is a cult and fantasies of an enhanced self are common features of daydreams. Many of us see our faces not as reflections of who we are, but as objects to be altered to conform to who we would like to be. Hairstyles are changed to enhance and flatter. Beards are grown to add interest, maturity and to conceal nature's 'errors'. Make-up is applied to imitate famous models, fashions and styles. In fact, for many adults in the modern world some degree of awareness of self-image for motives of social and sexual attraction is an accepted fact of life.

Most of this is harmless, of course. But for the actor it is an attitude to appearance which needs to be balanced by an understanding of what is really there. I have found relatively few actors to be obsessed by their appearance. Contrary to the stereotype, they do not continually strive to look wonderful. But they *do* know what they look like.

When we look in the mirror, many of us see a blurred image. We see what we are accustomed to *want* to see. To realize the true shape and structure of our faces, we need to go beyond the automatic defences of our 'vanity system', and experience our faces in a different way. We need to see our faces with our fingertips.

At the Royal Academy of Dramatic Art I ask actors to shake their hands about for a minute or two to release tension. Blood flows into the hands, and the fingers; those marvellously sensitive antennae become tingly and charged with feeling. One is reminded of Woody Allen's carnal wish to be reincarnated as Warren Beatty's fingertips.

Eyes closed, actors explore their faces. Fingertips stroke, probe, slide and slither over the skin, feeling for lines, texture, fat and bone, hair and hairlines, details of ears, lips, eyebrows. Putting on a deep frown changes everything: tension of skin over the nose, across the forehead, shape of lips, jaw, position of hairline. We think of a frown as only the lowering of eyebrows. But our faces register emotion, and emotion is all-encompassing.

A broad smile felt with our fingertips reveals puffy, apple cheeks, tightly stretched lips, creases near the eyes, flared nostrils. We usually don't realize that our own faces are doing all this work, giving all this away.

Two actors sit close, opposite one another. One has his eyes closed. The other places one forefinger on the bridge of his partner's nose, another forefinger on the bridge of his own. Then with his eyes closed too, he carefully and lightly traces his own features and, simultaneously, those of his partner. It is a revelation. In contrast with those of others, our own noses seem to take a strange and rambling journey from top to tip, or the length of the upper lip becomes a cause for merriment, much longer or shorter than realised. The partner turns out to have ears twice the size of your own.

It is an adventure. It is an exploration of your face as it really is. We are generally aware of our appearance and that of the people around us, but 'looking' with the fingertips reveals many surprises. It shows you your real face.

Drawing the Line

Antony Sher looked at me, eyes narrowing like an artist measuring perspective. I shifted uncomfortably on his couch, trying to improve my posture without his noticing. 'If I was to do a drawing of you,' he said thoughtfully, 'I'd be observing things about you and sketching lines on paper. If I was playing you as a character I'd do the same thing except I'd be using my body and voice instead of lines on paper. I think that's what all actors do. They sketch characters and colour them in with themselves.'

Anyone who has seen Antony Sher's marvellous drawings and sketches (which have been exhibited) would realize that when he is drawing he is doing a great deal of interpretation. It is not only external image that is captured by his drawing pen; it is the internal essence. And he uses his body not as a three-dimensional pictorial representation of someone, but as a creative interpretation of their inner nature.

The 'artist's' approach to observation has been noted by other actors. Rip Torn, for example, says that when he is working, 'I have a great deal in common with painters. . . . I do paint characters. I select my elements by the way I choose to walk, the way I move, the way my voice operates, the actual pitch of it, the sound of it. I select those in the same way a painter takes colors from his palette to create an impression. So while my identification is instinctive, my selectivity is conscious; that's where the artistry comes in.'[7]

Few of us draw after we have left school and for many, art lessons have simply demonstrated to us our inability to faithfully represent on paper the objects around us. Children who cannot produce a sketched facsimile of an object or person end up thinking they 'cannot draw'. As a tool of the way of the actor, sketching opens eyes afresh, if done in the right way. Or rather, the wrong way.

At RADA piles of drawing paper are handed out and felt tip pens for each actor. I explain that I am going to ask them to do some drawing. Groans. Moans. Denial of any shred of artistic talent. Impossible task. As the protests die down, I give my instructions. I want them to work in pairs and taking it in turns each actor is to draw a picture of his partner's face. Renewed groans, at higher volume. Threats of mutiny. I raise my hands in hopes of quelling the rebellion and announce that there is one very important rule to be followed in this exercise. When drawing the partner's face, the artist must *not* look down at the drawing. At no time must the artist take his eyes from his partner's face. I tell them that if they once forget the rule or submit to temptation and glance down, then they must begin the drawing all over again, turning the page over for a fresh start.

This, of course, violates all our understanding about the way to draw something. If there is not constant checking between the object being drawn and the lines on the page, how can you hope to have an accurate representation of the person? The drawing will not look like the subject and is therefore worthless.

But this is where we make the mistake common to so much of our perception. We become used to the idea that the way we *see* the world is a more or less accurate reflection of reality. Research in psychology has, however, demonstrated the extent to which we 'create' what we see, transforming the optical image in the brain into a shape and structure we recognize.

The way in which the actor works as an artist is not to produce a photographic likeness of a character, but to sketch an outline which captures the essence, and reveals the truth about a person. This necessitates *fresh* perception – recording details free from the habitual assumptions we make in forming brain images. Looking at someone with insight, as a 'sketch artist', draws on the same perceptual sharpness as observing someone as a basis for a role. Or in learning about life.

The problem with drawing a face is that faces are such familiar objects. We suffer from face overload and take them for granted. We are so used to reading facial expressions for the purposes of social interaction, that we forget to see the face as a mask. A revealing mask, which projects the deepest realms of the person 'underneath'.

Actors are always willing to have a go. They crawl into position in pairs, arrange or argue briefly as to who will be the artist and who will be the model for the initial drawing, and they start. The results of this exercise are almost always astonishingly effective. The drawings do not look at all like the ones we did at school. They look like Picasso. Strong, vibrant, impressionistic; inaccurate in some details but stunning in the way they capture the *essence* of a person. Total concentration on the contours of the face of another person seems to summon deep truths that escape us in our daily lives of casual glances, furtive eye contact and carefully maintained interpersonal distances.

After several partners and lots of drawings, an art show is organized. Pictures of each person, by different artists are collected together. And dominant features, often unexpected and surprising ones, occur over and over in the various drawings. Actors leave with a collection of drawings of themselves, reflections of their inner beings, tucked under their arms.

This is not a book of practical exercises, but it *is* so easy to sketch people. It can be done on the back of an envelope, a paper napkin in a restaurant, a shopping list retrieved from the pocket, a theatre programme. Or a pocket sketchbook and pencil can be a treasury of observation. But the rule must stand. For the pictures to be any good to your observational powers, they have got to be terrible in conventional terms. At first, anyway. . . . And all drawing must conform to the golden rule: no looking down. All attention goes into the subject being sketched.

Afterwards, people look different in the street. The way they hold their faces seems almost like conscious expressions, even grimaces, which become more 'set' with age. But even in very young people, the face is already reflecting the deep pools of experience within.

Facing reality.

Observation for a Character

In the film *Kramer vs Kramer*, Meryl Streep plays a woman who deserts her husband and then demands custody of their child. But at that point in her life she felt inadequate to play the part, 'How could I play her? I'm not a mother. I wasn't married at the time'.[8] To compensate for this lack of experience, Meryl Streep wandered for days around Manhattan's East Side, where the character was supposed to live, soaking up observation and atmosphere and forcing herself into the imagined personality.

There are some experiences in life that need to be experienced first hand to know the full weight of them; vicarious 'knowing' from the outside is simply too superficial. However, we also know that being a fully experiencing participant in something can sometimes be limiting, even blinding. We are so overwhelmed by the all-encompassing nature of an experience that we find it difficult to gain perspective, to see into it clearly. The filling of an otherwise empty channel with researched, vicarious experiences can sometimes work very effectively. Streep says, 'Sometimes if you live outside an experience, you have greater insight than if you're in it.'

Observations like this are consciously undertaken to build a role. The actor's knowledge of others, their behaviour, milieu, attitudes and habits, becomes a further extension of the actor's knowledge of himself.

Of course, there are lots of ways of observing. Bruce Dern, for example, says, 'I'm a people-watcher. I'm an observer, an astute student of the human condition. Not sociologically, but individually.' He describes Jane Fonda as a sociological observer, 'She looks at things in groups and in classes and in bunches: this group of people, that group, them, their. I'm never concerned with anything but him or her.'[9]

Antony Sher revels in this aspect of his work, 'One of the things I love about being an actor is that we're constantly being exposed to new things; and we're lucky that way, because someone who works in an office would get the things in life that they find interesting and would stick to those things. And we're constantly being thrown into situations when we have to play people who are into different things than we are. One is opening one's self, to some extent, to a different field. And I love that.'

Sher told me about his role in the TV series based on Ray Bradbury's novel, 'In the TV series I did, *The History Man*, I played a sociology lecturer. When I started I knew nothing about sociology, and though I was finding out about the subject for only a short period of time, I found the research interesting. If it hadn't been for the role, it is a subject I would never have investigated in a million years.' Sher also delighted in the detailed research necessary for one of Mike Leigh's plays,

Goosepimples, in which he played an Arab, 'I can tell you everything about Arab social behaviour from what they have for breakfast to how they go to the toilet, which again is hardly what one would normally know.'

As well as dealing with what the actor already is, the process of preparing a part can be enormously stretching because it has the effect of putting the actor in a range of situations outside his immediate experience.

Charlton Heston has played a number of roles which required the acquisition of specific skills. Perhaps best known is the now legendary chariot-race in *Ben-Hur*, surely one of the most memorable action sequences in modern film. For that role Heston had to undergo weeks of training until his chariot racing abilities reached competitive level. There have been other roles which required a high level of skill, less celebrated perhaps but significant nonetheless. *Counterpoint* is one of Heston's favourite films. 'I have always enjoyed classical music, and in it I played an American orchestra conductor captured by the Nazis in 1944. I spent four months learning how to conduct – which was longer than it took me to learn driving the chariot in *Ben-Hur!*'

Heston remembers vividly his experience of painting the ceiling of a chapel in his portrayal of Michaelangelo, 'It was astonishing to have at my disposal a full-scale replica of the Sistine Chapel, complete with ceiling and wet plaster, and a copy of the scaffolding that Michaelangelo designed. Using it did give me some sense of the man.' Heston described to me with amusement a recent flurry of excitement in the academic world, 'when some art historian decided that Michaelangelo did not lie down to paint the Chapel. I'm the only one alive that ever tried it, and I'm telling you he lay down.' But he admitted, with the wry humour of the only person alive that has tried it, that painting the ceiling of the Sistine Chapel lying or standing are both impossible, 'If you stand, and tilt your head to look up, the paint falls in your mouth. And if you lie down, the paint falls in your eyes. Both techniques have their drawbacks. . . .'

Ironically, actors who are conspicuously successful have their freedom to observe curtailed. With fame it becomes impossible to enter many of the ordinary social settings, because one is instantly recognized. Meryl Streep has pointed to this difficulty, 'The soul, the source of what I do, is observation. But since I became famous I can't watch people – because they're watching me. It is absolutely impossible.' 'It seems to me,' she says, 'when you become famous, a lot of your energy goes into maintaining what you had before you were famous, maintaining your sense of observation, being able to look at other people. If they take away your observation powers, you're lost.'[10]

The crucial importance of living a 'normal' life, extends to the problem of avoiding allowing wealth to elevate one to a pampered position, with life's menial tasks all performed by servants. Meryl Streep does most of her 'ordinary living' chores, 'I've always been afraid to let go', she explains. 'If you lose the understanding of what it is to live day-to-day how can you act anything but movie stars or kings and queens?'

Glenda Jackson recognizes the potentially distancing effect of fame, in which the pressures are to live a life divorced from the mundane. It is easy to be driven into 'inhabiting a very select world of people in which you simply see the same people over and over again. The further you take yourself away from ordinary life, the more difficult you make it for yourself as an actor. And to say that because of your chosen profession you have to be excluded from, for want of a better phrase, the real world, strikes me as being absurd, because you can't actually do your chosen profession if you totally lose touch with the real world.' 'My private life has to be ordinary', she says. 'In acting you have to present recognizable human beings. And to do that you have to try to keep in touch with the basic problem of real people's lives.'

A common stereotype of famous actors is that they live exotic and pampered lives, cocooned from the rest of the world by the trappings of luxury and phalanxes of personal assistants. No doubt there are actors who allow this to happen, but many are determined to avoid it. Far from living in a 'fantasy world', they are determined to live in the 'real world'. While we fantasize about living like famous actors, they struggle to live like us.

Seeing

Fundamental to our experience of life are assumptions about the way the world is. Assumptions so deeply embedded in our cultural upbringing that they seem to us as if they are absolute reality. In seeing, for example, the eyes supply the brain with sensory data about the external world. But to make any sense of this data, the brain has to interpret and organize it according to our conceptual models of what the world looks like.

The perceptual experience of basic objects (table and chairs, for example) is a result of the brain imposing structure on a stream of visual data, but people have a high level of agreement amongst themselves as to what visual configurations constitute 'table and chairs'. But when we deal with much more complex judgements of experience, such as the character of a person, our structuring of information is very variable from one individual to another. It is affected by our beliefs, prejudices, loves, fears, interests and blind spots. We see what our needs allow us to see.

While our view of other people, and our relationship to them, can change according to our moods, or the state of our own lives, nevertheless each individual tends to approach life with his own fairly 'set' structures. We tend to see, and judge, ourselves and others in ways that for each of us are predictable.

We see the world along our own channels – and channels can easily become ruts. So, even when it would be good for us to see people in fresh and different ways, we cannot because, regardless of the sort of 'information' we receive from people, we each tend to structure it according to our own perceptual and emotional frameworks. We see a varied and everchanging social environment in our same, favourite old ways.

But for actors this is anathema. If an actor were to see people in predictable ways he would play wildly different characters as if they were similar. Actors need to keep the structures they place on 'social information' as flexible as possible. Parts of the actor's life – like observing the details of people's behaviour, becoming aware of faces by feeling or drawing, and learning the skills and habits which punctuate the lives of others – all these and the many other techniques of 'actor observation' keep the channels clear of ruts. This enables the actor to live his own life more flexibly.

Antony Sher reckons that 'even the more superficial observations of people's lives broaden one's spectrum, and I think it spills over into actors being very open, very broad-minded, very liberated people.'

Seeing with freshness and clarity. Facing reality.

CHAPTER 9

Dream: Images of Power

'THE FEAR OF vampires, and the nightmares about vampires, are tied up with the desire for vampires'.

Klaus Kinski believes that we need vampires. Talking of his role as Dracula in the film *Nosferatu*, he says, 'There is a human desire to give yourself, to be taken, to give love without any limit . . . it's natural to be attracted by the vampire. We are drawn to things we don't know – but which we feel.'

The way to communicate such deeply experienced human emotions is, Kinski reckons, through the use of images, like those that give such power to the films of director Werner Herzog, 'I believe people comprehend more by feeling than by words. That's why I like Herzog's films. He communicates directly from the screen to the audience. There is nothing separating the person on the screen from the person sitting in the cinema, nothing separating my eyes from the eyes of the audience, nothing separating my soul from the soul of the spectator.'[1] Films communicate in images of high emotional potency. As Jack Nicholson says, 'It is a primitive eye that watches the film even in the most sophisticated person.'[2]

Indeed, actors in 'primitive' societies used this power of imagery to literally carry people 'out of time' into a mythological world. Peter Brook, talking about his 1985 production of the *Mahabharata*, at the Avignon Festival, says, 'A myth as opposed to any story is a series of events and images told in narrative form which works on the reader on many levels. A commonplace example would be the imagery we know from the Gospel . . . the image of Christ being nailed to the cross is no simplification because that image alone for thousands of years has been rich in the infinity of layers of meaning for people. . . .'

While the words of spoken language basically deal with a single idea at a time, symbols can combine the most disparate elements into a unitary expression. The adage that a picture is worth a thousand words intimates the powerful information-carrying capacity of images. 'This has always been said and known to be the truth about fairy stories', Peter Brook continues. 'If you just dwell on the essential, the apparently naive imagery of a fairy story, behind it you find layers and layers of meaning which are not intellectual meanings, but explanatory meanings, meaning that is evoked by the flow of images.'[3]

Today, tragically, the concept of myth is devalued and little understood. It is contrasted, unfavourably, with fact. People will say of something they do not believe, 'That's just myth'. But stories carried by powerful imagery are the stuff of myth, and we absorb them greedily and ignorantly from film and theatre; even the truncated narrative and heavy-handed symbolism of television commercials carry meaning we barely understand consciously.

Simplicity and Silence

Liv Ullmann thinks that images are crucial today because Western media saturation has led to word 'overload'. There is so much talk, on television and radio, and in the press, that it becomes a babble of noise, 'Sometimes the best words create images of their own. But we are so full of noise, we really need to see what is in the pauses. The truth behind the words. That's why I think the understanding of imagery is more important than words.'

She feels that images communicate at many depths of meaning, but they need to be presented cleanly and simply. Since both acting and watching performances are based on recognition – the identity with human experience which bonds people together – she speaks of aiming for a performance which communicates 'everything' with a single movement of the head, 'I think the greatest pleasure is that you as an actor have made the character so real that in the end, when you just do that movement of the head, the audience are already with you.'

Theatre, film and television, at their most effective, take us into an 'imaginal' state of mind. We contribute our imagination to the action in a myriad of ways, and we can sometimes be so absorbed in something that it feels as if we have been in another world. Coming out of a theatre or film our minds may be alive with images from the show for hours, with particular images occurring occasionally for days, or weeks. Famous scenes we have witnessed in films or theatre are sometimes permanently in our memory bank, remembered much more readily than many scenes we have seen in 'real life'.

In stage work, Liv Ullmann aims to keep her performance simple, because that leaves more lasting images, 'What I try to do now is to leave people with some clear images, which will come back to people days, weeks, even months after the performance. It's the imagery which makes you understand even after the words have been forgotten.'

'The wonderful part about acting is that you can convey these very, very complex things quite graphically,' says Geraldine Page, describing her work as a way of communication through images. 'Quite often I've tried to explain things to people who I thought were quite sympathetic, and I'd talk and talk and then realize that they hadn't comprehended a single word I'd said. . . . But if I walk on the stage with a certain attitude, people will understand immediately. . . .'[4]

Their immediacy, the way they stay in your mind, and the many layers of meaning they carry gives images their power.

Fantasy

Fantasy is taboo. In the secular, instrumental world of today, to indulge in fantasy is to dwell in a 'realm of unreality'. It is considered to be a waste of time. An indulgence.

Liv Ullmann decries this, but thinks it important to distinguish between different sorts of fantasy. 'I think there's good fantasy and bad fantasy. The bad fantasy is what you see on television – the commercials that tell you if you use this hair spray, a fantasy life will follow – your husband will come home on a white horse. That is a dangerous fantasy because that is not how life is.' This is the sort of fantasy that we all recognize as unreal, and the promotion of unrealistic expectations about life Ullmann considers dangerous and frustrating, '. . . People live in anguish because they've based their whole lives on unreality.'

But she considers that there is 'good fantasy', which is a recognition that in human terms there is no 'objective, real world', but rather one in which we interact creatively with our environment, colouring it with our own contribution to the active process of perception, 'Good fantasy is . . . the wonder of a flower of a season when the trees get their leaves, and you make it alive. . . . And that is a wonderful fantasy because it enriches what is already there with what is already in you. Even in reality there are lots of beautiful dreams.'

We tend to forget that fantasy is an ever-present element in everyday perception. Instead, to indulge in fantasy is sometimes even considered pathological. In psychiatric terms, 'If . . . the gratifications of reality are insufficient, thinking may not be controlled by the demands of reality but may serve as a regressive or substitute satisfaction. Such musing is known as fantasy. . . . The psychotic patient may live simultaneously in two unrelated worlds – one of fantasy and one of reality.'⁵

We all have a stream of inner consciousness which consists of memories – images of events past; anticipation – images of expected future events; and reality – related thinking, coping with immediate events in the external world. And we all have, in addition, *unrealistic* images which are not directly connected with the 'objective' world in which we live. In their private, inner world, most people experience fantasies about love, sex, success, happiness, material wealth and revenge. In other words, we all live simultaneously in the world of fantasy and reality.

Caughey has described how, 'We do not live only in the objective world of external objects and activities. On the contrary, much of our experience is inner experience. Each day we pass through multiple realities – we phase in and out, back and forth, between the actual world and imaginary realms.'

He points out how we awake in the mornings after spending hours in the image-laden world of dreams, and how, in our early morning routines, we frequently drift off into an internal stream of reverie – moments from the past, imagined scenes from the day ahead. Travelling to work, most people are only partly aware of the familiar route, 'Much of the time we are "away", lost in anticipations of the hours or years ahead or in fantasies about how things might otherwise be . . . and so throughout the day, hour after hour, day after day.'[6]

This world of inner fantasy is intensely personal and emotionally potent. And inevitably the stream of inner images affects dramatically the way we see the external world of supposed reality.

Of course, there are people who become lost in the world of fantasy, and who cannot find the way back to the equally important realm of rationality. Psychiatry functions to help these people. But these unhappy extremes should not seduce us into thinking that 'sanity' means living a totally rational, fantasy-free life. A totally rational person would be insane.

Fantasy is integral to our whole way of life – not some aberrant, time-wasting indulgence which can be forgiven if practised only during leisure hours. Fantasy is psychologically a fact, for all of us. In its own way, fantasy is reality.

Being Childlike

'People still go to the theatre; still go to museums and see new artists. They will seek it out and take the risk in droves. And it's not just because they are trying to escape. It's because they are trying to *enter*.' William Hurt objects to the common assumption that to watch a play, film or television drama is an 'escape' from reality, a vacation from the important things in life. Rather, he says, it is a conscious wish to *enter* the world of the imaginal; a complementary, equally important dimension. And when people have entered the world of imagination they are, according to Hurt, in a mental environment in which they can create communal events with their shared imaginations, '. . . The mask comes to life. And what do people believe? They believe their imagination. The life that is happening is the life of the imagination. That is the mind of the actor.'[7]

Children enter this world frequently. In fact, we often associate 'make-believe' with children, forgetting that as adults we make-believe all the time in our minds. We carefully avoid expressing this fantasy life externally, afraid we might be thought 'childish'.

'You must become as a little child again', says Laurence Luckinbill. 'It's the difference between being childish and childlike. . . . It's never having given up asking the basic questions. "Why am I a man?" What would it be like if I dressed completely differently and ran a vegetable store or tried walking backwards. . . . I do things like that and other people who are actors do, too. It's not peripheral to us; it's fundamental. It's what life is . . . that kind of experimentation.'[8]

Games of make-believe, the hallmark of childhood, are also the central aspect of the actor's world. But most adults, when asked to get up and play-act, feel a bit silly. A group of children, asked to walk backwards to discover the sensation, would probably cooperate readily. But with adults, self-consciousness paralyses. Embarrassment inhibits.

And yet for many people, the liberation which accompanies a party – whether it is organized games, dancing or whatever, is the license to 'forget yourself' and play with abandon. We allow ourselves to behave, under certain circumstances, in a manner familiar from our childhood. And we enjoy it. It is a release, a liberation.

Childlike ways of asking questions mean that we have to strip from ourselves layers of accumulated material which has channelled our thinking. Most adults 'learn' along well-drilled lines. The child, on the other hand, is more open to totally new ways of doing things because he has not built up so many defences. Our defences serve a purpose of course. We all have vulnerable areas of our lives and we protect those areas with specifically developed defences. But they get in the way of allowing us to re-examine ourselves. We protect ourselves from ourselves.

Liv Ullmann told me about her view of theatre as a place where people can go as an audience or actor, and return to the childlike view of the world, 'I think acting is tremendously important because the theatre is one of the few places people can still go and suddenly unlearn something they have been taught. Unlearning is, I think, very important.' Ullmann feels that this childlike state is not only for the audience, but is the state that she, as an actress, should seek. 'It's the innocence of childhood – when we were still open, when we could paint a tree and let it look any way we liked. It was the time before somebody came and said a tree looks like this and you must paint it so.'

She sees the return to a childlike perspective not as an escape – she lives very fully in the 'adult' world – but rather as a renewal of her flexibility and freedom. Time spent in the childlike imagination refreshes the decisions made as an adult, 'Now both the past and the present are part of me. I can mature and find values that have to do with this world. . . . Now I can use what I want of my (childlike) fantasy, incorporate it into my living. My choices – of who I want to be – are bigger in some ways today. At the same time, of course, there are many fewer tomorrows than there were three years ago when all of tomorrow was ahead. Now there are a lot of yesterdays, but if I use yesterdays wisely all the tomorrows can be enriched.'[9]

To enter this world we have to drop some of the restrictions of adulthood. To overcome the enculturated idea that to indulge the imagination is 'foolish'. Not appropriate for adults.

The actor transcends the paralysing bonds of social approval. Far from constantly seeking societal acceptance, as is the common stereotype, actors seek to lead audiences on a journey back into themselves. In order to do that, actors have to accept themselves – and take the risk that others will, while watching their work, nevertheless designate what they do as childish, embarrassing, shameful.

Janet Suzman, talking about Glenda Jackson, says, 'The thing about Glenda is that she has no sense of shame; and I mean that admiringly. She feels she has nothing to be ashamed about. She accepts herself as she is and expects others to do the same.'[10]

Glenda Jackson is in good philosophical company. D.T. Suzuki, the Zen Master, says in his foreword to *Zen and the Art of Archery*: 'Man is a thinking reed, but his great works are done when he is not calculating and thinking. "Childlikeness" has to be restored with long years of training in self-forgetfulness.'[11]

The way of the actor provides just such a training.

Images of Power

The actor lies on his back, eyes closed. His breathing is slow and rhythmic. He is in a trance, deeply involved in a fantasy trip. I ask him to imagine stepping through a large door, and to describe to me what he sees. After the briefest of intervals, his face suddenly goes slack, and an expression of surprise takes over. He starts to speak, 'It's amazing . . . incredible. It's a huge, sort of . . . studio.'

'Studio?'

'Yes. There's equipment all about. Cameras and mikes, tapes and so on.'

'You mean a film studio?'

'Yes. A film studio. Only strange. Everything is plugged in, ready to go. It's just that there's no one here to work anything.'

Suddenly he exclaims, 'That's incredible. There's a *huge* screen – a projection screen. But there's nothing playing on it. Wait. There's something starting . . .'

I saw his eyes moving under the lids, but he didn't speak. I prompted him to tell me what he could see.

'It's sort of an underwater scene. It's beautiful. The colours are just fantastic. They keep changing.'

His voice and facial expression clearly denoted awe and excitement. 'It's the most fantastic thing I've ever seen', he continued. 'There's a fish. A huge, multicoloured fish. It's magnificent.'

His voice was trembling with excitement. I was surprised and rather startled by his sudden passion.

'The fish is going up a tunnel', he went on excitedly. 'It's swimming slowly up a tunnel. Beautiful. I want to follow it. I want to go into the water and swim up the tunnel after the fish.'

Some time later, we sat in the pub, Albie talking, me listening. He was raving about the fantasy images. He said it was like a trip he never wanted to return from. Better than any dream. Better than anything.

Images are very powerful experiences. A visual or sound image can influence us in ways different from but as equally effective as the written or spoken word. Our normal reliance on our mental processes to control our lives is one of the first things to change in the way of the actor. Intelligence is still required, of course, and the process of rehearsal and performance requires considerable mental involvement. But this needs to be *balanced much more* with the intuitive. In western culture, this does not mean *adding something*. The intuitive faculty is always there, but we override it with mental functions. Often instead of allowing our intuitive levels to operate freely and guide our behaviour naturally, we try too hard to analyze and consciously direct our lives.

In the past twenty years, a variety of psychological studies have shown that the left and right sides of our brains specialize in different types of activity. The left side of the brain appears to be concerned largely with 'rational, sequential thought, and with linguistic faculties such as reading, writing and speech.' It 'analyses, abstracts, counts, marks time, plans step-by-step procedures, verbalises, makes rational statements based on logic.'[12] And in most modern societies, we value these 'left brain' activities very highly. Too highly. For as psychologist Peter Russell points out, 'When we say that someone has "a good mind", we usually mean to imply that they can think logically, reason well, and express themselves clearly – all predominantly left-brain activites.'[13] But the other half of the brain is there to be used also.

Increasingly, scientists are beginning to realize that the right side of the brain is equally complex, equally important. For it appears to be more concerned with visual-spatial functions, emotional appreciation, and perhaps with intuitive thought.[14] The right brain sees things that, 'may be imaginary – existing only in the mind's eye – or recall things that may be real. . . . Using the right hemisphere we understand metaphors, we dream, we create new combinations of ideas.'[15] And one of the most crucial capabilities of the right brain is imaging, in which the brain is able to apprehend, understand and conjure up images.

The right and left halves of the brain do not seem to work together at the same time. One or the other predominates. Both are needed in the way of the actor, for all of the functions listed above are part of the process of creating a performance. But the left brain seems to predominate most the time – so the actor reserves specific spaces of time in which the right brain is dominant. And analysis gives way to intuition. One way to work with, and begin to trust the intuitive, is to learn to work in the language of the intuitive – images.

Many actors find that they work best in a visual sense. John Hurt, for example, 'I'm not a great reader at all. . . . I think the real root of the matter is that I have an emotional approach to life and my mind is entirely visual. Hence my original training as a painter before taking up acting.'[16]

Imagination is, of course, a central core of the actor's talent. But the development of imagination is not, as some might think, merely encouraging a rich fantasy life. Acting is *action*, and in workshops the emphasis is on the *power* that can be generated by working with images.

In workshops actors develop the ability to create imagery so intensely that it can increase the strength of the body threefold. Three chairs are set up so that two are facing each other at about 5 or 6 feet apart, and a third is between and at right angles to them. An actor lies across the chairs, feet on one, head on the opposite chair, and bottom supported by the middle chair. The actor then enters a concentrated state of mind, and visualizes an iron bar passing through the body. The image builds up to such an extent that the actor thinks of nothing else, and feels his entire body supported by and suspended on the imaginary bar.

When I judge the actor to be ready, I slowly remove the middle chair, and the actor is able to keep his body suspended across the space. The body is rigid; there is no trembling or shaking, and no visible physical effort on the part of the actor. We have had actors 'suspended' so rigidly that a person can sit on the actor's unsupported stomach, and lift their feet from the ground. The vivid image of the iron bar enables the muscles of the body to be coordinated to generate sufficient strength to easily support the weight of a second person across the space between the chairs.

The ability of states of mind to affect the operation of the body is now becoming well-established in medicine. In cancer therapy, for example, success has been obtained with 'visualizations', a technique in which the patient creates mental images of the interior of the body, and especially the cancer cells which are seen as attacking that body. The patient then visualizes his or her own white blood cells coming in and destroying the cancer cells. The precise details of the imagery may vary considerably from one patient to another, but the principles of the visualization are the same.

Actors are supreme visualizers. Sometimes, it helps them to get through a performance even when quite ill or seriously injured. Lynn Redgrave says, 'It's mind over matter: it's like those yogis who lie on a bed of nails or walk on hot coals; it's like natural childbirth. When you're concentrating very hard on something else, you are unable to feel pain. I've seen people, and I've done it myself, hobble to the theatre, sprint their way through a performance, and have to get on crutches as soon as they're off. I haven't ever broken anything, but I've had cuts, sprains, hurts, whatever. And I literally didn't feel pain at the time.'[17]

Dreams

Dreams are considered to be the 'royal road to the unconscious' in classical psychoanalysis, but few of us pay much attention to our dreams. Dreams are often mundane, sometimes interesting, only very rarely fantastic. And the vast majority of people remember very little about their dreams at all.

This is because the spirits are no longer talking to us.

Centuries ago, worldwide, dreams had an 'other-world' significance. They were messages, warnings, adventures from a separate realm. Most cultures envisaged this realm as the spirit-world – spiritual forces which represented all the knowledge that could not be encompassed in our rational minds.[18] Far from being a primitive superstition, this was a sign of wisdom. Now we assume that the world of the rational, by which we mean positivistic, cause-and-effect, logical, operational thought, is the only *really* valid way of perceiving and understanding the world. It is, of course, extremely valuable. As a scientist I would not question the benefits to humans of the advances of scientific medicine and technology. But we are faced with a human world playing with nuclear annihilation, turning a blind eye to massive starvation, pursuing a life of luxury for some at the expense of others. We are realizing the limitations of science, medicine and technology. Like an orchestra with only one instrument, we keep searching among the same simple tunes for the answers.

Dreams are now seen mechanistically. They are 'white noise' in the brain, or at best communications between one part of the self and the other. But, personal content apart, it is the *structure* of dreams which is important. For they usually appear in fragmentary, half-finished narrative, incongruities between how people look and what they say, shifting identities of dream characters, unpredictable sequences of events, strange relationships between people. Dreams are held together by connections which are emotionally powerful, but logically inconsistent. Like life.

While we fool ourselves into believing that life can be controlled, as if it were a vast machine built by robots, we are forever surprised by the happenings, shocks and surprises, frustrations, coincidences and complexities of our daily lives. This is because life, both personal and collective, is much more like dreams than like the particular style of waking, rational consciousness we inaccurately, and dangerously, label 'reality'.

Traditional cultures realized this and made provision for it by paying special respect to the actor shaman, the person who could induce us to enter the world of dreams through the inspiration and skills of his public performance.

The language of the dream is the image. It is a language that actors still understand. Liv Ullmann, working for UNICEF, writes in her book *Choices* about the starving in Africa. But she does not write in detail about the economics, politics, logistics, important though these all are. For she is trying to *move* people and get them compassionately interested in the tragedy of people in desperate need. So she presents an image. She describes a little boy in Somalia, 'An image of a child. . . . A little boy who grabbed my finger and aimlessly led me around in a refugee camp. A little naked boy with an empty plate and eyes – oh – a hundred years old, and a tiny behind as wrinkled as an old man's.' She walked around the camp with him, '. . . my finger clutched in his hand, my eyes on his little head of soft black hair covered with dust. (He) is almost certainly no longer alive in the desert of Africa, with his empty plate. And his wrinkly, tiny behind, and old, old eyes.'[19]

The rational is crucial. It will help us to grow the food to feed the starving. But the rational will not *move* us. We need the world of the dream. Images of power.

CHAPTER 10

Death: Living Near the Edge

FILMING *The Emerald Forest* almost killed Powers Boothe. Deep in the rain forests of Brazil, John Boorman was directing a scene in which Boothe, in character, was supposed to be injured and almost drowning under a waterfall. Charley Boorman, playing the role of his son, had to try to help him. But Boothe suddenly seized up and could not move. John Boorman describes what happened, 'We were shooting some distance away. Charley was desperately trying to keep him afloat and calling to us for help. We could not hear his cries against the roar of the waterfall, and kept on shooting, thinking how convincing their acting was. Powers could not move a muscle. Only Charley kept him afloat.'

Eventually it became clear that Boothe's acting was so convincing because he was really drowning, 'We realized and . . . went in and pulled him out. Powers needed oxygen and it was a couple of hours before he could get on his feet.'[1]

Crossing a busy city street can be dangerous, admittedly, but few of us reckon to be put in physical and even life-threatening danger in the course of our daily work. Excepting perhaps police and fire officers. And actors. It doesn't happen every day, of course. Or even very often, but often enough to make a difference. When we see how actors respond to the risk, it is clear that there underlies it all a conscious acceptance of the risk.

John Boorman recalls another incident similar to that which almost killed Powers Boothe. It happened while Boorman was filming *Deliverance*, also set in wilderness surroundings. Actor Ned Beatty was sucked into a whirlpool, 'He went under and it was forty-five seconds before he re-emerged downstream. We all dived for him. It was terrifying.'

But it is Beatty's bravado in the face of the horrifying accident that gives a glimpse of the way actors live 'near the edge'. Afterwards we asked him what his thoughts were when he believed he was drowning. He replied like a true actor, "I thought, how the hell will John be able to finish the film without me? Then I realized that the crafty bastard would somehow find a way. It made me so angry I was determined not to drown." '2

It begins to sound a little like wanton risk-taking. Is it because actors find work so hard to come by that they will undergo any dangers demanded of them? This is probably part of the truth. But there is more to it than that for the same attitude prevails in actors long after they have scaled the peaks of success. It is more than a passive acceptance of the risks. It is a determination to defy and transcend them, and to work on in situations where most of us would throw in the towel and check into the hospital.

For example, John Cottrell catalogues some of the damage sustained by Laurence Olivier over the years, '. . . a full-thrust sword wound in the breast as Hamlet, untold sword slashes about the hands and arms and head, innumerable falls from horses including being thrown headlong into a lake, a broken ankle in *Theater Royal*, a torn calf muscle in *The Beggar's Opera*, an arrow between his shinbones when filming *Richard III*, a torn cartilage as Crookback on stage, and an electric shock through a scimitar entering a studio dimmer. Only luck saved him from more serious injury when he dived into a net during filming of *Fire Over England* or when he was left hanging by one hand from a piano wire some forty feet above the stage in *The Critic*.'3

The *Richard III* incident illustrates vividly how the actor works through injury. Olivier, in character as the King, galloped on horseback towards a camera mounted on a small hill. A master archer was ready to shoot the King's horse from under him. The arrow was fitted with a real warhead. On being struck, the horse was trained to roll over 'dead', but the horse was protected by an armour suiting of half-inch cork covering hardboard, and beneath that a plate of steel. At the crucial moment the arrow was fired, Olivier was urging his horse up the hill. In the process he jerked his left leg forward.

Bernard Hepton, an actor in the film, saw what happened. Olivier's 'own armour was made of rubber and wouldn't stop a paper dart. The arrow sank deep into his calf. . . . Everyone fell silent while Oliver just sat there, motionless, the blood gushing from his wounded leg. But when Tony Bushell, the associate director, ran over to him, he simply asked, "Did we get that in the can?". "Yes," said Bushell. And Larry still sat there on his horse, discussing in matter-of-fact fashion how they might use the shot to the best advantage. And not until then, after several minutes of business talk, did he finally say, "Now get me off this horse and find a doctor, will you?" '[4]

I asked Charlton Heston for his views on the physical challenges and risks of the actor. He admitted that such an attitude was very much a part of his approach to work. 'I've never missed a performance or a day's shooting, or half a day's shooting', he said. 'I was bitten by a poisonous spider in Malaya last year, which is more poisonous than a Black Widow. And when they bite you, you don't feel it because they inject you with anaesthetic, so I never did see him. My hand swelled up, oh, about (indicates double size) and I couldn't use it. I was quite sick for a couple of days and the hand was swollen for four weeks. The producer came downstage and said, "Chuck, maybe I should put on the understudy." I said, "If you put on the understudy I will kill you. You follow what I'm saying to you?" He said, "Yes, that's very clear." '

Heston points out that this attitude, rather than being silly bravado, is necessary for the work they have to do, and once accepted, the risk of physical injury brings with it a mental toughness. For serious injury can finish a career, 'I think an actor, even a successful actor, has to come to terms with the fact that employment is eternally temporary and can come to an end at any time. Any part can be your last part. If you are badly hurt or disfigured or become unable to walk without a limp or to see or hear voices or if you even have a serious heart attack, in fact become unviable. It's rather like being an athlete for life, whereas with most jobs you can cruise beyond that. And in consequence you have to come to terms with that with a certain mental toughness.'

Facing a daily world in which one's faculties of survival are kept in trim, one's physical and mental alertness are given an edge which invigorates, refreshes, energizes, and shows a *commitment* to 'living near the edge'.

Preparation

When Meryl Streep did *The Taming of the Shrew* in Central Park, she insisted on 'wearing four-inch heels, so that she would be the same height as the actor who played Petruchio. This was on a raked stage, with concrete all around, platforms you had to jump up and down on. It was terrifying to watch.'[5]

What prevents this high-risk behaviour from being sheer lunatic bravado is the preparation many actors put into the physical side of a role. Sometimes the challenge to be met is not so much the risk of an accident, but rather the amount of energy and stamina required by a performance.

Many actors are careful to keep fit. Rip Torn, for example, likes to go to the gym every day, particularly when he is working. 'The best actors, and I've talked to many about this, feel a similar need', he says. 'Olivier, for example, used to work out at a gym; he felt that that was the single most important quality for an actor – physical strength. Keep in very, very good health, good shape. And Michael Redgrave, writing in his book, said that he found it obligatory to work out, whether it be running, or swimming, or weights, or fencing. He needed a physical work-out, then a nap.'[6]

Indeed Lynn Redgrave, when asked about the qualities necessary to be a good actress, puts physical fitness at the top of her list, 'Stength and stamina – good health. I put those before talent. . . . Acting is tiring: it requires a lot of work, a lot of muscle, an enormous amount of voice. As I've said, you have to blow something up while making it look normal, and do that for eight shows a week . . . acting is just hard, hard work.'[7]

Dustin Hoffman, at the age of 46, wanted to wait ten years before playing the part of Willy Loman, in Arthur Miller's play *Death of a Salesman*, so that he would be nearer the age of the character. Miller warned him against waiting, saying, 'A lot of actors have come to grief over this role, because it is just so darn big. You won't have the physical strength for the role at 56.'[8]

Hoffman was aware of the problem. The part of Loman had been played by many actors, but notably by Lee J. Cobb and this fine actor had found the role exhausting. 'After a month, Cobb's voice started giving out', Hoffman says. 'He was overweight and a smoker. After four months he had to be replaced, he couldn't take the punishment any more.' So Hoffman went into training for the role, 'Jogging, just eating a salad during the day.' He gave up smoking, drank only one cup of coffee a day and virtually no alcohol. For long periods each day he remained almost silent, saving his voice. He also took naps before performances. 'It's just like being a boxer', he said. 'Boxers always take naps before a fight.'[9]

The sporting analogy is apt. Acting is a physically demanding profession. The notion that acting consists of a comfortable stroll on a stage for a couple of hours each evening, or sitting around a film set waiting to shoot 30 second scenes, ignores the physical energy and commitment required. Films involve long hours of work and can last weeks in difficult locations. Make-up sessions can be long and arduous. Stage work is done under great stress of public performance; lights are hot, the vocal demands tiring. Evenings full of sustained physical and mental concentration, almost every night for weeks, even months on end, can be very debilitating.

The exhaustion resulting from even one demanding performance can be considerable. Ian McKellan says of playing Hamlet, 'There is a passage where you are on stage for an hour. You are the machine for every theme and you have to fuel that machine somehow. Then right at the end you have got to do all that bloody fighting. You are certainly ready for death after that.'[10]

The work of the actor can sometimes push him close to the limit of his physical capabilities. Near the edge.

Performance Risks

Accepting the physical risks of acting is the least of the actor's challenges. Many people would choose to do something physically threatening in preference to something psychologically frightening. At school, risks of injury in sport could be accepted more readily than risks of failure in giving a speech on Parents' Day, or at Graduation. Performance pressures dig deeply into sources of fear.

Ralph Richardson characterized the risk-taking actor involved in a major role as being rather like a jockey, 'You know you have a famous horse which many great jockeys have ridden. You make all possible preparations, but then there is always a 25 per cent chance that you won't get over the jumps. You know that and you are frightened. What makes you a professional is that you are used to being afraid. You accept fear.'[11]

The fear of failure can be crippling. But it is the actors themselves who set the standards which are so hard to reach. Lynn Redgrave talks about how rare is the truly great performance, 'I feel that seeing a really great performance on the stage is one of the most wonderful experiences you can have. . . . And while there's lots of good work about, those nights when you're present at something extraordinary are very rare; one can remember them on one hand. . . . It's a very elusive thing to achieve.'[12]

Glenda Jackson is one of the people who have achieved it more often than most. She explained to me how good acting gets more difficult with experience, rather than easier, 'The longer you do it, the harder it gets because all you ever really learn are the difficulties of it. It doesn't ever become any easier, and your own awareness of the possible pitfalls increases, so that's the one thing that you learn.' Glenda confirms Lynn Redgrave's statement about the elusiveness of great performances, 'It's very, very easy to do it badly, and it's very, very hard to do it well – the complete realization of a performance and production the way you imagine it the first or second time you read a play. You always go out wishing it to be the best it's possible to be.'

And yet many actors seek roles which test them harder, challenge them further, push them nearer the edge. The urge to test the boundaries are not restricted to young actors who are establishing their capacities. Professional risks seem to be taken by actors who would seem to have nothing to gain from them – people who are so well established that they could continue to 'do their thing' for a long time to come with no danger of work drying up. Meryl Streep, after phenomenal success playing contemporary women in all her previous major films, said to her agent, 'I've got to do something outside Manhattan, outside 1981, outside my own experience. Put me on the moon; I want to be somewhere else. I want to be held in the boundaries of a different time and place.'[13] The result was that Meryl Streep played an Englishwoman, in a historical drama, and produced her award-winning performance in the film *The French Lieutenant's Woman*.

Perhaps even more remarkable for an established actor, Charlton Heston made his theatre debut in London's West End in 1985. I asked him why he had risked the critical purgatory of such an act, when he was such an established film star, and had stage acting opportunities in the theatre world of Los Angeles. He was keen to avoid a self-serving or pretentious answer to the question. But he had to admit that his life as an actor is fuelled by danger and risk-taking, and that the 'personal fitness' that comes from fighting the odds is very satisfying. He needs to test himself from time to time against difficult challenges.

All the major, taxing roles are worthy tests, 'To undertake one of the killer parts, to take risks, is to keep yourself in trim, to test and thus extend your capacities. To keep in a literal sense from getting fat-headed; to keep the blubber off your brain. Those parts are hard to do. You've got to watch your step every inch of the way. And again, with all the great parts, Macbeth, Hamlet, Othello, you finally drop to your knees exhausted, in the upper reaches of the snow-covered slopes, like a leopard who has ventured into the high altitude of a mountain.'

Performance Battles

'I had a terrible stage fright and it wasn't based on whether I'd be good or not, it was based on what the people would think of me.'[14]

This admission from Shirley Maclaine points to perhaps the most powerful phenomena in the 'near-the-edge' world of the actor: the stress of performing before an audience. As Helen Mirren says, 'Everybody's frightened of having to talk in front of people. Anyone who's had to stand up and recite a poem in class or make a speech to the mayor on Speech Day has found it the most horrific, terrifying, sickening experience.'[15]

For most actors the tension of public performance does not disappear with experience. Actress Elizabeth Wilson says of Meryl Streep: 'When Meryl's on stage, there's a look in her eye of a real fighter. But though you don't see it when she's

performing, Meryl suffers greatly before an opening. She per-
spires, she paces. She gets more nervous than anyone I know.'[16]

When I asked Antony Sher about the stress of public performance he admitted, 'The terror of taking a play in front of an
audience is extraordinary. . . . I heard that someone has done a
study of stress and discovered that the adrenalin an actor uses
just on an ordinary night – let alone a first night – is equivalent
to the adrenalin experienced by someone involved in a car
crash. It is a very unnatural thing for one person to step up in
front of a thousand other people and be watched for a period of
time. I think that must put all sorts of peculiar strains and
stresses on the actor that are simply not experienced in most
other professions.'

One of the results of this stress is to exert tremendous
pressure on actors to deliver what the audience wants. While at
one level this is what the actor wishes to provide, the pressure
sometimes undermines the actor's ability to deliver. Liv
Ullmann talks about times when the actor feels she is losing the
audience. 'Often you do all the wrong things', she says. 'You try
to do more, which of course makes it less truthful. You give up
and do less which makes it even less truthful. Sometimes you
make a third try – start to be glib and do things that you know
are safe.'

Actors like to be liked, as much as any of us, and it is here that
they are vulnerable. For the audience is like a large-scale
judging panel giving instant reaction to the quality of the
actor's work. Under pressure, the temptation for actors is to try
to ingratiate themselves with the audience, 'All actors do that
at times because we're a little vain, we don't want to go down
the drain. At those times you try to look very pretty or you try to
be funny with ones that are really sweet and charming. You try
to make the audience fall a little in love with you. A lot of actors
do that, including myself when I really get insecure. You aim
for surface things. But if you can't reach an audience, it's best to
do nothing.'[17]

While an audience can be a tremendous boost, support and
wave of energy for an actor, the reverse is also true. It can be
just as threatening for an actor as it would be for many of us: an
object of fear. This is hardly surprising. As the theatre historian
Southern points out, a single individual may address another

individual without nervousness. But even between individuals, '. . . . if the one addressed is more influential or powerful than the one addressing, or can destroy him, then an element of nervousness, or at least deference, may colour the address.'[18]

But we are here dealing with a single actor addressing scores, hundreds, even thousands, 'Whenever an individual addresses a group – even the most easy and complacent group – then he is facing a strength that is capable of overpowering his own, and this is true not only from a physical point of view but also from a psychological point of view.' To handle a psychological power greater than one's own entails a raising of perception and response which we call 'nervous'. It is almost a biological reaction. Like an animal, the actor allows himself to be cornered, and there he performs and does battle with the audience. This is a sense of living with danger which creates a tremendous vitality and energy. But there is no doubt that there are elements of hostility involved – it is indeed a battle.

Marlon Brando talked of this 'battle' with the audience. He admired actors who controlled what they 'gave out'. For example, 'Spencer Tracy is the kind of actor I like to watch. The way he holds back, holds back – then darts in to make his point, darts back.' He refers to Jacob Adler, his acting teacher from early in his career, in New York, 'Old man Adler, old Jacob, he taught me something once that I've never forgotten. To hold back twenty per cent and you're always being honest with the audience. Try to show more than you've got to give and they catch on right away.'[19]

Simon Callow has identified the aspect of competition, even aggression, that exists between the actor and the audience. 'There's no getting away from the fact that theatre contains an element of hostility. Every actor knows that. Standing on the stage is an aggressive act. It says: Look at *me*. Listen to *me*. It says I'm interestng, I'm talented, I'm remarkable.'[20]

Callow points out that the audience naturally responds to this as a challenge, ' "Oh yeah?" says the audience. "You'd better prove it – why should you be up there instead of me?" . . . the audience in the theatre is . . . thrilled by the risk he is taking, but unconsciously longing for him to fall. At the very least, the fact that he *might* fall is a large part of their enjoyment.'

He identifies one of the battlegrounds on which this fight

takes places as the content and style of the performance. 'An element of control is always involved in the actor's relationship with the audience. They will sometimes try to make it a different kind of play to the one you're trying to give them, and in general it will be a less rich one.'[21]

And the source of the battle? Callow reckons it is because actors are trying, in a performance, to get 'the audience to surrender their armour and open themselves to their deepest anxieties.' To be challenged to enter into a new experience is in itself threatening, and is something audiences often resist.

Glenda Jackson concurs with Callow's analysis. She says that the audience has the hostile presence 'because audiences essentially want to see what they've seen before – they don't want to be anything other than confirmed.' She also indicates that there is an aspect of power in an audience watching an actor, an aspect which encourages the audience to want the actor to be submissive, 'They would like you really to say to them "Please love me". You can crawl on your stomach to an audience and they absolutely adore it.' Like Liv Ullmann, Glenda emphasizes how strong the pressure can be from an audience, and how important it is for an actor to resist it, 'You have to actually go out there and say, "Now listen, this is how this author sees the world and you may like it or you may not, but I am going to present it to you as honestly as I can. And if you dislike me while I'm doing it – tough!" '

Living Near the Edge

Psychologists have studied people's responses to challenge and risk in their lives.[22] They have found that the majority of people prefer to avoid it, seeing impulses 'as forces requiring control, and perhaps in some sense as threats to general personal stability.' These people wish to maintain inner equilibrium, 'a state of high psychological inertia – impulses undergo a series of delays, censorships and transformations before they are permitted expression'. The main reward for this attitude is the security it achieves. There is nothing intrinsically wrong with this approach to life. Except that many people avoid challenge and excitement *without realizing it*.

Often our lives will become dull because we never go near our capacities. We operate so deeply inside our 'secure zones' that we even begin to lose the appetite for novelty. But dull lives do not happen by chance. Rather, our pattern of accepting or avoiding challenges determines the level of stimulation we live with.

Psychologists found that people who say 'Yes' to a challenge were individuals who actively search for emotional excitement in their environment – novelty, movement, change, adventure – these provide the external stimuli for their emotional lives Furthermore, these people were found to respond quickly to internal stimuli. Their inner impulses were allowed ready and full expression, and their lives had a positive energy and vitality. The reward for their approach to life was excitement and adventure.

We improvise life. There is a limit to the extent to which life can be controlled, and although people often take great pains to plan for all eventualities, something unexpected always happens. That is one of the few certainties of life – there are no certainties.

Living 'near the edge' keeps a person sharp, aware, creative, ready to respond to life's surprises. And the way of the actor is to live with challenge. We often fall into the trap of thinking that actors cavort before audiences because they need the attention and applause. But we seldom think 'Do they need the danger?' I think they do. I think we all do. Perhaps not to the degree risked by the actor. But closer to it than some of us are accustomed to venture.

Actors in traditional societies were expected to transcend physical and psychological death. In a sense, the two were seen as one and the same experience. This was because when an actor shaman was marked out early in life, usually by his sensitivity to altered states of mind which were believed to be amenable to discourse with the spirits, such as telepathic dreams, vivid visions, trance states and so on, his days were numbered. As himself, that is. For becoming an actor shaman meant allowing the former identity to die, in order to be reborn as a person who had access to the secrets of life. Part of the training entailed rigorous physical challenges, including fasting for long periods. Sometimes, initiation included trials of commitment and courage. The drowning traumas suffered by Powers Boothe and Ned Beatty during filming sound characteristic of the sorts of things demanded of traditional initiate shamans.

The physical effort, along with induced trance states, prepared the future actor for a guided journey into himself or, in metaphorical terms, a journey to the land of the spirits. Here, depending on the cultural or tribal context, the individual would suffer 'physical' death in various ways at the hands of the spirits. In northern Europe, for example, this might entail the experience of being bodily cut to pieces by magic dwarfs, manifestations of the powers of the Earth, and then being reconstructed with the body of a shaman.

The future actor shaman underwent psychological and 'physical' death and rebirth as dramatic acknowlegement by himself, and by the community, of his commitment and new status as a person able to incarnate the spirits. And since the actor was someone who often manifested the 'dead', in that he could perform as the spirits of the departed, it was considered essential that he had in initiation entered, himself, into the realm of the dead.

Today, of course, it is very rare for people to undergo such demanding and personally transforming experiences. But the principal is provocative: that to live 'near the edge', to be aware of boundaries of experience, encourages the individual to live to the full. We do not need to go beyond the boundaries necessarily, but to test them was, and is, a test of one's commitment to life. People who *have* been very near to the edge, surviving a serious accident or illness, for example, tend as a result to live more fully. Awareness of death introduces one to the fullness of life.

Even today, the way of the actor is physically demanding. It involves the taking of risks, the acceptance of the fear of failure, and coping with the psychological power of a mass audience. Glenda Jackson, talking to me about the actor's relationship with the audience, characterizes it as a situation soaked with fear, 'You risk the whole of yourself – I mean, you do actually take your life in your hands and walk out there to see if that ravening beast is going to snatch it from you or allow you to keep it for a little bit longer. Actors commit so much to the work – it is *so* important to them, that acting always puts you in a life and death situation. And fear is a great energy.'

The acceptance of danger, challenge, risk – living near the edge is a great energy.

CHAPTER 11

Charisma: The Power of Presence

GARY COOPER AND Charlton Heston were having dinner together in London. It was the late 1950s and Cooper was still one of the biggest film stars in the world, the archetypal western hero. Heston was just beginning his film career. 'I was making a film with Cooper here in England', Heston said. 'Coop and I were both here without our families, so we sometimes took meals together. On this occasion we were over in Berkeley Square at a steakhouse called *The Guinea*; quite small and crowded, but very good.'

Also seated at a table in the tiny restaurant was a table full of 'Teddy Boys', the 1950s' English version of Hell's Angels, with Edwardian style dress rather than leather and motorbikes. The sadistic toughness and threatening demeanour were, however, the real thing. 'They were making their presence felt noisily,' continued Heston. 'Eventually it came time for us to leave, and Cooper was a little ahead of me as we weaved our way through the narrow aisles between the tables. As we passed the table of Teds one of the young toughs said derisively, "There goes that big cowboy star". Cooper stopped. Seconds ticked by. Cooper turned slowly, seeming to fill the room with his presence. Fixing his adversary with a icy stare, he drawled, "When you say that . . . *smile*." ' Heston paused in his narrative to savour the memory, the image of Gary Cooper standing, feet apart, challenging a table of thugs. 'Now, I don't know whether the kid knew that was a line from Cooper's classic film *The Virginian*, but suddenly we weren't in a restaurant in London, we were standing in the middle of a dusty street in Abilene. And nobody at the table moved. There were no smiles. They just sat, very

very carefully. Coop stared at him for as long as twenty seconds, turned on his heel and walked out.'

Outside the restaurant Cooper climbed into the back of his Rolls Royce, and straightened the crease in his trousers. Heston joined him. 'I climbed in beside him and I said "You delivered that line very well, Coop." He narrowed his eyes and drawled, "Well . . . I've had a lot of practice." '

Heston and I laughed at that story. Gary Cooper was a big man and it is amusing to think that the table of young machos suddenly realized that they were taking on more than they had bargained for. But Heston's point is that Gary Cooper filled the restaurant with the presence he wanted to create. He seemed larger than life. 'If you look at actors like Laurence Olivier or Ruth Gordon, they create a sort of super-reality', Heston continued. 'I don't mean that they are supernatural figures, or superhuman or mythic, but that they fill the stage and screen more than the average person would. Gary Cooper was like this. He was generally dismissed as an actor, but in his element, within his range, you could not take your eyes off him. And in the restaurant he showed that he could command the same attention in real life.'

What is this ability to create a 'super-reality'? Often it seems to be labelled with the catch-all term 'charisma'. In other words, we know it when we see it, but don't ask us to define it. But what is charisma? One way to explore it is to look at the phenomenon of movie actors.

Personality Stars

It would be surprising to meet an urban dweller in a Western country who had never heard of Robert Redford. Or Meryl Streep. Or Marlon Brando. Or any of the very long list of actors, a list which would certainly include Clint Eastwood, Charles Bronson, Sylvester Stallone, Charlton Heston, Glenda Jackson, Liv Ullmann, Shirley MacLaine and many more. Their fame is phenomenal. Roles in films are the source of their power. These people are actors, but they are also 'stars'. They are a continuing and important presence in people's lives because they are 'stars'. They have 'fans', a diminutive for 'fantastic', which derives from the Latin 'fanaticus' – 'someone inspired to frenzy by devotion to a deity', or 'a person possessed'.[1] For most people, 'stars' and 'celebrities' play a significant part in their imagination. Asked to list people one either knows or has heard of, most people in Western countries list more 'stars' than individuals in their 'real' social world. Despite the lack of face-to-face contact with these unmet people who figure in our 'imaginary' social world, we nevertheless feel strongly about them. We are attracted by their images, repelled by them, identify with them, imagine ourselves in social, personal or sexual relations with them. In the world of our imaginations they are people.

So what is a star? Downing suggests that, 'A star is someone whom the audience wishes to see doing and thinking certain things, someone who sums up, through a series of cumulative performances, an approach to contemporary reality which the audience can share. A star is a *social construction*. And certainly, stars have "charisma".' For successful 'personality stars' there are restrictions on the sort of acting that is possible. 'Stars have to be partially predictable; they can show off different facets of the persona they have come to represent, but they cannot easily abandon the persona altogether.'[2] It is the 'persona', or public face presented in performance, to which the public become attached. These star actors represent something like the 'spirits' of actors in traditional cultures and the actor takes on a kind of supernatural significance. The characters, or performance extensions of the actors' personalities, seem to crystallize our feelings about sexuality, codes of behaviour, life-style and image, manifested as in Noh and other traditional forms of theatre. The actor takes on an almost supernatural significance. Over the years, there have been a number of very powerful 'spirit' actors: Jimmy Cagney, Gary Cooper, Humphrey Bogart, James Dean. The actors may personally be rather different from their screen image, but their image shows little variance. A clear example is Clint Eastwood, whose personal demeanour is quite different from the hard, cold *Man with No Name* of the spaghetti westerns and his later incarnations in the *Magnum Force* movies. But the audience knows before going to see the film what 'spirit' is going to be incarnated by the actor Clint Eastwood.

Young actors, especially American men, attempt to develop this 'star' personality presence. Rip Torn has identified this tendency as happening even in the drama schools, and links it with the availability of work for actors, 'In the schools, character acting is not even taught any more. You are taught, instead, how to present your own personality. People figure that that's the way they'll get the commercials, that's the way they'll become a star – just by playing themselves.'[3]

Estelle Parsons, who achieved public prominence for her performance as Clyde Barrow's sister in the movie *Bonnie and Clyde*, is an accomplished stage actor and director. She complained that she recently ran into difficulties in directing a play, because the actors were unwilling to move away from personality projection, 'There's not a lot of work for people who want to play characters; they tend to stay at a very low-income level and low-profile level. So, if you play yourself, you're going to get further ahead and ultimately be much more successful.'[4]

However, many actors become trapped playing typecast characters. Liv Ullmann feels that some 'star' actors, who could take more risks with their choice of roles, are overly-concerned with maintaining their image as personality actors. She identifies this timidity, mostly among male actors, as reflecting an uneasiness, an insecurity about being an actor. It results in the need to compensate by projecting an unchanging, virile image, 'Many men actors are really ashamed of their profession. And they really take care of their image. Look on the screen: they are all so virile. What Jack Lemmon did in *Save the Tiger* was very unusual, or Erland Josephson in *Scenes From a Marriage*. Mostly, they are all bigger than life. And that's not only because they're men but also because they're men actors.'[5]

Presumably these actors personify a spirit that speaks volumes to a need deep within America and the other cultures around the world where their films are very popular. With the exception of Woody Allen, there are few film actors with the strength and power that it takes to manifest a 'weak' spirit as a personality actor. The success of Allen's films underscores the need for his sort of 'spirit' to be represented.

Sometimes, actors are identified by the public with the 'personality' of their roles even when this is uncomfortable for and unintended by the actor. A clear example is Marlon Brando's portrayal of Kowalski in Tennessee Williams' *A Streetcar Named Desire*. The public took the brutal, physical domineering Kowalski as the personality of Brando. But the actor says of the character, 'Kowalski was always right, and never afraid. He never wondered, he never doubted. His ego was very secure. And he had the kind of brutal aggressiveness that I hate. I'm afraid of it. I detest the character.'[6]

In a similar case of 'mistaken identity', Gene Hackman was trapped by the role of tough New York police detective Popeye Doyle. In *The French Connection*, Hackman's performance was so mesmerizing that the public responded as though Hackman *were* Doyle. 'I watched Eddie Egan (the New York policeman on whom the role was based), and I tried to do the physical stuff', says Hackman. 'There's a certain New York street guy, you know, the way he walks, the way he talks, the way he bounces. It was very, very tough for me. People think I'm like that, but nothing could be further from the truth. I was amazed at the violence in those men's lives. It would scare the hell out of me.'[7]

Brando and Hackman eventually liberated themselves from the stereotype. There are also many actors who play a wide variety of roles and achieve star status nevertheless. Dustin Hoffman, for example, turned down scores of parts offered to him which were carbon copies of his film breakthrough as the disillusioned college student in *The Graduate*. And the part he eventually chose to follow this film was as a New York down-and-out character called Ratso, in *Midnight Cowboy*. Hoffman is a technically fine actor, but he is also a 'star'. He has 'charisma'. His success suggests that the presence of personality actors as fuelled by professional image and type of role is only part of the story. Why is it that some people are more 'watchable' than others, so that on the stage or screen people cannot take their eyes off them? What is it about these people that attracts us?

Personal Magnetism

One obvious answer is that we are attacted by good looks. Female actors in particular are often required, especially in films, to have a sexual attraction which commands the attention of the audience. But this is too simple. There are many charismatic actors who do not fit conventional notions of physical attractiveness and yet who have a magnetic quality which makes them eminently watchable: Barbra Streisand for one. Sam Waterston suggests that, 'Personal mannerisms don't work any better in the movies than they do in the theatre. But the person, the person-ness or personality of the actor is what makes people want to go to see him. Audiences wanted to see Barbra Streisand in the movies. Because "By golly, there's somebody." '8

Richard Burton was such an actor. Very early in his career, Burton attracted attention while playing the very minor stage role of a man scrubbing a floor. The scene was a romantic duologue between John Gielgud and Pamela Brown, the centrepiece of the play. Burton had to scrub and interpolate a word or two. 'The first time we went through the scene,' said Gielgud, 'he felt immediately, without any direction, exactly where he should matter in the scene and where he should obliterate himself. He never changed it.' Richard Leach, another actor in the production, says that when Burton was on his knees and scrubbing, 'You couldn't take your eyes off him. There was an inborn arrogance. He just did it. But because he is who he is, it was totally compelling.'9

In a BBC television interview, Burton recognized the quality of presence. 'Put ten actors on a stage together, and there will be one who everyone notices.' But while Burton believed that there are certain actors who are utterly compelling to watch, he saw no way to predict the degree of an actor's charisma just from their physical characteristics. He thought that 'the charismatic actor could be beautiful, tall, arresting, but could also be short, fat and bald.'10

Anthony Quayle, who directed Burton in a number of productions, saw in Burton 'an appearance, a voice and a magnetism that came once in twenty years to dominate and attract and fascinate an audience. Olivier had it when he was very young. It's a kind of animal quality.' Quayle realized that Burton's attractive quality was not just old-fashioned pin-up sex appeal, but nevertheless this was the nearest familiar characteristic that could begin to capture it, 'Maybe it's something to do with sexuality. . . . It's some peculiar quality which interests men and excites women, a latent power to disturb. You hardly need open your mouth if you have it.' Anthony Quayle also identifies another thread to this charismatic quality, 'Usually it comes with success – the success gives you the authority. You're not having to be friendly, not having to be anything. You can just *be*. . . . It's pride, a funny quality, and Burton had it before he had the success.'[11]

So what can we make of these qualities? Perhaps 'animal' and 'sexual' imply inborn physical attributes. A sense of natural attraction. But authority, pride and mystery are psychological qualities. They sound like reflections of an actor's attitude to life and Anthony Quayle associates authority and pride with the freedom *to be*. Not to be constantly checking that one is gaining approval from others. Inner confidence. Assurance.

To be 'charismatic' is not the same thing as to be liked. In fact, perhaps, charisma is partly the strength to resist the need to be liked.

Mystery

Another factor was identified by Kenneth Tynan as mystery. Writing about Burton in the 1950s, when he was playing Othello, Tynan said, 'Within this actor there is always something reserved, a secret upon which trespassers will be prosecuted, a rooted solitude which his Welsh blood tinges with mystery.' Burton later explained something of this aspect of himself and his work in interview with Tynan, 'I don't think anyone wants to help you particularly. Despite the agonies of a first night, and the nervousness and so on, you really have to look after yourself. I think that particular loneliness, solitude, the idea of carrying on your own private room, is not unique to actors, though all actors have it, a little more than most.'[12]

Similarly, writer David Nathan, in his biography of Glenda Jackson, notes her quality of aloneness. He quotes Hugh Whitemore as saying, 'Glenda has got the reputation of being a tough, ballsy actress and her voice is very strong and clear. . . . But she has all the qualities of vulnerability and a sort of loneliness. She's a marvellously lonely actress.'[13] Glenda Jackson plays a wide range of stage and film roles, but each is suffused with her own particular appeal.

This sense of having an inner mystery, separateness, inaccessibility deep down seems to be a quality that *attracts*; it pulls the audience towards the actor. It is a quality which demands the participation of the observer, and this energy direction is perceived as vulnerability or mystery.

Heightened Reality

While there are undoubtedly some actors who 'have it', charisma is often not a quality that is forever present, beaming from a person like a 24-hour lighthouse beacon. There are actors of impressive presence in performance who, in private life, relax almost into anonymity. Alec Guinness, for example, is well-known as a person who can fade into the background in private life, and yet in performance he seems, almost effortlessly, to assume tremendous charismatic qualities. John Hurt, too, can go virtually unnoticed in everyday life. When he was playing his universally acclaimed role of the flamboyant homosexual Quentin Crisp, in *The Naked Civil Servant*, Hurt claimed that he could enter a pub dressed in the outrageously gaudy garments of Quentin Crisp, but would be ignored. That is, until he went into character, 'became' Quentin Crisp in his mind and body, and as a result suddenly attracted enormous attention. Laurence Olivier, similarly, does not carry his stage presence around with him. His wife, actress Joan Plowright, says, 'You know people would be rather amazed to see Larry at home just with the family. He is so *ordinary*. . . . He doesn't get recognized at all.'[14]

When writer David Thomas went to interview Klaus Kinski, he was stunned by the actor's presence because it was so different from what he had expected, 'When you first meet the actor who was Aguirre, you are amazed to find so slight a figure (5′ 7″, 140 lbs.). You expect a tyrant who could drag cannon over mountains and tame a jungle with willpower.'[15]

So what is it that enables these gifted actors to summon up, or create, the spellbinding presence that permeates their performances?

A number of actors have referred to the necessity of being able to produce some sort of concentrated reality in performance. Lynn Redgrave considers that on stage, 'You have to be able to make something you're blowing up appear real to fifteen hundred people. There's nothing natural about it, yet you have to make it look natural, and it should feel natural to you.' And she emphasizes that this is the case also in films, 'Even film acting, which is so hung up on being natural, is not natural at all. If the camera's on you very close and you're going to sit down, you have to sit down like this (she lowers herself onto the chair very slowly). That's not natural and it's not truthful. It *appears* on the screen as if I had a perfectly natural sit-down at a perfectly normal speed. But it isn't at all. And if I think it's truthful for my character to cross the room in a great fury, I'll have to check that at a certain point because the camera won't be able to follow me.'[16] In performance she is presenting a kind of *heightened* naturalness.

Lynn Redgrave also points out that there are a number of ways of behaving on stage which might be truthful for the actor, or even the character, but which are not heightened sufficiently to satisfy the needs of drama. For example, she says that it might be truthful to pause for ten minutes on stage because the character has a sudden thought, but the demands of the playwright and the interest of the audience militate against this, 'So you have to look for another truth, because that one is not interesting theatrically. You have to find a combined truth – one that's true for you, that says something to the audience and that best puts forward the play.' In other words, the truth being performed has to be not only valid for the actor, but also for the play, film, or situation: a *heightened* truth.

How is this possible?

Sam Waterston has commented on the creation of presence in performance. He feels that the visibility of the actor is a matter of making the life of the character, everything he thinks, feels, does, *matter a lot*, 'Basically, I think that you've got to get into the character, try to understand him, figure out what he means by everything he says, and try to make it all matter a lot. Trying to make it matter a lot is terribly important. Everybody's visibility is increased greatly in proportion to how much their work matters to them.' Waterston points out that this principle applies to daily life too, not just to performance, 'You see that happen all the time in life. There's a crowd of totally anonymous people, and somebody wants something very badly; that person doesn't have to raise his voice, but he starts to glow, and he becomes interesting.'

Waterston explains this point through the language of emotion seen instrumentally. He says that if he is to act something with the emotion of anger, it is not effective, in action terms, to say, 'I'm going to do this angrily.' Instead, he translates the emotion into action, 'For instance, if I say to myself, "I must get you to allow me to take that chair home with me", and if I make those stakes very high, and if you continue to refuse . . . then that may make me mad.'[17] Waterston explains that this is a much more effective approach dramatically than merely summoning up 'angry' emotion.

Jack Nicholson holds similar views. He explains that he does not go into a scene thinking 'This character should be sad.' Instead he translates the emotion into terms of action, 'I go in knowing he wants this, and the environment is that, and this is how he's going to approach his problem, and I try to make it even more important than it would be to the character, and that creates feeling. Whatever feeling trying to achieve those ends creates, that's the emotion.'[18] To describe these approaches to infusing action with presence is not, of course, to assume that it is easy. In everyday life we pull back from translating emotion into action. Simon Callow has expressed this point cogently, 'For me the biggest problem was to show myself wanting something. To want anything is to put oneself into a position of frightening vulnerability; and then to pursue a course of action to achieve that want is to show oneself at one's most naked.'[19] It is a kind of emotional vulnerability which shows clearly through the masks and disguises we adopt in daily life.

In performance, this was demonstrated clearly by John Hurt. In *The Elephant Man* Hurt played the role of the unfortunate person who was born with a skin condition and deformities which led to his being exhibited in freak shows as 'the elephant man'. For this part, Hurt was very heavily concealed under layers of make-up which virtually obliterated his natural features and freedom of bodily expression. Reflecting on this experience, Hurt has said, 'Acting that's really tough is like that in *The Elephant Man* where you're trying to project something out through that make-up. . . . It's a question of thinking right.'[20]

Spontaneity

'In acting, it's best when you don't really know. Unpredictability is the most arresting quality that an actor can have.'[21] Jack

Nicholson points here to one of the least understood aspects of exciting acting: unpredictability, spontaneity, surprise. How do actors achieve these qualities? The answer, ironically, is preparation and planning.

'I hate the idea of acting being some kind of mystical process', says Glenda Jackson. 'It isn't. I mean you do as much as an individual can do; you clear the undergrowth, you get rid of the stuff that isn't useful, you discard the ideas that aren't quite right. You do everything you can, both physically and mentally, to be ready for something else to happen. That's what the performance is: is something else going to happen?'

Glenda Jackson likens the preparation for performance as essentially *preparation for the spontaneous*. For something magical, something extra, something special to take place on stage very hard advance work is crucial. Spontaneity is not a kind of easy, spur-of-the moment facility that an actor has, but rather is a state of possibility engendered by comprehensive preparation. With reference to the 'Is something else going to happen?', she says, 'I suppose there is a kind of mystery element in that, but I don't like the idea of it being entirely a process that is without any kind of guiding sense.'

Liv Ullmann agrees, 'I'm always very well prepared when I come to the set. I know my lines. I don't come with hangovers. When I'm working, I go to bed early so I'm prepared in the morning.' But although she lays the groundwork carefully, she does not try to work out her emotional work in advance, 'Emotionally I don't prepare. I think about what I would like to show, but I don't prepare, because I feel that most of the emotions I have to show I know about . . . I can show them.'[22]

It is important at this stage to allow instinct, intuition to take over, to use what has been prepared, to allow one's natural juices to flow. This means being alert and open to what is happening, and to be ready for spontaneity – living in the moment. Geraldine Page says that, 'The training that I have is in my brain and it works on material in not-so-conscious ways. I have all sorts of complicated, computerized knowledge stored away in the back of my mind. When I do wing it, a lot of work has been done that I wouldn't have time to sit down and explain to everybody.'[23]

Estelle Parsons explains that this open attitude is not the

same as being relaxed, 'Preparedness is more a matter of openness and concentration than relaxation, I think. It's being receptive, being prepared to accept anything. If you are a closed person, you have to get rid of the blocks. To me, relaxation means a certain lethargy, a laxity – I would think you can be very relaxed and very blocked at the same time.'[24]

Meryl Streep talks in similar vein, 'I don't like to analyze the character I'm playing too much and for films I don't like to rehearse a lot. . . . I like acting to be as near to life as possible, when you don't know exactly what is going to happen. . . . That way you have the chance something spontaneous will happen to make the character come alive. I suppose it's working by instinct, really.'[25]

Concentration

'Working by instinct' is a highly disciplined process. It takes supreme concentration. In the film *Kramer vs Kramer*, Meryl Streep plays the part of Joanna, a mother who goes to court for custody of her child. The scene in which she gives testimony at the custody hearing is a wrenching sequence and Streep plays the character in a state of controlled, high emotion; Joanna cries visibly in spite of herself. The director of the film, Robert Benton, recalls Meryl Streep work in filming that particular scene, with amazement. 'We must have shot that scene from seven in the morning until six at night, over and over again. First in close-up, then a medium shot, finally a long one. Later in the day we shot only Dustin reacting to her on the stand. During this last take, all 30 people in the room were facing Dustin. I happened to be watching Meryl as well. She had the same intensity as she had when she first did the scene.'[26]

This is concentration of a high order. But to get behind the compelling presence of Meryl Streep, we have to consider more closely the *kind* of concentration being shown. It is more than conscientious attention to the business of her working day. It seems to be concentration of a particular kind.

Film director John Boorman is struck by the importance of concentration to the presence of an actor. Filming *The Emerald Forest* in Brazil, Boorman worked with actor Powers Boothe, 'Powers is a very penetrating actor, with great concentration. Powers . . . is quiet, reclusive, saving himself for the role, conserving all energy. We speak of an actor having "presence", and it means exactly that. What all good film actors have in common is concentration, the ability to focus all their attention, intellectually and emotionally, into the character and scene.' He goes on to note, 'Most of us are always partly somewhere else, thinking of what will or what has happened. Being "self-conscious" is allowing part of oneself to be aware, to stand back and observe the situation instead of being totally in it and of it.'[27]

Unfocused awareness dissipates. Concentrated awareness generates a presence that people can *see*. As Sam Waterston says, the essence of acting is 'being a person who is *visible*. . . . People can see you.' [28] But what is it that people see?

Charisma

The large, carpeted rehearsal room is strewn with actors. Fifteen bodies lying flat on their backs, eyes closed, meditating. Outside, three floors below, the London traffic rumbles by. Inside, the hiss and sigh of deep, rhythmic breathing fills the room with an organic sound, pleasant yet eerie. With each succeeding breath each actor imagines breathing in a colour. Any colour he wishes. This workshop is the culmination of three weeks of intensive training in creating vivid imagery, and we are working on the power of presence.

We had discussed the dynamics of 'charisma', the factors which might give an actor the compelling attraction of a shaman, magician, performing mystic. The actor's ability to draw the gaze and spellbind the mind. Was it concentration? Will? Authority? Are there non-verbal cues in body posture, movement or gesture which signal to us that we are watching someone special? Certainly it seems to have only marginal connections with conventional physical beauty. Is it something we see in the eyes? Or a feature of the face which attracts us?

Probably all of these factors are present. But is it possible that there is another crucial, unrecognized dimension? Something beyond the physical, but yet communicable on some extraordinary wavelength? We set out to explore.

Each time the actors breathe in, the imagined colour gradually fills their bodies. Oxygen becomes a psychological force and soon is converted by the mind of the actor into a physical force, or rather, an energy which unites the physical with the psychological. Hopefully, it will provide a concentrated centre, from which the actor can draw fully on his energies, like the concept of energy, 'chi', which integrates the mind and body. It is not a theory or an abstract concept. It is the driving force behind a karate chop crashing through a pile of bricks. In principle, we want that power in the stage presence of an actor.

After forty minutes of intensive, guided meditation, I ask the actors to imagine that ripples of light are radiating out through their skin, like small waves of water from a pebble lobbed into a still pool – to get the energy moving from the centre. 'Extend the colour beyond your body boundary, and allow it to shimmer around you as an extension of the energy your breathing has created.'

After a time, when everyone has had a chance to 'extend' their concentration in the form of an imagined colour, I tell them they can stop working and sit up. We were to discuss how they felt. Rehearse and improvise with the concentrated energy they had developed. To see what we could do with it.

Silence. No movement, no signs of breaking concentration. Suddenly, someone over on the side of the room sits bolt upright in one movement. It is Martin, and his body is rigid, his legs straight out in front of him, his eyes still closed. But I also see something else: something which shakes me to the core. Around his body shimmers a broad band of light, bright turquoise and pulsating like a heartbeat. The band of light travels from the ground at the base of his spine, up his back, over his head and face. For some reason it stops under his chin.

I am stunned. I have never seen anything like it. Blinking my eyes rapidly, I break my gaze and look out of the window. Lazy afternoon sunshine glints from the passing cars in the street below. But when I look back at Martin, the band of light is still there. So vivid and tangible that I feel as if I could walk over and grasp it. Breaking my gaze again, I survey the other actors. Some are stirring, slowly stretching themselves to wakefulness. The space around and above them seems highly charged, shimmering as if with electricity. But that could be my imagination. And so, surely, was the band of colour around Martin. I sucked in a long breath, filled my lungs and breathed out slowly and steadily. Apprehensively, I glance back at Martin, expecting the colour to be gone. It is still there. Every bit as vivid as before, still visible up his back, over his head and stopping just below the chin.

I spoke before I had time to think. 'Martin's got a blue aura', I blurted out, half in amazement, half in excitement. The moment I spoke, Martin opened his eyes and swore loudly. 'That's incredible', he gasped. 'Blue is the colour I have been working on all week.' I had had no knowledge of the colours individual actors had been using in their meditations.

The room was in immediate uproar. Actors rushed to sitting positions, clamouring for me to read their auras. Others stared in wonder at Martin, some asking him what had happened. Those who had still been deep in meditation struggled up amid the noise, startled. Martin was shocked and thrilled. He felt he had learned to project his presence so strongly that the colour had been visible.

I have no corroborative witnesses for this event. Martin's blue aura had disappeared the instant he opened his eyes, and no one else in the room had seen it. It is of course possible that I saw a powerfully projected figment of my own imagination; that it was pure chance that I had seen the colour exactly matching the one the actor had been working on; a fluke that the colour had remained so vividly even after I had twice broken my gaze, and that it was the sound of my voice that had broken the hallucination rather than Martin's opening eyes that had removed his 'externalized' concentration. There was no way I could prove anything, for this was an acting work-shop, not a controlled scientific study.

And yet there is an array of research evidence which suggests that there may well be more to it than a mere imagination and that there is something about people which is out of the range of consciously perceived perception and yet within our range of experience.

Some psychics claim to be able to read the 'aura' which supposedly projects around the body, and recent research has attempted to photograph this band of light. At first, the concept sounds strange to us because in western culture we are so accustomed to thinking of the skin as the outer layer of our being. But heat exchange with the surrounding environment is continuous, and it is not difficult to conceive of an extension of energy around the body.

The idea of the human aura originated in ancient times and is depicted in the sacred images of Egyptian, Indian, Greek, Roman and Christian art. Actor shamans in traditional societies, including western cultures in centuries past, worked with manifestations of energy which looked like auras.[29]

Recent research began in Russia when machines were designed which can photograph the energy emanating from living things, from the human body to plants. In 1974, the discoverer of this camera, Semyon Kirlian set up his own laboratory, while research projects on Kirlian-designed machines were established in other Russian centres. The photographs thus obtained are studded with luminous dots and flares, and a Leningrad surgeon, Dr Mikhail Gaikin, observed that the position of the glowing energy spots emanating from the human body corresponds with the standard points used in acupuncture.

Whether these 'Kirlian auras' have any connection with the psychic auras of tradition remains to be established. But it certainly seems possible that we are just beginning to understand a dimension of energy which has been unknown in western science, but familiar for centuries to mystics and psychics.[30]

And actors.

Traditional actors were considered to be people of great presence. Like modern actors, their personal magnetism was enhanced by reputation. But they were also people who exerted a strong influence on others, mostly through the strength of their character and will.

Many actor-shamans appear to have been enigmatic, mysterious and strange. Yet their performances were very well rehearsed. Spontaneity was supported by preparation and concentration. But perhaps more than anything the quality of energy is the factor that brought the power of presence to actor-shamans. For they healed, and it was believed that they transmitted an energy to the patient. An energy that drew upon the support of the spirits – concentrated personal resources from within. And it is concentrated energy which is the factor lending the power of presence to anyone with the commitment to claim it for themselves. That means focusing on what one wants or needs and investing that goal fully with all the energy at one's disposal.

The way of the actor is not an esoteric discipline divorced from everyday life. It *is* everyday life, heightened and lived to the full, with an awareness of powers beyond understanding. Glenda Jackson says that acting is the sense of life being lived 'second by second, beat by beat'.

In the acting of our everyday lives, the performances that constitute our selves, some situations seem more 'dramatic' than others. Theatre, and life, are more interesting when we are caught up in dramas, heightened emotion, compelling conflicts and passions. This is because all our energy is thereby focused on what we are trying to do. We seem awake, alert, alive – in action.

The times of our lives when we are fully engaged, involved and drawn into action, are times when we 'forget ourselves'. Literally. For quite often the most exciting moments of our lives are lived so fully in the moment that they cannot be recalled to conscious memory. We were *so* involved in action that the experience has been transmuted into our own beings without the 'distance' from the event necessary for conscious memory. Our minds do not bother to record the details of such full experiences; we are too busy living to make notes.

Actors live in the moment. Fully. But in everyday life we rarely risk complete contact with the present. Robert Benedetti suggests that we prefer 'a sense of comfortable continuity, which is achieved by blurring the lines that separate the present from the past and future. The past, in memory, and the future, in expectation, can both be controlled by our consciousness, but the present can be met only on its own terms. Although you can never specifically isolate it, you can put yourself in touch with the unending *flow* of the present.'[31]

Filling the present moment. Living now.

CHAPTER 12

Soul: Liberation from the Body

THE FIRST TIME Shirley Maclaine floated out of her physical body, it happened while she was asleep. It seemed to her nothing like a dream, 'It felt more real than a dream. I felt I was suspended over the Earth and I dipped and flowed with the air currents just like a bird. I floated over countries and mountains and streams and trees . . . my being concentrated and expanded at the same time. I had the sensation that this was actually happening, that my body was irrelevant and that *that* was part of the experience. The real me was floating free and clear, filled with the peace of connection to everything that was.'[1]

Some years later, one night in the Andes, Shirley Maclaine sat in the healing waters of a sulphur spring, 'I breathed deeply. . . . My head felt light, I physically felt a kind of tunnel open in my mind. It grew like a cavern of clear space that was open and free of jumble. . . . I became the space in my mind. I felt myself flow into the space, fill it, and float off, rising out of my body until I began to soar. I was aware that my body remained in the water. I looked down and saw it. . . . My spirit or mind or soul, or whatever it was, climbed higher into space. Right through the ceiling of the pool house and upward over the twilight river I literally felt I was flying . . . no, flying wasn't the right word . . . it was more gentle than that . . . wafting seemed to describe it best . . . wafting higher and higher until I could see the mountains and the landscape below me and I recognized what I had seen during the day.'[2]

This experience is, of course, literally 'outside' the boundaries of reason. In Western scientific culture we assume that our conscious and unconscious selves live within, or are even synonymous with our physical body. And to exist externally to the body violates our conception of our selves.

For most of us in everyday life, the sensation of operating from a control centre within the physical body is paramount. We think of ourselves as an individual entity quite separate from everything and everybody around us. We live according to the assumption that our identity is coterminous with our body, and that 'I' am 'in here' while everyone and everything else is 'out there'. This viewpoint is so deeply ingrained in the way we are brought up that it conditions every other perspective we develop in life. It comes as a shock when we hear of people who believe it could be otherwise. Who would believe, for example, that the self can exist *outside* the body, as we did, in western culture, centuries ago.

We are all familiar with phrases like he 'jumped out of his skin', 'I was beside myself with excitement', and so on. They survive from times past, when we believed that a certain state of consciousness could be achieved in which the person was literally out of their body. But while this sounds strange to us now, there are still ways today in which we can understand our selves as extending beyond the boundaries of our skin. When we are in a room with other people, for example, we exchange body heat, recycle air, micro-organisms, and so on. In biological terms, the skin is what *joins* us to everyone and everything else, as much as it separates. It is permeable; all sorts of things pass through it.

But what of our psychological selves? Here we also exist independently of our body. For example, at any given moment it is likely that someone is thinking about us; a friend, lover, acquaintance, work colleague, relative. And the way we exist in other people's minds has, of course, no geographical boundaries. That part of us which occupies the minds of others can be all over the world at any one time.

If this is the case, where is the innermost core of our being? The essence of ourselves? And how is it connected with our body?

The part of the 'self' that exists independently of the body used to be called the 'soul'. Because it has religious connotations which have lost the power of meaning for many, the idea of the soul has faded in recent years. But in the world of acting it still carries validity. Klaus Kinski, for example, talks of the 'soul to soul contact' between himself and film audiences, a concept which for him expresses a level of communication he hopes to achieve, a realm beyond the mere 'interpersonal'. Liv Ullmann talks of the truth of acting as the 'discovery of the soul of another human being'.

The soul represents something at once greater and more concentrated than the self – it is the *essence* of the person. From the point of view of this discussion, the interesting thing about the soul as a concept is that it allows an image of an aspect of one's nature that is not bounded by physical notions of existence. Although we sometimes still talk of 'the heart' of a person, especially in referring to an emotional quality of feeling or courage, most of our references to the 'self' are restricted to the little 'person' who lives between the ears and behind the eyes, and from whose vantage point we peer out at the world through the two convenient apertures we call 'eyes'.[3]

This sense of a 'self', located in the head, is for most of us the control box from which we live, from where we make decisions about our behaviour. This sense of self dominates – it is thought of as in a proprietal capacity relative to the rest of the body. We speak, for example, of 'my arms' or 'my legs' as if they were somehow separate from, but owned by, the self. Yet the self cannot escape the body. We are limited by physical boundaries. And because this body-bounded view of our selves is so fundamental, it underlies all other aspects of how we live. . . . That is why, in the way of the actor, it is important to be liberated from the body.

Centre

Every actor works from a *centre*. Not so esoteric as the soul, for the actor's work is practical, the 'centre' is a working, moving base for action. Often it is not used consciously, rather it is an intuitive guiding source of energy from which the actor works, acts and lives. In the actor's world, performing off-centre, or without centre, lacks directness, truth, power. Since this is true also of life, living from the centre is a way of being we can all use.

Like 'soul', 'centre' is difficult to define, too slippery to pin down effectively in words. This leads to confusion even in the actor's world. But in workshops and rehearsal, actors can be helped to locate a physical and psychological source of power within the body (for most actors, between the heart and solar plexus). Working from this centre alters dramatically the way a person functions. Most importantly, it ensures that the actor can live from a personal base that is not restricted only to the head. Of course, the brain remains a crucial locus of thought, decisions and reflection. But moving the sense of *self* into the body balances and harmonizes, because in the West we do not employ a developed understanding of energy (except in the narrow physical sense). The centre provides a focus for both taking in and expressing energy. It is the source from which a person's energy flows. It is a concept familiar in the East, and illustrated in the martial arts. In the West it is a pivotal aspect of the way of the actor. And acting from the centre is the key to a liberation from the body-bounded self.

Extending the Self

Kirsten Hughes lies on her back in the middle of a very large rehearsal room. A studio theatre, in fact. She has her eyes closed. I talk her through a relaxation procedure which slows her breathing, relaxes her body and clears her mind. Each succeeding breath becomes slower and deeper than the one before. I ask her to imagine that with each succeeding breath she is taking in a colour, any colour she chooses. With each intake of breath a ball of the coloured light is forming in her body. A bright, vivid ball of light at her centre. It is the centre of her energy, her body, her mind. This psychological process, in which the colour is a powerful visualization, concentrates mind and body very powerfully.

I ask Kirsten to imagine a pebble being dropped into her ball of colour, as if into a pool of water. Ripples spread out and around, and the colour passes through her skin and gradually spreads around the room. She continues to breathe powerfully. The colour ebbs and flows until it fills a huge space outside her body.

Eventually the colour fills the complete interior space of the theatre. And this colour is the extended self of Kirsten. The room is filled with her energy. Her body and my body are inside her extended self. We are inside *her*.

I ask Kirsten to stand up, keeping her eyes firmly closed. Taking her by the arm, I lead her around a tour inside herself. She discovers the environment, the space, inside an extended self. It is huge. We walk faster. Her eyes are tightly shut, I am leading her at a good walking pace, and she reports to me on her sensations – where it feels warm, where cold. And she tells me when she feels she is passing through the centre of the space, from where the energy has arisen.

Kirsten begins to feel at home inside herself. She is striding around confidently in the space. I let her arms go and she walks with no guidance. She is safe because she is not walking in alien territory. Something that is not her. Everywhere she goes is space that is hers. Her self. No longer confined by her body. Extended. Expanded. Exhilarated. The boundaries are stretched. Until she walks near a wall and I shout 'Stop!' Then she sets off in a different direction, continuing the voyage inside Kirsten.

Eventually, she begins trotting across the space, eyes still closed. I guard the edges and shout when she is in danger. She is running inside herself. She runs again. And again, faster. Soon she is running at high speed across the room, with me to meet her near the boundaries. It is terrifying and thrilling to watch. And the sense of exhilaration and liberation that comes from running uninhibited, blindfold, in extended inner space, is incredible. The feeling of confidence that accompanies *becoming* the space around oneself, filling it, owning it, is tremendous. And when two or more people are present, the space is shared in a way more exciting, more fully, than before.

Finally, I guide Kirsten back to the centre of the room. She lies down again, and I direct her breathing back to normal. She leaves to go straight on to a rehearsal for the production she is in. Her fellow actors told me the next day that they were stunned by her work in the rehearsal. They had never seen her performing with so much confidence.

Confidence in a self extended beyond the body.

Flying

'I think there are occasions on a first preview or a first night when it does seem like a parachutist having to launch himself into mid-air – you have this terrible feeling that you actually cannot take that next step. You have to force yourself to. I've never jumped off an aeroplane, but it must be something like that, with the sense of you *knowing* the parachute's going to open, it's going to catch you, you're going to land alright. It's just that unnatural thing of stepping off into mid-air.' Antony Sher recounted this experience of 'flying' as something that has happened to him many times. It is a common experience among actors, who talk of being on a 'high' during a performance, 'winging' it, and so on.

Most of us know what it feels like to fly, because we have experienced it in dreams. We are familiar with the exhilaration and terror. But for actors, it is a part of their working life.

Sam Waterston describes such an experience. It happened while he was playing the role of Lucky in a production of *Waiting for Godot*, 'I had a revelation in the last performance of the play that ignited the whole character and illuminated it in a great flash right while I was standing on the stage.' But it was the emotional high, literally, that accompanied the inspiration which is relevant here. 'It was like an ecstatic experience. . . . The only other time I've had an experience like that was when I was skiing once.' Waterston was skiing in Austria for three weeks, 'I skiied every day, all day long. I actually began to get pretty good. Towards the end of the time I was skiing parallel down the mountain, and I was going about sixty miles an hour. . . . Everything was just working perfectly, and I wasn't thinking about it any more and suddenly, I had a sense of taking off. It was like flight. And the same thing happened when I was doing that play.'[4]

This is exactly the sort of ecstatic experience described by the traditional actor-shaman, who considers flying to be a state of heightened awareness. In shamanism it is the ecstatic state in which the shaman transcends his physical body to journey to the land of the spirits. And while the actor-shaman soars in his imagination to the spirit-world, Waterston soars in his imagination in finding the most truthful characterization of *his* spirit, his role.

Sam Waterston likens acting to, 'Being able to safely fly – that's what you try to get. As opposed to wanting to fly something, you want to fly!'

In traditional cultures actors experienced this state of out-of-body at almost every performance. For the actor-shaman was believed to journey to the land of the spirits in a disembodied state, returning to deliver messages from the spirit world. Indeed, it is said that primitive actors were, literally, able to fly.[5] This is based on the fact that their performance costumes were often made of feathers and other bird-like features, but we should exert caution here, because traditional societies do not maintain the sharp distinctions between reality and imagination that we do in the West. They have a more sophisticated understanding of metaphor in the myriad areas of life which require creative perception.

In traditional societies, *experiental* reality is considered to be as important as material reality. And this is surely right. For when people imagine a scene or an event, what goes on in their mental and emotional experience is very similar to what goes on if the corresponding event actually happened. The imagination does not rely on external material reality for its power of effect. In other words, the actor-shaman *feels as if* he is flying, even though his physical body remains grounded. He is flying in spirit, experientially. Like Antony Sher and Sam Waterston.

Out of the Body

In the Royal Academy of Dramatic Art, by four o'clock in the afternoon, the actor was in a light trance. He was lying on his back, eyes closed. I sat next to him. There was no one else in the locked rehearsal room. Soft sunlight streamed through the window and splashed golden swathes of colour across the beige carpet. Inside the room, the only sound was the rhythmic, slow breathing of the actor as he deepened his trance.

'Just relax', I murmured. 'When you feel ready, I'd like you to allow yourself to come out of your body.'

The actor lay absolutely still, except for his eyes which moved about under the lids. 'Take your time', I instructed. I knew that if he tried too quickly and failed, he would lose confidence and the project would fail. 'Take your time, and when you're ready, allow yourself . . .'

'I'm out', he interrupted in a strange, eerily croaking voice. 'I'm on the floor.' He was speaking with some difficulty.

'You're floating along the floor?'

He nodded very slightly. 'Yes', he whispered.

We sat in silence. I hardly dared to breathe. My eyes scanned the floor. I thought I saw movement halfway to the window, but then realized that it was the movement of dust in a pool of sunlight.

'I'm going out . . . under . . . the door.'

I looked over at the door: large, old, solid and, most significantly, firmly closed. Under the door I could see a narrow crack of perhaps one inch between the base of the door and the carpet.

'I'm . . . going . . . down the stairs.'

I was suddenly struck by the absurdity of his journey. If he was indeed outside his body he would surely be travelling through walls. Yet he was reportedly descending the central staircase which leads down to the RADA lobby. I could hear the pounding of feet as people raced up and down the staircase, and in a wave of panic, I wondered whether a travelling astral body could be trampled to death.

The actor was silent again.

'Where are you now?' I whispered.

'Lobby. . . . In . . . the lobby.'

RADA has an entrance lobby with a reception desk, just inside the front doors, and opening out onto the main staircase. It is usually a hive of activity, with people rushing to and fro. Presiding over the entrance lobby is 'Uncle John', RADA's giant receptionist, who ensures that students arrive on time and don't leave before time. Little did he know that an astral body was sneaking past his desk.

'I'm outside!' he burst out excitedly. His face was beaming, animated.

'Tell me what you can see', I said, ready to put some gentle tests and controls on the experiment.

'I can see the doors. RADA's doors.'

The Georgian building has two rather unusual and attractive front doors. 'Can you describe them to me in detail?' I persisted.

There then followed the most astonishingly detailed description of the RADA doors – far more intricate and precise than anything from normal memory, 'There are five bolts in the right upper panel, and six in the lower panel. The brass handle is up on its hinge. There is a deep scratch across the left hand panel, extending to the divider strip at the bottom.' And so on. I was staggered by such convincing detail. He talked about the doors slowly, but precisely, for several minutes. Then he broke off as if distracted by something. I watched his face closely.

'I can . . . go up', he muttered.

'Up?'

'I can float up.'

'Take your time: float up slowly. Tell me what you can see.'

There was a short silence. I imagined him floating up the outside of the building.

'I can see us. I can see us . . .'

I snapped my head around to the window, expecting to see something – I knew not what. An apparition? A ghostly presence of some kind? I could see nothing but the blue afternoon sky lazing above the buildings. I glanced back at Bill's face. He seemed calm still, though there was activity behind his eyelids. He appeared to be scanning a scene of some kind. He went quiet again. His breathing became shallower and slightly faster.

'Where are you now?' I said gently.

'On . . . the . . . roof.' He was having trouble speaking again, but he was clearly excited. 'It's great . . . I can see . . . all around London.'

His voice trailed off. His face remained relaxed. I decided to push the experience a little further. He seemed to be confident and strong. 'Would you like to fly?' I suggested calmly. 'Would you like to jump off the building and fly?' My intonation was clearly aimed at encouraging him to try it.

But he lay absolutely still and silent for a few seconds. Then he spoke rapidly and urgently, 'I want to come back. I don't want to fly. I want to come back.' The colour was draining from his face fast.

I talked him down, rather like an air-traffic controller. 'Take your time, Bill. We'll get you down nice and easily, nice and safely. Take it slowly, and just drift gently down the side of the building . . .'

His eyes fluttered under the lids, his breathing remained shallow.

'I'm . . . coming . . . down', he croaked.

'Tell me when you're coming in the door.'

'I'm coming . . . up . . . the stairs', he said finally. Obviously he had successfully negotiated the front doors and was well into the building.

'I'm back', he breathed.

In the RADA bar, an hour later, the actor started on his second pint of beer. His eyes were shining, every sinew of his body taut with the experience he had just undergone. He sincerely believed that he had travelled out of his body. We discussed it. There seemed to be three levels of explanation for the visually intense journey he had taken. The most basic, which neither of us believed, was that he might have simply imagined the entire experience. Actors develop a vivid imagination as a necessary part of their work: given the psychological requirements of the set-up, it was just conceivable that the entire experience had taken place in his mind. But how would this explain the detail he was able to summon up? We went outside the building, walked across Gower Street, and looked back at RADA. The door was exactly as he had described it, down to the last bolt. The cracks in the masonry were precisely where he had claimed.

We decided that the second ordinary explanation for the experience was that under light hypnosis he had recalled details about the building that he had stored in his memory without being consciously aware of it. Eighteen months of going to RADA meant that he had approached the front of the building hundreds of times, and while being generally unaware of it, must have registered many sense impressions, including details about the front door, and even cracks in the masonry which were just visible across the street.

The third explanation, least acceptable, but most satisfying, was that he *had* indeed travelled outside his body in some form. But how could this be possible?

The *experience* of going out of the body is surprisingly common. Research has indicated that a significant proportion of the general public have at least once felt as if they were leaving their body, usually under uncontrolled circumstances.[6] While asleep, for example, though the experience differs markedly from the standard dream state. But the *nature* of the experience is what is under dispute. Is it paranormal? Do people *really* come out of their bodies? Is it a vivid fantasy, or is there a sense in which consciousness can exist at a distance from the body? There has been little serious study of this phenomenon, since it falls outside the rigid boundaries of conventional science supported by the funding agencies. But some of the studies that have been done have proved intriguing, if not conclusive.

For example, Karlis Osis, of the American Society for Psychical Research, developed a study in which he invited a psychic, Keith Harary, to demonstrate to researchers that when he travelled out of his body it was something more than a dream or vivid fantasy. Harary stayed in one room, periodically inducing states in which he went out of his body and, while in them, 'visited' another room to see if he could make his presence there felt by the experimenters. They were not told when he would enter the room out of his body; they were required only to report any unusual feelings or sensory images. At the end of the first session, it was found that the experimenters' reports of these experiences were significantly more frequent during Harary's out-of-body periods. Even more remarkably, Harary directly influenced the behaviour of a kitten which was in the other room with the experimenters. The kitten stopped meowing when, at the precise moment of being out of his body, Harary stroked it.[7]

In Charles Tart's laboratory in California, a person who could induce such states at will managed to float out of his body, rise from the couch where his physical body was strapped to scientific measuring devices, and in his disembodied state read accurately a five digit random number which had been placed on a shelf high on the wall. Attempts to explain away the results of this study end up with statements such as, 'It was only telepathy'.[8]

William Hurt is another well-known actor who has described an experience of travelling out of his body, 'I was acting once, and I went and sat in the back row and I just watched myself acting'. Hurt considers that this sort of experience is part of the role of the actor as a psychic explorer. He says, 'You get power from the freedom of experience. . . . You just jump from a higher place. But you *have* to jump.'[9]

The way of the actor extends many personal boundaries, and

the boundary of the body is an important one to breach, because it allows for a freer, extended sense of self. Even the experience of going out of the body can be a transcendent one. Shirley Maclaine described her experience of 'flying' as a special event, an ecstatic time which profoundly affected her life. Whenever she felt 'displeased or lonely or out of sorts or strung up and nervous', she thought of that experience and of how peaceful she had felt when she floated out of her body.[10]

Vivid fantasy or paranormal event – extending the self beyond the body boundaries can be a liberating experience.

CHAPTER 13

Powers: Psychic Sensitivity

IN THE AUTUMN of 1955, Alec Guinness went to Los Angeles to make his first Hollywood film, *The Swan*, with Grace Kelly and Louis Jordan. He arrived 'tired and crumpled, after a sixteen-hour flight from Copenhagen'.[1]

When Guinness had refreshed himself at his hotel, he was taken out for dinner by Thelma Moss, then a Hollywood screenwriter. Guinness says, 'We arrived at three restaurants of repute at each of which we were refused admission because she was wearing slacks'. This was after all the 1950s!

They finally arrived at an Italian bistro, frequented by actors, where Thelma was sure they would be welcomed. But the restaurant proved to be full. No tables were available. 'As we walked disconsolately away', says Guinness, 'I became aware of running, sneakered feet behind us and turned to face a fair young man in sweatshirt and blue jeans.' It was James Dean. He introduced himself and offered to let Guinness and Moss join his table. 'We followed him gratefully, but on the way back to the restaurant he turned into a car-park, saying, "I'd like to show you something." '

Dean led the way to a car that 'looked like a large, shiny, silver parcel wrapped in cellophane and tied with ribbon', and announced proudly that the car had just been delivered to him, and that he had not even driven it yet. Alec Guinness reacted very strangely to the presence of the car. So strangely he still cannot explain it himself. 'The sports-car looked sinister to me', he says, 'although it had a large bunch of red carnations resting on the bonnet. "How fast is it?" I asked. "She'll do a hundred and fifty", he replied. Exhausted, hungry, feeling a little ill-tempered in spite of Dean's kindness, I heard myself saying in a voice I could hardly recognize as my own, "Please, never get in it." I looked at my watch. "It is now ten o'clock, Friday the 23rd of September, 1955. If you get in that car you will be found dead in it by this time next week." ' Dean was taken aback.

Guinness apologized, shocked by what he had said, explaining that it was due to lack of food and sleep. They joined Dean at his table, the evening went well, and they eventually parted 'full of smiles'. No further reference was made to the new car.

But Guinness was troubled. Disturbed. Concerned, 'In my heart I was uneasy with myself.'

And at four o'clock in the afternoon of the following Friday, James Dean was dead. Killed while driving the car.[2]

Attitudes to those phenomena which are now regarded as paranormal have undergone numerous changes in the course of history. But in traditional societies today, and Western societies in the past, the actor-shaman was regarded as the prime exponent of paranormal powers. In fact, his role in tribal communities was to use his abilities to communicate with the spirits (literally the powers beyond the normal) on behalf of the people. Future shamanic actors were selected for training and initiation often on the basis of extraordinary experiences in childhood and adolescence – experiences which indicated a sensitivity to communications from the spirit-world, along channels usually not accessible to the general populace. Alec Guinness' premonition of James Dean's death would, in traditional societies, be considered normal for the way of the actor.

The paranormal occupies an uneasy place in life today. Surveys have shown that it is accepted as valid by the majority of people in Western cultures, but it has had a mixed reception in the scientific community. Partly this is because acceptance of the 'paranormal' would devastate many of the most established scientific theories, and partly it is because most phenomena falling into this category have proved very difficult to catch within the nets of normal scientific enquiry.[3]

This is true of very many of the most important elements of life – science has not proved, for example, that people can love each other. The very nature of love is such that it is almost impossible to measure scientifically, and in the laboratory becomes reduced to 'interpersonal attraction' and other more circumscribed categories of behaviour. But we do not stop loving each other because science cannot measure, analyze and prove its existence.

Nor do we stop communicating in ways which use intimate channels because they defy scientific exploration. Reports of coincidence, telepathy, precognition and clairvoyance appear annually in their thousands. But mostly they are random. Unpredictable. Spontaneous. We have no way of inducing or controlling these intimate levels of communication. But the way of the actor comes close to it. For it uses and encourages levels of sensitivity beyond those normally thought possible.

Intimacy

'. . . There is a curious kind of intimacy that actors have among themselves which is specific entirely to the work.' Glenda Jackson is talking about the closeness that develops between actors working on a production. She feels that the nature of the way of the actor means that, '. . . on an acting level you can quite easily break through all those social barriers that keep the world spinning. . . . It's often the case with actors. You have close relationships with them and then you never see them for years and it doesn't make any difference, you are still friends.'[4]

Lynn Redgrave has described a similar experience, 'There is something about combining with a group of people in a common cause that is very lovely. There's a sort of intimacy that you feel, even though you don't know each other very well. What's nice is that . . . you can meet twenty years later and pick up as if you have never left them. I don't know if there are too many other jobs where that happens, and so I think actors are very lucky.'[5]

It seems as if the preparation, production and performance induces a kind of ritual closeness. The project being created necessitates cooperative interchange with fellow actors which transcends the usual 'friend-formation' processes and, like an encounter group, suspends some of the boundaries we place on the ways and levels with which we communicate with one another.

Often 'togetherness' is consciously encouraged. Recently, John Carlisle took on the role of Ralph Nickleby in The Royal

Shakespeare Company's revival of their tremendously successful *Nicholas Nickleby*. The directors, Trevor Nunn and John
Caird, took the first week of rehearsal for the read-through of
what is essentially two plays. John Carlisle reflected on the very
large company, which would be touring around the world with
the production, 'We are going to be working and living together
(on tour) for the next eighteen months. This mix has *got* to
work!' He described the second week of rehearsal in which
Nunn and Caird set exercises to 'break down barriers'. For me
the most successful exercise is where you act as a mirror to your
partner. We were asked to alternate as mirrors to each other
while John or Trevor called out different emotions and movements to us. It is impossible not to feel closer to someone when
you have been showing them your anger, hate and love, and felt
it reflected back at you with the same intensity of feeling.'[6]

Exercises such as this can be contemplated in group therapy
or experiential 'encounter group' settings, but the thought of
practising them in one's place of work – the office, factory floor
or even the family home, underlines the high level of emotional
contact actors achieve with their co-workers.

Of course much of this intimacy comes through the work.
There is hardly a need for the verbal exchanges of personal
information which underpin the process of communication and
ordinary friendship. As the playwright Strindberg commented
a century ago, 'No form of art is as dependent as the actor's. If
he does not get the support of his fellow actors, his performance
will lack resonance and depth. He will be held in check and
lured into wrong inflections and wrong rhythms. That is why
rapport among actors is imperative for the success of a
play.'[7]

The openness and receptivity of actors is, in the hothouse of
acting work, often transferred to one's colleagues – especially
fellow actors and, sometimes, directors. The focus on high-
pressure work, along with the necessity for working cooper-
atively, makes for powerful levels of communication. Certainly
some actors feel that the amount of *giving* to their co-workers is
very high. George Segal has said, '. . . After you've played a
scene you walk away because it's over and when the film is over
there's a great emptiness because part of acting is giving
something of yourself to the person you're acting with, even if

it's only in terms of the character you are playing. And what you give they take away with them.'[8]

When Marlon Brando met his co-star Maria Schneider, at the beginning of filming *Last Tango in Paris*, he began his relationship with her by leading her to a nearby bar, where he told her, 'We're going to go through quite a lot together, so let's not talk. Just look at me in the eye as hard as you can.'[9]

Sensitivity

I found Liv Ullmann almost impossible to interview. She spoke fluently, had interesting things to say, and was warm, charming and friendly. But the trouble was she was so receptive, so interested, so open that I had difficulty in resisting talking about my own ideas and myself. I had the feeling, being with Liv, of being recognized as a person, contacted with genuine warmth, and being invited to meet her halfway with her receptivity.

A similar observation was made by Virginia Wright Wexman, whose interview with Ullmann was published in *Cinema Journal* in 1980. She said of her time with Liv Ullmann, 'Though she had already been interviewed several times that day, she remained extraordinarily attentive, responding with unaffected enthusiasm and sensitivity. Months later, on reading Joan Didion's account of her own attempt to interview the actress, in which the roles of interviewer and interviewee were subtly switched, I was reminded of that afternoon.'

Wexman takes this obviously common observation of Liv Ullmann's sensitivity one stage further, 'Ullmann's aura of sympathetic receptiveness to the personalities around her sets her apart from the stereotype of performers who are self-absorbed narcissists. It is tempting to believe that this quality has made a substantial contribution to her astonishing capacity to imagine herself living other lives, playing roles which are not simply versions of herself but empathic renderings of the world around her.'[10]

Liv Ullmann values highly a trust in people and situations, a willingness to explore, go along with things to find out. She says, '. . . If tomorrow turns out to be wonderful it's because you've allowed tomorrow to be completely open and full of faith. To me that is the positive aspect of innocence.' However, this path to self-knowledge, while deeply rewarding and often positive, pleasant and exciting, also has its dangers. Opening up to experience allows for emotional highs, but one also has to accept and suffer the lows. Negative experiences hurt, and perhaps that is why for most of us our range of experiences is narrower than for actors. Many people avoid the disappointment and therefore miss the highs.

Liv Ullmann says, 'I'm open enough for good things to happen to me because I allow bad things to happen to me, also. If you are open, if you trust, if you believe in tomorrow, you also allow a lot of disappointments because you believe so much in tomorrow.' Ullmann sees receptivity, openness, trusting to experience to be something that is an *everyday* attitude, 'Every day is a choice of how to live'.

Many other actors make a choice in favour of receptivity; it is the way they live and the way they work. Sybil Thorndike, for example, says of Laurence Olivier, 'Larry's got such an enormous sympathy for people. That's what makes him such a frightfully good actor . . . he's so deeply, deeply sympathetic and genuinely emotional. His kindness to anybody in any trouble is extraordinary. It's one of his chief characteristics and the reason that he's such a wonderful comedian – because he can get inside anybody and see whether they are troubled.'[11]

This active empathy is a positive openness to people; a willingness to take in their emotional states, their states of being.

Another fine actor who chooses the richly rewarding but also the disappointing and negative sides of sensitivity is Marlon Brando. A remarkable description of Brando's sensitivity and the way it translates into his acting is provided by Eva Marie Saint who acted with him in the classic film *On the Waterfront*, 'Marlon had an incredible sensitivity to everything that was around him', she recalled. 'He was like an open wound. What he was never got in the way of the role that he had to play. It became such a natural part of him that he didn't have to put it on. When you work with other actors, something happens in the eyes as they start to assume their characters. The eyes grow grey and glassy, the way a snake looks just before it is going to shed its skin. Actors *start acting*. But Marlon never did. He *was* Terry Malloy.'[12]

The stunning result of Brando's sensitivity is on film to admire, and can be as much admired today as when the film was released over two decades ago.

Of course Brando's image as a person was at that time anything but sensitive: he was identified as uncouth, belligerent, arrogant. Later, Brando said of himself, 'I just put on an act sometimes, and people think I'm insensitive. Really, it's like a kind of armour because I'm too sensitive. If there are two hundred people in a room and one of them doesn't like me, I've got to get out.'[13]

The director Elia Kazan, sensing Brando's insecurities, suggested that Marlon might try psychoanalysis. Brando did undertake analysis; his thoughts on this and his sensitivity give an important clue to the way he perceives the process of 'sensitivity', 'I was afraid of analysis at first. Afraid it might destroy the impulses that made me creative, an artist. A sensitive person receives fifty impressions where somebody else may get only seven.'[14]

This is not necessarily a 'paranormal' faculty, of course. But it is an openness to signals, communications and energies from people which makes close communication possible.

Something of this high degree of intimacy and sensitivity can be seen at work in the experience of Dirk Bogarde. While filming his acclaimed performance as von Aschenbach in the film *Death in Venice*, Bogarde formed an intense, close working relationship with his director Luchino Visconti. The degree of communication that developed between them was a combination of the sensitivity of actors and the intimacy of the dramatic working environment. 'My relationship with Visconti was extraordinary', recalls Bogarde. 'We seldom spoke. . . . We sat a little apart from each other, admitting each other's need for privacy, but never more than a metre away. Incredibly we had no need of speech together. We worked as one person. I knew, instinctively, when he was ready, he knew when I was.'[15]

This is communication of a very high order and it is exciting to be reminded that it can happen between people in a working environment. It is communication within the bounds of normal understanding – Bogarde and Visconti exchanged nods, winks, raising of eyebrows and other subtle sign language to communicate but in the complexity of a film set they had obviously forged a powerful communication channel between them. Many of us have experienced moments like this with people to whom we are very close – but it must be rare in most working or social environments.

Traditional actor-shamans were considered to be 'psychic'. Their sensitivity was to those aspects of life which lie beyond the normal senses – the mysteries, the unknown, the forces which work powerfully but are unseen. These forces were manifested as 'spirits', and actor-shamans were open to communication from these beings.

Actors today manifest the 'spirits' of people. As we have seen, these bear important similarities to the primitive spirits, but the modern actor's sensitivity is to other people. Observing them. Understanding them. But also being open to subtle realms of communication from people – fellow actors and people in general.

It takes strength to be open in this way, for interaction with others, if not overtly supportive, is often seen as a threat. Many of us are cautious, on guard, protecting ourselves from unwanted intrusions. But actors have to develop degrees of openness that can be employed in their work.

At RADA, working with a group of actors who had rehearsed together every day for several months, we developed an exercise to consciously open these channels of communication with one another. And some of these trials were so successful and powerful that the communication approached that between Bogarde and Visconti, and even that unexplainable psychic contact between Alec Guinness and the ill-fated James Dean.

Psychic Sensitivity

Two actors face each other across a large rehearsal room. One of them is blindfolded. In the space between them a pattern of chairs is scattered across the room as a barrier. If the blindfolded actor were to walk straight across the room, he would fall over the chairs. On a given signal, the sighted actor guides his blind partner across the room towards him by giving verbal instructions, 'Two steps to the right; one step forward, two to the left . . .' and so on. Most couples communicate well at this level, though it is not as simple as it sounds. People can take bigger steps than expected. Or fail to heed instructions closely enough. It requires concentration.

Later in the day the pairs of actors have a more difficult job to do. The sighted actor guides his blindfolded partner across the room through barriers erected after the blindfold was put into place, using only *vocal* sounds. The guide can use any sounds he wishes to make with his mouth, but must not use words. The exercise is perfectly feasible, but requires a rapid build-up of communication between the two actors, a working language devised between them while the exercise is in progress. Some people invent sounds which are immediately clear. Others seem to have a more obscure bent. Whatever they do invent has to be used consistently, and has to be responsive to the blindfolded partner's reactions. A sound meant to indicate 'turn right' can easily be taken by the partner to mean 'turn left' or even 'step backwards'. The sighted partner must immediately see this and make the necessary adjustments. Most pairs are able to work effectively. Blindfold actors get across the room with a minimum of accidents. Interpersonal concentration increases. Actors are tuning in to each other's communication channels.

Eventually, the most difficult and exciting stage is reached. The sighted actor is to guide his partner across the rehearsal room, and safely around the barriers, using only concentration. No sound cues are allowed at all. And the blindfolded actor is instructed only to be open to messages from his partner which will come directly into his mind or body. I first devised this workshop as a way to test, challenge and stretch actors' ability to concentrate on their partners. A danger in acting is that an individual actor performs without reference to those around him. Yet, when we tried the exercise, we were astonished to find that some of the actors were able to perform as well using only concentration as using words. They walked safely through the barriers almost without hesitation. Others moved slowly and carefully, as if collecting information or waiting for 'telepathic' signals from their partners. Others had no success at all, and hit the barriers repeatedly.

On one occasion I work with a group of six actors who have tremendous success. People circumvent barriers with such ease that we are simultaneously exhilarated and a little afraid

of the power we are tapping. At the end of the session, they urge
me to attempt to go through the barriers. I select a partner, am
blindfolded, and then wait while the barriers are put in place.
The chairs are placed on the ground very softly, and I can gain
no sound cues to the location of the barriers.

I am given the signal to proceed. Although there is little
danger of serious injury, the exercise feels very dangerous. The
space in front seems threatening, barriers lying in wait. After a
long pause, I start walking forward, slowly. One step. A second
step. I feel no sensation from my partner, and have no idea
where the barriers lie. I take a third step, and suddenly sense
danger. I know, with certainty, that if I take another step, I
will hit one of the barriers The threat is directly in front of
me, as if there is something physically dangerous just a foot or
two away. I am still not aware of receiving any messages from
my partner, and I have no idea in which direction to move.

I rotate my body in an arc, keeping my feet rooted firmly to
the ground. Everywhere, every direction, feels dangerous.
Then I locate space to my right and slightly forward which feels
safer. I sidestep carefully into the space, and hit nothing. I take
another sidestep, crossing the room at a diagonal, and keep
going. After perhaps a dozen steps, I begin to grow apprehensive. The area to my right begins to grow less inviting. I feel
that if I step any further I will hit something. I need help, but
am getting no. communication at all from my partner. I swivel
my head, trying to build up in my mind a picture of the barriers.
My mind is a blank. I try to read messages from my partner,
but can hear or visualize nothing.

Then I realize that I am doing all the work with my brain,
furiously attempting to pick up any words, pictures, images,
messages. I decide to shut off my brain and try to feel through
my body. Immediately, I experience something quite astonishing. A strange and disturbing sensation, as if someone is
pulling at my belt buckle. It pulls me forward and to my left. I
follow the direction of the pull, sidestepping slowly, and then I
hear quiet gasps from the others in the room. Either I am doing
well, or I am about to step out of the window. At the same
instant, I feel a touch on my arm. I take off my blindfold, and
see that I am standing next to my partner. I turn to look at the
room, and realize why the others are so amazed. Across the

room run two long parallel lines of chairs, set out to form a V-shaped corridor covering the whole width and length of the room. I had walked exactly along the corridor without touching a single chair. And the likelihood of my doing that purely by chance would have been very small indeed.

Actors today do not usually think of themselves as psychic. But really they should. For as Charles Marowitz points out, 'When people sense what we mean without any outward sign from us, we assume they are *psychic*. Actors are attempting to be psychic all the time. They are transmitting thoughts, experiencing desires, exerting wills, inducing states – and sending out all variety of emanations to an audience who, for their part, are physically comprehending – or not – depending on the strength of the actor's signal.'[16]

Telepathy means literally 'feeling at a distance',[17] and this is precisely the relationship between actor and audience.

But, of course, it is not only actors who are working on a plane akin to the psychic. It is all of us. For if we are receiving 'messages' from the actors, we are opening our channels of communication beyond those of the normal senses, or at least in a combination of the senses which constitutes something different. Marowitz again, 'An audience's radar sees more than it is shown, and what it does not see, it can sense; and what it does not sense, it can imagine. Confronted with such elaborate scanning-devices, the actor can conceal nothing. . . .'[8]

Actors seek to be open, sensitive and intuitive. Degrees of receptivity to others are valued. If we learn from the actor that there are degrees of communication beyond those within our normal awareness, then we have benefitted. And it could be just the beginning. After all, in the case of Alec Guinness, it led to psychic powers.

CHAPTER 14

Energies: Intimate Communication

THE DRAG QUEEN talked dirty right from the beginning. For when Antony Sher starred in Harvey Feinstein's play *Torch Song Trilogy*, he had to play an opening scene in which he is presented to the audience immediately in the 'professional persona' of his character: a drag queen. He is alone on stage talking to the audience. The monologue is very funny, but also 'strong stuff' with pungent references to the sex life of a drag queen. And when I sat in the audience in London's Lyric Theatre, this scene provoked laughter which bordered on the nervously hysterical. Sher told me how the audience reaction felt like a palpable entity he had to work with, 'Sometimes that first speech can be quite alienating – people must know roughly what the play is about before they come, but somehow they find themselves listening to this man who is talking dirty to them, and the house audience sometimes recoils.'

The play focuses on the life of a gay man, and although the New York production went through a period of playing to gay audiences, before reaching a much wider public, in London it attracted mixed audiences from the beginning. Sher says he could tell instantly from the reaction to the first lines of monologue, 'Just how gay the audience is. Some nights I really have to pull out the charm and relax them. But where there is a large percentage of gay people, they warm to the monologue immediately. They think "Ah, another man in a dress!" '

Part of this 'reaction' from the audience is vocal and easy to read, 'It's very interesting what this play does to different audiences, and it causes vocalized reactions that I've never experienced in the theatre before. People shout out – get so involved . . . you know, normally in the theatre there are two kinds of noises: there's applause or there's silence. Here you get all sorts of different variations.'

But the total response to the dialogue adds up to more than noises from the audience. Sher says it's an 'atmosphere', a 'feeling' that comes in waves from the auditorium.

Simon Callow has described a similar experience in audience 'sensitivity', when he played the character of Mozart in Peter Shaffer's *Amadeus*, at the National Theatre, 'I had again the experience I've only had on two or three previous occasions: a hunger from the audience, a feeling that they were getting something they'd done without for too long. Everyone who appears in the play feels the same thing: there's a magnetic pull coming from the auditorium . . . not one performance of the two hundred or so that we did failed to ignite an electric charge in the audience. . . .'[1]

So what *is* the nature of the actor's relationship with the audience? Where does this energy come from? Theatre can be a cauldron of powerful emotion though often framed and made safe by the neat rows of seats, uniformed ushers, predictable bars and tiny sweet counters. But if we peel off the layer of genteel decorum and peek underneath, we see something much more primitive, much more powerful, and so dangerous that it has had to be smothered by 'polite society'.

The Audience Experience

Each individual has their own bubble of space surrounding the body which we seem to regard as 'territory'. It is an area which is charged with sensitivity. When this space is invaded, in the normal run of everyday life, we try to reduce the tension by avoiding eye contact with the people who have entered it. And when we are in situations where the space is difficult to protect, in crowded trains, lifts and so on, we retreat into an internal world of reverie, glazed eyes, and a denial of the presence of others around us.

In an audience people voluntarily put themselves in close proximity with strangers, which is a stressful event both physiologically and psychologically. Seats usually face in one direction and therefore eye contact is minimized, and rules of the game are usually observed so that one does not turn around in one's seat to look directly at the people seated behind. Nevertheless, space is invaded. It is intimate. A full theatre is a mass of overlapping 'bubbles', in which each person has allowed those seated adjacent, front and back, into his own space. Being in a theatre audience is a tactile experience. But since the members of an audience are participating as one in the same event, the commitment goes beyond mere sharing of 'body bubbles'. The members of an audience have an affinity with one another because they have tacitly agreed to share an emotional journey, a dramatic experience. To the extent that the experience is shared and is known to be shared, then the other people in the room are not so much strangers. Friendship is the willingness to share experience with another, and so audience togetherness is a form of sharedness, and friendship.

Of course, most of us have been members of audiences which did not feel at all like this. People can resist the sharing. But for those performances described by Sher and Callow, the 'audience experience' was surely exhilarating. It is probably heightened still further by the lessening of tension of being one person in a group of strangers who have become 'friends'. By recognizing that they are *with* you, in appreciation of the play, you belong to them, and they belong to you.

Actors, the catalysts of this group experience, are well aware of the importance of the 'audience experience'. 'They're the missing ingredient that you're working towards, and only when you finally have an audience do you have a play. They're part of it. The live theatre is special in that it's the only medium that depends to that extent on an audience.' Lynn Redgrave points out that ballet and opera are ruled by the music and will tend to go on regardless of what the audience does or does not do. 'But the participation of the audience in theatre is essential, and what they bring to it or don't bring to it alters the nature of the performance.'[2]

In contrast, she points out how the influence of watching television, which is a very different process, has resulted in a deterioration in the ability of people to *participate* as a theatre audience, 'It doesn't matter what people do in front of a television set or movie screen because their participation is nothing. That's why it's lovely and very relaxing to go to a movie or watch TV; you don't have to join in. And that's why a lot of modern audiences are difficult to play to; they don't know, for example, that if they talk, the actors can hear them, or their fellow audience can hear. People are so used to talking through a TV performance.'[3]

There are interesting dynamics in film audiences, too, but obviously theatre is the medium in which actors are conscious of immediate audience reaction.

Liv Ullmann feels that audiences 'give as much as the people on the stage. An audience is much more part of a production than they know. They can give in their silence, because in the silence you can hear their listening. They can give in their laughter because you hear in their laughter that they're sharing the joke. They can give very much by just smiling because you can hear on stage when a smile goes through the whole theater. And they give through crying because you can hear if an audience has tears in their eyes – it's a kind of movement.'[4]

This responsivity is because the audience *cares*. Liv likens it to talking to an individual, 'If you feel that person really wants to listen – even if what you're saying is not very special – you say it with more heart. . . . That's what makes people flourish – they need someone who recognises them.'[5]

It is this element of recognition which begins to bring us closer to the true nature of theatrical energy. For it sounds very like the experience Simon Callow had on playing in Martin Sherman's play *Passing By*, about two young homosexual men who fall in love. '. . . It was extraordinary. The tiny Almost Free, smallest of all the fringe theatres, was packed every day with men who . . . were deeply moved. It was a touching story; but it wasn't that. It was as if a secret that had been kept for too long were finally being told to people who knew it individually but had never seen it acknowledged . . . the actors were acting, as it were, on behalf of the community. . . .'[6]

Communal Ritual

For centuries, the role of the actor in traditional societies was to act on behalf of the community. The actor-shaman heals himself by going into the world of fantasy, the imaginal, the spirits. And this world contains the secrets which we all know, individually, deep down in our unconscious, but which need to be *shared* publicly. Acknowledged.

To journey into the dreamworld of the imagination is to enter the psychological state in which these secrets may be encountered and understood intuitively. In traditional societies this journey was considered to be a renewal, a process, to which the audience must contribute. Not only in 'suspending disbelief' to render the drama more effective, but also by positively contributing imaginal commitment so that the audience is in a state amenable to messages from the spirits. Sometimes, the spirits had harsh things to say, and the traditional audience had to have the strength and will to remain open, vulnerable to painful news.

Sometimes today we see and hear things in theatre and film that are painful, that we would prefer to avoid. And just as the primitive actor had to draw the audience into the performance, and engage him fully, so do today's actors.

The audience needs to *enter* the performance and fill it with their fantasy, their imagination. Liv Ullmann talks about the importance of allowing an audience to do that, believing that actors should not get 'in the way for the audience; let them be creators too. Let them come in with their fantasy.' To make this possible she believes that the actor should not do too much on the stage. She says that if she allows some quietness around her, then people can contribute their imaginations to the performance, '. . . the audience and I must create it together. If I'm a little more quiet and I allow you to interpret in me what has been silent, you will have better experience than if you've had a very busy lady all over the stage. . . .'[7]

While there is a basic parallel between traditional and modern theatre in the actor – audience interaction, there are crucial differences in what we see as the *purpose* of the whole enterprise. For today theatre is considered as entertainment. It falls into the category of culturally uplifting entertainment. Stress-reducing activities, if practised in moderation, are after all generally sanctioned.

But the role of the actor in traditional society was radically different. For regular contacts between the spirit world of deep, intuitive truths and the general public was not only considered to be entertaining. It was *necessary*. It maintained the balance of the natural order. And to live too fully in the rational, secular world of everyday events, without contact with the mysteries underpinning life, was feared, because it led to individuals and communities becoming cut off from the meaning of life.

A healing performance by the actor-shaman, carried out in front of an audience comprising the whole community, was aimed not only at helping particular, sick individuals. The performance was for the community as a whole. It was a communal ritual in which the actor brought the public into contact with the powers of the imaginal world, both within themselves individually, and in a shared sense as a group. In traditional societies acting was a ritual which released communal energies, and invoked the spirits. It still does.

'Theater is, apart from the church and the concert hall, one of the few places where people can still meet around an event – an event which tells them something, opens their eyes. And it's an experience shared with a lot of other people. It's not sitting alone in front of a television set or with a newspaper.' Liv Ullmann feels that this shared experience happens less and less in our world today, and is something actors can give people. 'The audience can share our experience, our interpretation of words, of life – what it is to be alive.'

Her notion of energy in theatre focuses on shared emotion, 'Everything that is shared is basically what the human person is longing for and where he grows the most. Love is shared. It's almost like a mass of positive energy that floats out because many people release it together.' This is what she sees happening in the theatre, '. . . with an audience when you start to breathe together, laugh together, cry together. This makes more laughter and more breathing, although you are not aware of it because you are doing it with somebody else. If you had been sitting alone in the audience, you wouldn't have laughed so easily, maybe your tears would have been more silent. It enables; sharing enables people to come out with their feelings.'[8]

Ben Kingsley describes it as a kind of contagion, which implies a process of shared excitement, 'The buzz you get from saying a line . . . can, if you work hard, become contagious, the thrill can be passed on and shared.'[9]

And Glenda Jackson develops the notion of shared theatrical experience. She says, 'I'm not interested in theatre that is merely a spectator sport. The most exciting and, to me, the only valid reason for having a theatre is that, upon occasions, you can create a microcosm of society.' And she told me, 'When it works at its best, you have two groups of strangers who come together into a space that belongs to no one, and out of that you create a whole, you create a unit and it is an experience that will never be repeated in exactly the same way. It can happen again with another group of strangers, but it is an entirely specific evening.'

In a general sense, Glenda Jackson considers this experience of coming together to be the main reason for having theatre, '. . . My social view of the purpose of theatre in any society that wishes to consider itself well-balanced and productive is to provide the shared experience, that extraordinary coming together of a group of strangers and, by that act, losing their strangeness. It may last no longer than it takes you to walk through an exit door, but that experience when it happens is undeniable and that, as an idea of what it is to be a human being in the company of other human beings, is very valuable.'

She emphasizes that it must be a live performance to generate this sort of environment, 'It is a process whereby the audience is actually working as hard as the actors, because you have that energy that is shared. Not only that, but it is all concentrated on that particular lit area. The energy goes off the stage, into the auditorium and then is sent back to you. When that happens there is a real sense of bonding, of sharing, of being a unit and what the actors do is enhanced by what the audience do. . . . It feels like a microcosm of what an ideal society would be like – a total sharing of energy. Of course, occasions where it happens fully are very rare, but it is one of the main reasons for acting.'

Estelle Parsons agrees, and emphasizes some of the points she thinks are necessary for generating this atmosphere, 'I think the essential ingredient is that it should be alive. It should be a communion of souls in the same way as religion.'[19]

These views are very like those characteristics of traditional societies. But how does this process of community-focused energy happen? Director Charles Marowitz suggests that there is '. . . the quintessential centre inside the actor through which he establishes contact with an equivalent centre in the audience. On one level this is thought-transference which is an essential part of all acting; on another it is . . . spiritual contact; that is, the establishment of communication with unseen forces.'

But we do not normally think of theatre as a place of 'unseen forces'. How do they arise?

'Think for a moment with what difficulty a medium tries to establish contact with a spiritual force', Marowitz suggests. 'There is the ritual of the seance, the darkened room. The holding of hands round the table, the group concentration, the exhortation to invisible presences to materialise or give a sign. . . . The theatre works on a similar principle (social ritual, darkened room, communal presence, intense concentration, evocation of non-existent people and events).'[11]

While we do not use the language of mediums to discuss this process, we get near enough to it. Marowitz points out, 'When a performance can be said to "work", it is because it produces resonances which critics subsequently refer to using words such as "magnetism", "magic", "spellbinding" and "hypnotic".'[12]

In Charles Marowitz' view, the real focal point of the drama is not on the stage, nor in the auditorium, but in a 'state of consciousness which bridges the two areas. It is a plateau of sensibility in the audience which the actor reaches by climbing through himself and his material.'[13]

Sam Waterston, acting on Broadway, describes the relationship between himself and the audience in similar terms, '. . . There was a sensation of incredible communication, which neither I nor they were really responsible for. It was just taking place in the air between us. . . . It was like a group experience. . . .'[14]

Energies

This communal ritual is fuelled by the actor's energy. Al Pacino considers that energy is produced by actors rather in the way of 'emotional' athletes, 'You work hard; . . . and then the emotion comes up and out. It's exercised and exorcised.'[15]

Of course, not all actors can produce sufficient energy for the theatrical ritual. Rip Torn comments, 'There are some people who are very fine movie actors, but who only have an acting power for the camera at a distance of five feet, close up. They don't have that force on the stage. They don't have that kind of energy.' He compares the energy used in a normal conversation with a stage performance, and points to the quality of intensity as a distinguishing variable, 'It's not just making it large. A lot of times it's the intensity. Stage energy is a more intense energy than we need for talking here.'[16]

Certainly actors seem to be aware of an energy quality in performance. Antony Sher's performance of Richard III was one of the most widely acclaimed theatre performances of recent years. One of the things that struck me about his performance was that the impact seemed to reach across the rows of seats and filled the large auditorium. It had the power that one associates with small, intimate theatre. I asked him about what reaches the audience, 'I'm aware of the importance of energy', he said, 'I'm conscious of feeling the need to send out an energy.'

Actors do work with considerable physical energy. Ian McKellan, on playing Hamlet quite early in his career, was struck by the purely physically demanding nature of the role, 'There is a passage where you are on stage for an hour. You are the machine for every theme and you have to fuel that machine somehow. Then right at the end you have got to do all that bloody fighting. You are certainly ready for death after that.'[17] The amount of energy built up and expended, physically and mentally, must be tremendous. After each performance of *Hamlet* McKellan needed three hours to unwind.

Sometimes, the build-up of physical energy expenditure can be exhausting but somehow necessary; a release for the imagination. Judi Dench says, 'Sometimes it helps if you've been rehearsing all day. Then you go past that barrier of tiredness. It can be just marvellous then – because then the audience doesn't see the actor energizing. You're using overdrive. And on those occasions, sometimes, everything just drops into place . . . it can be thrilling.' Again, this build up of physical and mental energy to such a pitch can be gauged by the 'unwind' factor. Judi Dench says, 'You're all right for about an hour and a half, and then you feel pretty flat. . . . I can't go straight to sleep. I couldn't go home, walk straight up the stairs and get into bed and sleep.'[18] Essential though this energy output is, it does not quite capture the power of presence. Many actors *work* hard, but although it is clear that actors use a high pitch of physical and mental expenditure, it somehow seems an inadequate concept to describe what connects between actor and audience to make that actor so watchable. It takes more than physical and mental effort to create the presence of Gary Cooper dominating thugs in a London restaurant, or Richard Burton gripping audiences, Albert Finney rising above a dreary script and Meryl Streep providing compelling viewing on screen. We need to know more than that they put a lot of *effort* into their work, though that is an indisputable basis. It does not explain the almost hypnotic effect that actors can sometimes have.

After watching Liv Ullmann's performance in Harold Pinter's play *Old Times*, I asked her about her use of energy. 'Sometimes in a play you have a wonderful scene and it refuels you for the next scene. But in this play I do not have wonderful lines; they are very strange lines. So I think about the part as a dancer. I see the whole thing as a dance: she moves this way, then this happens; she moves that way and then that happens. And that is actually what gives me the energy because I had no other things to go on. I dance the performance and there's always a kind of wave to follow, to ride on and that in itself does give a strange kind of energy.'

So what is this strange kind of energy? We begin to get a little closer to it when Glenda Jackson talked to me about perform-ance energy, 'It's energy that makes all the difference between a live and a dead performance. The contact between the actor and audience creates a releasing of an energy that is there all the time if we knew how to facilitate it.' Clearly, she is not talking about simply physical, or mental energy. Rather, it sounds like an emotional charge between actor and audience that transcends the physical effort of the actor and the intellec-tual presence of the audience. To express *this* sort of energy, Glenda Jackson thinks, is something for which we have no adequate concepts in the West, 'One sees it very clearly in Oriental cultures – it's the capacity to be completely relaxed and completely energized at the same moment; the ability to invest an emotion or an idea, a gesture even, with all the energy that you have and be able to control it absolutely.' She thinks that this capacity is within everyone, 'but we don't happen to find ourselves in a culture where it is as highly regarded as in some others. You see that sort of balance rarely in our culture, but you see it very clearly in Oriental cultures. It's the thing the Chinese have of being able to fill everything with absolute energy. Look at their martial arts.'

In the West we are used to distinguishing the mind from the body, and we therefore have separate categories for 'physical' and 'psychological' or mental energy. An understanding of the ways in which one can combine these concepts in a single energy source characterizes a number of Eastern approaches to life and action. In some of the traditions of martial arts, for example, and in acupuncture, the systems of energy used are 'visualized'. While there may be some psychophysical correlates of these imagined energy channels, the more important point is that this energy, called 'chi', can be used in dramatically effective ways. 'Chi' empowers a karate expert to chop through bricks with his bare hands, and an acupuncturist to induce anaesthesia under which surgery may be undertaken while the patient remains conscious.

For many Westerners these concepts seem esoteric and alien. But actors are aware of, and use a unified energy rather like 'chi', in the everyday Western setting of the theatre. Klaus Kinski experiences this energy as a power passing through. He likes to open himself up, and 'let the power pass through me to the audience.'

Similarly, Sam Waterston experiences energy passing through him, and finds it an ecstatic state, 'When you get completely high from it, and it is the best that it is, you are in the grips of passion. I don't mean scenery-eating passion; I mean that things are passing through you. You are a pipe in a channel.'

As in traditional cultures, these modern actors are bringing to us powers from the beyond. Healing energies. Spirits. And proving yet again that the way of the actor is still a path to personal knowledge and power.

CHAPTER 15

Return To The Mystery

THE WAY OF the actor adds nothing to our lives. Rather, it *takes away*; blocks, restrictions, fears, boundaries and conventional views of self and experience.

Trusting our intuition and removing the constraints on expression is the actor's path to the release of inner potential. Acting is a good way to accomplish this liberation. For not only is the creation of a character a process that draws on experiences from within, it also completely engages attention in a manner that renders it impossible to keep all defences intact. Simon Callow, reflecting on his first totally involving performance, says, 'I had no time to think about my performance. . . . For the first time . . . I understood what playing a character was. It was giving in to another way of thinking. . . . *I was being in another way.*'[1]

So what is the experience of 'being in another way'?

Most fundamentally, the actor engenders a view of life in which the myth of a single, unified personality is exploded. We are each many 'selves', and actors recognize and give expression to the variety of inner personalities that we so often ignore or repress. Following on from the realization that we are each not one but many people, actors change themselves physically, mentally and emotionally. In response to roles, but also in ways visible outside the theatre or studio, in everyday life. While we may think we would like to change ourselves', actors do just that. Dramatically.

In preparing roles actors live fully in the present. For past experience is recalled, relived, and recreated in the preparation of a role. Both the dramatic and the ordinary from one's life is

valued, and given continuous expression. The ordinary becomes special, and the past becomes present. These are the two
main ingredients of *living life now*.

The way of the actor emphasizes the richness and power of
our own imagery, and the use of the intuitive. But this is far
from being a 'soft option'. Physical challenge and emotional
risk are strong spices in the actor's life. Living in the present
moment, taking risks, leads to a vivid presence and a full
expression of inner power.

The actor's path extends many boundaries, including the
boundary of the body. For the centre – source and focus of
energies – is expanded beyond the body and into the surrounding world. Strong energies are expressed, rather than being
contained, and lost.

Traditional actor-shamans were considered to be psychic.
Their sensitivity was to those aspects of life which lay beyond
the normal. Actors today still demonstrate degrees of communication beyond those we normally accept. Extending the
powers of communication is one of the central features of the
actor's gift to the world.

Of course, we are all actors. The ideas and insights revealed
by actors are available for all of us to experience. Not only by
'acting' – though with amateur theatre, acting courses and
workshops, that is an option open to many – but rather by
realizing the many areas of life in which we fail to invest fully
with our energy.

At the heart of all acting is the supposition 'if only . . .' . For
a performance, this means building oneself into a frame of
mind in which 'If only I were changed into that character I am
to play, how would I think and behave; what would be my
experience?' For the rest of us the same 'if only . . .' is asked
often in our minds, and usually answered only with fantasy. But
the way of the actor is fantasy realized, in real life. Above all,
actors reclaim for us the crucial realm of 'if only' – imagination
and fantasy.

At the very least, this can help us to feel better about life.
Marlon Brando reflects that 'Everybody has had the experience of feeling: Christ, the world is coming to an end. And you
go watch John Wayne riding across the prairie, and you see
grass blowing and the clouds, and he grabs the girl and they

ride off into the sunset. You went in there feeling awful and you came out feeling good. *He* made you feel good. That's not bad, that's not a bad thing to do in life. . . .'[2]

Film director John Boorman confessed that, 'When I started out making movies I used to feel guilty that craftsmen were using good timber to construct my fantasies when they could be building homes. There is a terrible arrogance about taking these resources and converting them into shadows, into nothing.' But then Boorman met the Indians of the Brazilian rain forest, people who valued the world of the imaginal, 'The Indians, with their music, dance and ritual, are constantly striving to escape their material lives into the spirit world. In making a movie we take the material elements of our society and transmute them into a stream of light flowing onto a wall, hoping that it will contain something of *our* spirit.'[3]

Just as the shamans of the Brazilian Indians manifest their spirits, so actors today personify *our* spirits. It is a perspective we have forgotten. In rediscovering the role of the actor, I believe we have rediscovered a part of ourselves – that part which connects with the unknown, the powers beyond, the secrets of life that can only *ever* be known through the intuitive faculties. For it is here, deep within our spirit, that art meets science and proves to be every bit as powerful.

It is easy, of course, to sound pretentious about art, because to encompass it in words we have to reach for vocabulary which sounds exaggerated. And some will consider the elevation of actors to a position of importance to be pretentious. Yet in a world in which, with the scientific toys of our much-vaunted rationality, we are busily constructing nuclear weapons, we cannot afford to reject any possible sources of insight into human nature.

I am trained as a scientist and I value the benefits of the scientific approach to knowledge. But scientists themselves are now beginning to realize that our rational world is, in reality, deeply irrational and that science has its limitations. Actors are more than just cultural luxuries, aesthetic appendages or up-market entertainers. On the contrary, actors are essential for maintaining our vital links with the imaginal world, our universal self, the part of us that unites with the rest of humankind. In our efforts to create harmony and reclaim individual and mass sanity, I believe that actors should be classified as a precious resource and protected as an endangered species.

Traditional actor-shamans personified the gods and so do modern actors, by creating, and manifesting, characters that speak to us from the depths of our imaginations. They create something tangible from material that is ineffable. In the words of Alec Guinness, who opened this book with his tale of psychic powers, 'Creating something out of nothing is rather God-like. Not that we *are* gods, of course. But maybe like little gods. . . .'[4]

Actors in traditional societies were the guardians of secrets and mysteries. They revealed what they could in performance, but they always knew more than they could show. This is still the case, for the actor deals with the very nature of reality, a reality which cannot be analyzed in words, but which is expressed in the actor's work. As John Boorman says, 'An actor's hold on this is as fragile as it is for the rest of us, perhaps more so. Yet from time to time he can focus these things in a way that breathes life into life itself.'

The way of the actor keeps us in contact with the mystery which lies at the heart of life.

Notes

Introduction: The Actor's Way
1. Guinness 1985 pp.34–35
2. MacLaine 1983
3. Eliade 1972
4. Boorman 1985 p.88
5. La Barre 1972
6. Halifax 1982
7. MacLaine 1983 p.4
8. Andrews 1983
9. Thomas 1973 p.91
10. Roberts 1985 pp.10–12
11. Kalter 1979 p.52
12. Brook 1972 pp.122–123

ACTORS
1. The Lost Tradition
1. Rogers 1983
2. Peachment 1984 pp.12–16
3. Waymark 1971
4. Cottrell 1975 p.357
5. Ferris 1983 p.131
6. Ward 1983
7. Thomas 1973 p.153
8. Morella and Epstein 1973 pp.142–143
9. Hayman 1971
10. McAsh 1985 p.22
11. Billington 1973 p.145
12. Billington 1973 p.144
13. Billington 1973 p.144
14. Mandelbaum 1960
15. La Barre 1979 pp.7–11
16. Bates 1983
17. Charles 1953 pp.95–122

18. Huxley 1974 p.263
19. Southern 1962
20. Mayer and Immoos 1977
21. Mayer and Immoos 1977 p.43
22. Johnstone 1981 p.149
23. Lewis 1971
24. Tyler 1985
25. Bowers 1960
26. Kalter 1979 p.191
27. Caughey 1984 p.40

2. Actors, Not Acting
1. Thomas 1973 pp.234–236
2. Cottrell 1975 p.390
3. Cottrell 1975 p.390
4. Stanislavsky 1949, 1961a, 1961b
5. Marowitz 1978
6. Kalter 1979 p.185
7. Marowitz 1978 p.14
8. Kalter 1979 p.21
9. Wexman 1980
10. Callow 1984 p.80
11. Wexman 1980
12. Kalter 1979 p.185
13. Cottrell 1975 p.390
14. Marowitz 1978 p.15
15. Sher 1985
16. Hay 1984 pp.9–10
17. Kalter 1979 p.156

3. But Is It Art?
1. Bonner 1984
2. Artaud 1977, Grotowski 1975
3. Roose-Evans 1984

4. Kalter 1979 pp.229–230
5. Thomas 1973 p.112
6. Callow 1984 p.92
7. Kalter 1979 p.204
8. Ullmann 1977 p.222
9. Boorman 1985 p.103
10. Goodman 1985 p.10
11. Thomas 1973 p.64
12. Peachment 1984 pp.12–16
13. Callow 1986 p.36
14. Kalter 1979 p.191
15. Boorman 1985 p.128
16. Boorman 1985 p.112
17. McAsh 1985 pp.22–23

4. And Aren't They All Mad?
1. Smith 1983 pp.13–14
2. Smith 1983 pp.13–14
3. Smith 1983 pp.13–14
4. Gray 1979
5. Norman 1986 pp.20–24
6. Braithwaite 1974 p.5
7. Downing 1983 p.9
8. Hay 1974 pp.9–10
9. Eliade 1972
10. Halifax 1982
11. Kalter 1979 p.144
12. Thomas 1973 p.153
13. Guiles 1982 p.76
14. Jacobi 1967
15. Singer 1972 pp.166–168
16. Cottrell 1975 p.400–401
17. Kalter 1979 p.71
18. Kalter 1979 p.61
19. Thomas 1973 p.28
20. Kalter 1979 p.105
21. Kalter 1979, p.187
22. Ullmann 1977 p.222
23. Kalter 1979 pp.201–202
24. Morella 1973
25. Morella 1973
26. Kalter 1979 p.71
27. Norman 1986 p.23
28. Kalter 1979 p.21
29. Kalter 1979 p.185
30. Lewis 1986 p.16
31. Morella 1973 p.114
32. Thomas 1973 p.251

33. Morella 1973 p.139
34. Thomas 1973 p.252
35. Morella 1973 p.140
36. Thomas 1973 p.252
37. Thomas 1973 p.253
38. Callow 1984 p.80
39. Kalter 1979 p.226
40. Kalter 1979 p.62
41. Perry 1974 p.8
42. Thomas 1973 p.153
43. Cottrell 1975 p.404
44. Johnstone 1981 p.83
45. Kalter 1979 p.22

5. Possession: Finding Inner Selves
1. Bogarde 1978 p.364
2. Kalter 1979 p.203
3. Thomas 1980 pp.22–27
4. Southern 1962
5. Lewis 1971
6. Cole 1975 p.42
7. Marowitz 1978 p.100
8. Kalter 1979 p.51
9. Owen 1983 p.22
10. Goodman and Rygrave 1979 p.55
11. Bonner 1984
12. Kalter 1979 p.71
13. Andrews 1983
14. Ullmann 1977 pp.96–97
15. Ullmann 1977 p.217
16. Ullmann 1977 p.217
17. May 1970
18. Caughey 1984 p.18
19. Johnstone 1981
20. MacLaine 1983
21. Burton 1967
22. Kalter 1979, p.151
23. Kalter 1979 p.152
24. Sher 1985
25. Conrad 1985
26. Brook 1972 p.123
27. Kalter 1979 p.108

6. Transformation: Changing Selves
1. Southern 1962 p.277
2. Hayman 1971
3. Hayman 1971

4. Griffin 1969
5. Kalter 1979 p.202
6. Wardle 1985
7. Denby 1981 p.26
8. Beauman 1985 p.9
9. Nathan 1984 p.45
10. Jung 1956 p.167
11. Bates 1971
12. Cottrell 1975 p.400
13. Kalter 1979 p.74
14. Ullmann 1977 p.208

7. *Rebirth: Reliving Life*
1. Hay 1984 p.10
2. Beauman 1985 p.54
3. Quoted in Benedetti 1981 p.4
4. Kalter 1979 p.62
5. Franks 1985
6. Shakespeare 1985
7. Hay 1984 p.10
8. Kalter 1979 p.73
9. Gussow 1984
10. Brenner 1984
11. Gussow 1984
12. Gussow 1984
13. Brenner 1984
14. Brenner 1984
15. Goodman and Rygrave 1979 p.55
16. Kalter 1979 pp.28–29
17. Andrews 1983
18. Grof 1979

8. *Seeing: Facing Reality*
1. Morella and Epstein 1973
2. Thomas 1973
3. Thomas 1973
4. Heilpern 1979
5. Ullmann 1977 p.224
6. Ullmann 1977 p.224
7. Kalter 1979 pp.50–51
8. Usher 1979
9. Kalter 1979 p.202
10. Rosenthal 1982

9. *Dream: Images of Power*
1. Gow 1979 p.22
2. Downing 1983 pp.163–164
3. Elsom 1985 pp.14–15

4. Kalter 1979 p.39
5. Caughey 1984 p.157
6. Caughey 1984 pp.119–127
7. Norman 1986 pp.20–24
8. Kalter 1979 p.109
9. Andrews 1983
10. Nathan 1984 p.28
11. Herrigel 1953 p.7
12. Edwards 1982 p.30
13. Russell 1982 p.193
14. Russell 1982 p.193
15. Edwards 1982 p.36
16. Universal 1967
17. Kalter 1979 p.85
18. Ullmann 1985 pp.103–106

10. *Death: Living Near the Edge*
1. Boorman 1985 p.183
2. Boorman 1985 p.183
3. Cottrell 1975 p.384
4. Cottrell 1975 pp.264–265
5. Goodman and Rygrave 1979 p.55
6. Kalter 1979 p.49
7. Kalter 1979 p.89
8. Brenner 1984
9. Brenner 1984
10. Waymark 1971
11. Cottrell 1975 p.379
12. Kalter 1979 p.84
13. Owen 1983
14. MacLaine 1983 p.318
15. Hayman 1971
16. Rosenthal 1982
17. Andrews 1983
18. Southern 1962 p.24
19. Thomas 1973 p.55
20. Callow 1984 p.56
21. Callow 1984 p.81
22. Couch and Kenison 1960

11. *Charisma: Power of Presence*
1. Southern 1962 p.40
2. Downing 1983 p.96
3. Kalter 1979 p.63
4. Kalter 1979 p.218
5. Wexman 1980 p.70
6. Thomas 1973 p.41

7. Ward 1983 p.43
8. Kalter 1979 p.157
9. Ferris 1983 pp.58–59
10. Ferris 1983 p.70
11. Ferris 1983 pp.69–70
12. Ferris 1983 p.60
13. Nathan 1984 p.78
14. Cottrell 1975 p.404
15. Thomas 1980 pp.22–27
16. Kalter 1979 pp.88–89
17. Kalter 1979 pp.149–150
18. Downing 1983 p.145
19. Callow 1984 p.20
20. Hutchinson 1980
21. Downing 1983 p.145
22. Wexman 1980 p.70
23. Kalter 1979 p.18
24. Kalter 1979 p.215
25. Rosenthal 1982
26. Usher 1979
27. Boorman 1985 p.167
28. Kalter 1979 p.156
29. Matson 1979
30. Matson 1979
31. Benedetti 1981 p.21

12. *Soul: Liberation from the Body*
1. MacLaine 1983 p.3
2. MacLaine 1983 pp.332–333
3. Watts 1967
4. Kalter 1979 p.144
5. Eliade 1972
6. Blackmore 1982
7. Inglis 1985 p.47
8. Blackmore 1982
9. Norman 1986 pp.20–24
10. MacLaine 1983 pp.3–4

13. *Powers: Psychic Sensitivity*
1. Guinness 1985 pp.34–35
2. Guinness 1985 pp.34–35
3. Bates 1985

4. Nathan 1984 p.64
5. Kalter 1979 p.70
6. Truss 1985
7. Benedetti 1981 p.119
8. Nathan 1984 p.64
9. Morella 1973
10. Wexman 1980 p.69
11. Cottrell 1985 p.402
12. Thomas 1973 p.93
13. Thomas 1973
14. Braithwaite 1974
15. Bogarde 1978 p.366
16. Marowitz 1978 p.103
17. Russell 1982
18. Marowitz 1978 p.101

14. *Energies: Intimate Communication*
1. Callow 1984 p.97
2. Kalter 1979 p.85
3. Kalter 1979 p.86
4. Andrews 1983
5. Andrews 1983
6. Callow 1984 p.47
7. Andrews 1983
8. Andrews 1983
9. Chambers 1978
10. Kalter 1979 p.220
11. Marowitz 1979 p.102
12. Marowitz 1978 pp.102–103
13. Marowirz 1978 p.105
14. Kalter 1979 p.145
15. Peachment 1984 p.14
16. Kalter 1979 p.47
17. Waymark 1971
18. Gow 1979 pp.12–17

15. *Return to the Mystery*
1. Callow 1984 p.23
2. Morella and Epstein 1973
   pp.142–143
3. Boorman 1985 p.229
4. Bragg 1985

Bibliography

Andrews, D. 'Actress Liv Ullmann: Life without barriers'. *Christian Science Monitor* 1983

Artaud, A. *The Theatre and Its Double* (tr. Victor Corti) London: John Calder 1977

Bates, B. 'Territorial behavior in primates: A review of recent field studies'. *Primates: Journal of Primatology* 1971 vol. 11 (3) pp.271–284

Bates, B. *The Way of Wyrd* London: Century 1983

Bates, B. 'Spooks classified: on present views of the paranormal.' *The Guardian*, April 25, 1985

Beauman, S. 'As you like it, as they like it.' *Sunday Times Magazine* June 1985 pp.51–54

Benedetti, R. *The Actor at Work* (3rd Edit) Englewood Cliffs, New Jersey: Prentice-Hall 1981

Billington, M. *The Modern Actor* London: Hamish Hamilton 1973

Blackmore, S. *Beyond the Body* London: Heinemann 1982

Bogarde, D. *Snakes and Ladders* London: Chatto and Windus 1978

Bonner, H. 'Interview with John Hurt'. *Mail on Sunday* 29 April 1984

Boorman, J. *Money into Light* London: Faber and Faber 1985

Bowers, F. *Theatre in the East* New York: Grove Press 1960

Bragg, M. Interview with Alec Guinness. *The South Bank Show*, London Weekend Television, 6 October 1985

Braithwaite, B. *The Films of Marlon Brando* London: Barnden Castell Williams 1974

Brenner, M. 'Death of a Salesman' (Dustin Hoffman). *New York* 26.3.1984

Brook, P. *The Empty Space* London: Pelican 1972

Burton, H. *Great Acting* London: BBC 1967

Callow, S. 'To Beebe or Not to Beebe.' *The Sunday Times* 6 April 1986 pp.36–38

Caughey, J.L. *Imaginary Social Worlds* University of Nebraska Press 1984

Chambers, C. 'Responsibility to the future: Ben Kingsley and Patrick Stewart in interview'. *Plays and Players* 1978 25 (10) 10–15

Charles, L.H. 'Drama in shaman exorcism'. *Journal of American Folklore* 1953 66 95–122

Cole, D. *The Theatrical Event*, Middletown, Connecticut: Wesleyan University Press 1975

Conrad, P. 'An actor possessed'. *The Observer* 23.6.1985
Cottrell, J. *Laurence Olivier* London: Weidenfeld and Nicolson 1975
Couch, A. and Kenison, K. 'Yeasayers and Naysayers'. *Journal of Abnormal and Social Psychology* 1960 *160* (2)
Denby, D. 'Meryl Streep is Madonna'. *New York* 21.9.1981, p.26
Downing, D. *Jack Nicholson* London: W.H. Allen 1983
Edwards, B. *Drawing on the Right Side of the Brain* London: Fontana 1982
Eliade, M. *Shamanism: Archaic Techniques of Ecstasy* (tr. W. Trask) Princeton: Princeton University Press 1972
Elsom, J. 'Brook's Latest'. *Plays International* 1985 *1* (2) 14–15
Ferris, P. *Richard Burton* London: New English Library 1983
Franks, A. 'Scofield on the couch'. *The Times* 30.11.1985
Goodman, J. 'The rise and rise of an unconventional hero' (Interview with John Malkovitch). *The Times* Feb 20 1985, p.10
Goodman, J. and Rygrave, M. 'The making of Meryl' (Interview with Meryl Streep). *The Observer Magazine* 4.3.1979
Gow, G 'Energy and rompishness and exquisite agony' (Interview with Judi Dench). *Plays and Players* 1979 *26* (9) 12–17
Gow, G. 'Incarnation' (Interview with Klaus Kinski). *Films and Filming* 1979 *25* (10) 22–24
Gray, P. 'A mother finds herself: The silent suffering of Meryl Streep'. *Time* 3.12.1979
Griffin, J.H. *Black Like Me* London: Panther, 1969
Grof, S. *Realms of the Human Unconscious* London: Souvenir Press 1979
Grotowski, J. *Towards a Poor Theatre* London: Methuen 1975
Guiles, F.L. *Jane Fonda: The Actress in her Time* London: Coronet Books 1982
Guinness, A. *Blessings in Disguise* London: Hamish Hamilton 1985
Gussow, M. 'Dustin Hoffman's "Salesman" '. *New York Times Magazine* 11.3.1984
Halifax, J. *Shaman: The Wounded Healer* London: Thames and Hudson 1982
Hay, M. 'The essential touchstone for Roger Rees'. *Drama* 1984 *3* (153) 9–10
Hayman, R. 'Helen Mirren'. *The Times* 11th September 1971
Heilpern, J. 'Interview with John Hurt'. *Radio Times* 233 19 May 1979
Herrigel, E. *Zen in the Art of Archery* London: Routledge and Kegan Paul 1953
Hutchinson, T. 'Interview with John Hurt'. *Now Magazine* September 26, 1980
Huxley, F. *The Way of the Sacred* London: Aldus Books 1974
Inglis, B. *The Paranormal* London: Granada 1985
Jacobi, J. *The Way of Individuation* New York: Harcourt, Brace and World 1967
Johnstone, K. *Impro: Improvisation and the Theatre* London: Methuen 1981
Jung, C.G. *Two Essays on Analytical Psychology* New York: Meridian Books 1956
Kalter, J. *Actors on Acting* New York: Sterling Publishing 1979
La Barre, W. *The Ghost Dance: Origins of Religion* New York: Delta 1972
La Barre, W. 'Shamanic Origins of religion and medicine.' *Journal of Psychedelic Drugs* 1979 *II* (1–2) 7–11
Lewis, I.M. *Ecstatic Religion: An Anthropological Study of Spirit Possession and Shamanism* Baltimore: Penguin 1971

Lewis, P. 'The pride and joy of Peter Hall.' *Sunday Express Magazine* 23 Feb 1986, pp.15–19 + 58–59

MacLaine, S. *Out on a Limb* London: Elm Tree Books 1983

McAsh, I. 'Take 2: People in camera.' *Films* March 1985 22–23

Mandelbaum, D.G. *Anthropology of Folk Religion* London: Charles Leslie 1960

Marowitz, C. *The Act of Being* London: Secker and Warburg 1978

Matson, K. *The Encyclopaedia of Reality* London: Paladin 1979

May, R. Psychotherapy and the Daimonic, In J. Campbell (Ed) *Myth Dreams and Religion* New York: Dutton 1970

Mayer, F. and Immoos, T. *Japanese Theatre* London: Studio Vista 1977

Morella, J. and Epstein, E.Z. *Brando: The Unauthorised Biography* London: Thomas Nelson and Sons Ltd, 1973

Nathan, D. *Glenda Jackson* Tunbridge Wells, Kent. Spellmount 1984

Norman, N. 'Hurt: The actor with the atom brain.' *The Face* 1986 *69* 20–24

Owen, M. 'Meryl Streep'. *Evening Standard* (London) 19.3.1983, p.22

Peachment, C. 'An American Buffalo in London' (Interview with Al Pacino) *Time Out* 1984 *733* 12–16

Perry, J.W. *The Far Side of Madness* New York: Prentice-Hall 1974

Roberts, P. 'Actor as Storyteller'. *Plays International* 1985 *1* (2) 10–12

Rogers, B. 'Streep draws the line'. *Sunday Times* 20.3.1983

Roose-Evans, J. *Experimental Theatre* London: Routledge and Kegan Paul 1984

Rosenthal, D. 'The mystique of Meryl Streep'. *Cosmopolitan* May 1982

Russell, P. *The Awakening Earth* London: Routledge and Kegan Paul 1982

Shakespeare, N. 'Strong in practice' (Interview with Sheila Gish). *The Times* 27 March 1985

Sher, A. *Year of the King* London: Chatto and Windus 1985

Singer, J. *Boundaries of the Soul* New York: Doubleday and Co 1972

Smith, G. 'The lives and deaths of Dustin Hoffman'. *Rolling Stone* 3.2.1983, pp.3–4; 51–52

Southern, R. *The Seven Ages of the Theatre* London: Faber and Faber 1962

Stanislavski, K. *Building a Character* (tr. E. Hapgood) New York: Theatre Arts 1949

Stanislavski, K. *An Actor Prepares* (tr. E. Hapgood) New York: Theatre Arts 1961

Stanislavski, K. *Creating a Role* (tr. E. Hapgood) New York: Theatre Arts 1961

Thomas, B. *Brando: Portrait of the Rebel as an Artist* London: W.H. Allen 1973

Thomas, D. 'The many faces of Klaus Kinski'. *American Film* 1980 *V* (7) 22–27

Truss, L. 'An actor bids farewell to peace of mind'. *The Times* 19.12.1985

Tyler, R. 'The hard sell behind television's soft soap'. *The Times* 17 December 1985

Ullmann, L. *Changing* London: Weidenfeld and Nicolson 1977

Ullmann, L. *Choices* London: Weidenfeld and Nicolson 1985

Universal Pictures Ltd News, 'Interview with John Hurt' 1967

Usher, S. 'Why Meryl's best performance had an audience of one'. *Daily Mail* 19.4.1979

Ward, R. 'I'm not a movie star, I'm an actor' (Interview with Gene Hackman). *American Film* 1983 VIII (5)

Wardle, I. 'Rape of the American Indian as seen from the reservation.' *The Times* December 19, 1985

Watts, A. *The Book: On the Taboo Against Knowing Who You Are* New York: Collier 1967

Waymark, P. 'Ian McKellan joins the Shakespearian acting elite'. *Daily Telegraph* 29.3.1971

Wexman, V.M. 'An Interview with Liv Ullmann'. *Cinema Journal* 1980 *20* (1)

Index of Names